Bartók's *Mikrokosmos*

Genesis, Pedagogy, and Style

Benjamin Suchoff

The Scarecrow Press, Inc.
Lanham, Maryland, and Oxford
2002

SCARECROW PRESS, INC.

Published in the United States of America
by Scarecrow Press, Inc.
A wholly owned subsidary of
The Rowman & Littlefield Publishing Group, Inc.
4501 Forbes Boulevard, Suite 200, Lanham, Maryland 20706
www.scarecrowpress.com

PO Box 317; Oxford; OX2 9RU, UK

British Library Cataloguing in Publication Information Available

The hardback edition of this book was previously catalogued by the Library of
Congress as follows:

Suchoff, Benjamin.
    Bartók's Mikrokosmos : genesis, pedagogy, and style / Benjamin Suchoff.
        p. cm.
    Includes bibliographical references (p.) and index.
    1. Bartâk, Bâla, 1881–1945. Mikrokosmos. 2. Piano music—Analysis,
appreciation. I. Title.
    MT145.B25 S88 2002
    786.2'189—dc21   2002066897

ISBN 0-8108-5163-6 (pbk.: alk. paper)

♾ ™ The paper used in this publication meets the minimum requirements of
American National Standard for Information Sciences—Permanence of
Paper for Printed Library Materials, ANSI/NISO Z39.48-1992.
Manufactured in the United States of America.

For Eleanor

Contents

PART ONE

Genesis

PART TWO

Pedagogy

PART THREE

Style

Preface

When Béla Bartók began the composition of *For Children* in 1908, he continued the tradition of important composers writing characteristic and consequential keyboard works in the form of teaching pieces, such as Bach's Inventions for his children and Notebook for Anna Magdalena Bach for his wife, and Schumann's *Album für die Jugend* op. 68 and other works for children. Bartók also composed teaching pieces for the *Piano School* (*Zongora Iskola*, 1913), a method for the first year of piano study, that he coauthored with Sándor Reschofsky, a colleague at the Budapest Academy of Music. In this publication appear technical and theoretical descriptions and instructions, of which a certain number replicate those used by Bartók in his early editions of keyboard works from the standard keyboard repertory (Bach and Beethoven for the most part).

In June 1926, following several years of compositional "stagnation," Bartók embarked on his "enlargement of the newly won means" of exploiting the percussive character of the piano by writing his Piano Sonata and "especially the *Mikrokosmos* pieces." Although Bartók dated the *Mikrokosmos* as 1926–1939, only three pieces were composed in 1926. Nos. 81, 137, and 146, originally intended for inclusion in Nine Little Piano Pieces, were written during October. Bartók did not take up the work as presently constituted until 1933, the year he began teaching his younger son. As he stated during a New York City radio broadcast on 2 July 1944:

> The *Mikrokosmos* is a cycle of hundred fifty and three pieces for piano written with a didactical purpose, that is, to give pieces, piano pieces which can be used from the very beginning and then going on. It is graded according to difficulty, and the word Cosmos may be interpreted, *Mikrokosmos* may be interpreted as a series of pieces in all of different styles that represent a small world. Or, it may be interpreted as a world, a musical world for the little ones, for the children [see the complete transcription in *BBGM*, 106–7].

Furthermore, in his preface to the work, Bartók also states that the first three books "differ from a 'Piano Method' in the traditional sense by the absence of any technical and theoretical description and instruction. Every teacher knows what is required in this respect and is able to give the earliest instruction without reference to a book or method." My own experience as a tutor of American children, adult beginners, and aspiring piano teachers was hardly in conformity with Bartók's assumption. In fact, my preparation for teaching the last four books required investigation of the small number of available Bartók publications, including his folk music essays. This research led to my doctoral studies at New York University in 1950 and the subsequent publication of my dissertation, *Béla Bartók and a Guide to the Mikrokosmos* (1957) and *Guide to Bartók's Mikrokosmos* (Boosey & Hawkes, 1971. Reprint, Da Capo Press, 1983). Other important outcomes were my appointment as assistant to the trustee of the New York Bartók estate (1953), curator of *NYBA* (New York Bartók Archive, 1963), and successor-trustee of the Bartók estate (1967–1984).

As the published and unpublished *Mikrokosmos* sources of *NYBA* grew, it became apparent in the 1970s that the interest of Bartók scholars had turned from pedagogical to theoretic-analytical studies of Bartók's compositional techniques, such as his folk music sources and musical language. Some scholars investigated the work by way of Schenkerian methodology, set-complex theory, and structural models; others have turned to equally untenable concepts in terms of atonality, polytonality, and Golden Section. In retrospect, there is an apparent connection between the appearance of a number of these studies and the publication of my *Guide to Bartók's Mikrokosmos* (1971) and, particularly, my edition of *Béla Bartók Essays* (1976).

Accordingly, the present book investigates Bartók's *Mikrokosmos* from three viewpoints:genesis, pedagogy, and style. Part One examines Bartók's life as pianist and teacher, and traces the development of the work. Part Two, a revision of my *Guide to Bartók's Mikrokosmos*, is devoted to aspects of technique and musicianship in the complete work, including Bartók's own comments, and is intended for piano teachers, students, and performers. Part Three is a theoretic-analytical study of selected pieces from each volume of the *Mikrokosmos*, based for the most part on Bartók's own principles of composition or findings from his folk music studies, and is provided as a source for composers, music educators, and students.

The dedication of this book to my wife reflects yet another grateful homage for her devotion to my welfare and support of my work. And I am indebted to my friend and colleague, Elliott Antokoletz, whose significant studies of Bartók's musical language have had great impact on my investigation of the composer's oeuvre.

Acknowledgments

To Boosey & Hawkes Music Publishers Ltd. (London), Boosey & Hawkes Music Publishers, Inc. (New York), and Universal Edition AG (Vienna), acknowledgment is made for permission to use music examples from Béla Bartók's *Mikrokosmos* for Piano and Béla Bartók's Music for Stringed Instruments, Percussion, and Celesta.

Abbreviations

BBA   Budapest Bartók Archívum

BBCO   Benjamin Suchoff: *Béla Bartók: Concerto for Orchestra: Under-standing Bartók's World.* New York: Schirmer, 1995

BBE   Béla Bartók: *Béla Bartók Essays,* selected and edited by Benjamin Suchoff. Reprint. Lincoln and London: University of Nebraska Press, 1992

BBGM   Benjamin Suchoff: *Béla Bartók and a Guide to the Mikrokosmos.* Ann Arbor, MI: UMI, 1957

BBGR   Elliott Antokoletz: *Béla Bartók: A Guide to Research.* 2d ed., rev. and enl. New York: Garland, 1997

BBL   *Béla Bartók Letters,* ed. János Demény. Trans. Péter Balabán and István Farkas, rev. trans. Elisabeth West and Colin Mason. New York: St. Martin's Press, 1971

BBLW   Benjamin Suchoff: *Béla Bartók: Life and Work.* Lanham, MD: Scare-crow Press, 2001

BBSE   *Béla Bartók: Béla Bartók Studies in Ethnomusicology,* selected and ed. Benjamin Suchoff. Lincoln and London: University of Nebraska Press, 1997

BC   *The Bartók Companion*, ed. Malcolm Gillies. Portland, OR: Ama-deus Press, 1994

BP   *Bartók Perspectives,* ed. Elliott Antokoletz, Victoria Fischer, and Benjamin Suchoff. New York: Oxford University Press, 2000

HFS   Béla Bartók: *The Hungarian Folk Song*, ed. Benjamin Suchoff. Trans. M. D. Calvocoressi, with annotations by Zoltán Kodály. Albany: State University of New York Press, 1981

LMBB   Halsey Stevens: *The Life and Music of Béla Bartók.* 3d ed. Prepa-ration by Malcolm Gillies. Oxford: Clarendon Press, 1993

MBB   Elliott Antokoletz, *The Music of Béla Bartók: A Study of Tonality and Progression in Twentieth-Century Music.* Berkeley and Los Angeles: University of California Press, 1984

NYBA   New York Bartók Archive (now in *PBA*)

PBA   Peter Bartók Archive, Homosassa, Florida

RFM.i–v   Béla Bartók: *Rumanian Folk Music*, ed. Benjamin Suchoff, trans. E. C. Teodorescu. The Hague: Martinus Nijhoff, 1967, 1975

SV.i–iii Béla Bartók: *Slowakische Volkslieder*, ed. Alica Elscheková, Oskár Elschek, and Jozef Kresánek. Bratislava: Academia Scientiarum Slovaca, 1959, 1970 (vol. iii is unpublished)

TFM   Béla Bartók: *Turkish Folk Music from Asia Minor,* ed. Benjamin Suchoff. With an afterword by Kurt Reinhard. Princeton: Princeton University Press, 1976

YFM.i–iv Béla Bartók:*Yugoslav Folk Music*, ed. Benjamin Suchoff. Albany: State University of New York Press, 1978

PART ONE

Genesis

1

Bartók as Pianist

Béla Bartók was born on March 25, 1881, in Hungary, "in a small place called Nagyszentmiklós, which now, together with the whole county (Torontal), belongs to Roumania."[1] Bartók describes his childhood with this brief account:

> My mother gave me my first piano lessons when I was 6 years old. My father, who was the head of an agricultural school, was gifted musically and active in many directions. He played the piano, organized an amateur orchestra, learned the cello in order to play in the orchestra, and composed some dance music. I was 8 years old when I lost him.[2]

Other accounts of Bartók's early years were written by his mother Paula Voit Bartók in 1921 and 1922.[3] At the age of a year and a half he brought her to the piano to play a piece he had listened to the day before. He shook his head until she played the composition he wanted to hear. At the age of three Bartók was able to beat a drum in time to his mother's piano playing; if she changed rhythm, he would stop momentarily and then begin again in the new rhythm. At four, using one finger, he played as many as forty songs on the piano, all of them from memory.[4]

Bartók's first piano lesson took place on his fifth birthday, March 25, 1886. Scarcely a month later, Bartók and his mother were able to play a four-hand piece for his father. The child's recurring illness interrupted the lessons, and it was not until he was seven that it was discovered he had absolute pitch. After his father's death, the family moved to another house in the same town, and his mother gave piano lessons to support the family. Bartók resumed his piano studies under his mother's guidance; however, she could not induce him to count aloud the rhythms he felt instinctively.[5]

In 1890, while the family was living in Nagyszőllős, a small town in northern Hungary, Bartók began composing music for the piano.[6] He performed there for a local organist and choirmaster,[7] who predicted a brilliant future for the young pianist, with the result that Bartók and his mother went to the Royal Academy of Music in Budapest for a professional opinion. Károly Aggházy, pupil of Liszt and a teacher at the academy, heard the boy play and, as a result of the audition, wanted him as a pupil. But Paula Bartók decided against a change, since her son was ending his studies at the local intermediate school. The next year Bartók entered the gymnasium at Nagyvárad (Oradea, Romania) where he lived with his aunt. Here he took piano lessons with Ferenc Kersch, a composer and choirmaster, who concentrated on teaching Bartók brilliant display pieces.[8]

Bartók returned to Nagyszőllős in April 1892, and on May 1 made his first public appearance as a pianist, playing the first movement of Beethoven's Sonata op. 53 ("*Waldstein*")[9] and his own composition, *The Course of the Danube*. For his efforts, the eleven-year-old pianist received much applause and seven bouquets, including one of candy.[10]

Beginning in 1893, the family settled in Pozsony where Bartók studied piano and harmony with László Erkel, acquiring a solid grounding in the music of the eighteenth and nineteenth centuries. He attended orchestral concerts and operas, composed music, and played chamber music in several private homes. In addition, he had the opportunity to play the piano music of Liszt and Wagner as part of the musical programs given in the city. He took over Ernst von Dohnányi's place as organist in the gymnasium chapel, and earned fees as an accompanist and piano teacher.[11]

> When my education at the Gymnasium (high school) was concluded the question arose at which musical academy I should continue my studies. In Pozsony, at that time, the Vienna Conservatory was considered the sole bastion of serious musical education, but I took Dohnányi's advice and came to Budapest and became a pupil of István Thomán (in piano) and of Hans Koessler (in composition).[12]

Bartók's autobiographical account omits mention that he was offered free tuition and a scholarship from the Emperor's fund to study at the conservatory in Vienna, following an audition played there in December 1898, and that he was to have been admitted to the Academy of Music in Budapest without examination as a result of an interview with István Thomán in January 1899. The next month Bartók became very ill and was unable to practice until his arrival in Budapest the following September. Despite Thomán's promise, the director of the academy refused to admit Bartók unless he passed the required entrance examination. Although the young pianist had been away from the keyboard for more than six months, his playing of a Beethoven sonata for the faculty jury resulted in his assignment to Thomán's advanced piano class.[13]

After the first week in his new lodgings in Budapest, Bartók wrote to his mother about the poor condition of the piano there; that "everything rings and buzzes, the pedal squeaks, etc."[14] He was constantly being interrupted by uninvited persons requesting him to "play something" during his practice periods. Then, in October, he succumbed to a bronchial infection and was forced to return home to convalesce.[15]

Fully recovered, beginning in January Bartók returned to his piano study with Thomán who was considered one of the outstanding piano teachers in Hungary at that time. During the year, Bartók attended concerts, operas, and receptions, and on 21 January wrote to his mother about a recital played by the celebrated pianist, Emil Sauer.

I have heard Sauer and seen him—he played in a truly magnificent style. That one piano could produce such unusual sonorities scarcely seemed possible. What is striking is his comportment. He lifts his hands a yard in the air, wags his head from side to side, ponders over each piece; then, as if realizing he must play something, he attacks it. At the end, he raises his hands high up and then lets them fall on his knee—perhaps these mannerisms are what attract the ladies.[16]

During his vacation in August, Bartók was stricken with pneumonia. Upon the advice of a physician, Bartók, accompanied by his mother, went to the Italian Tyrol to convalesce. It was not until January 1901 that the young student was able to resume practicing; shortly thereafter he returned to the academy to finish the year.[17]

In September he began preparation for his first public concert at the academy on October 21, 1901. A review of the recital states that:

First, Béla Bartók played the Liszt B-minor Sonata with a steely, well-developed technique. This young man has acquired extraordinary strength. A year and a half ago his constitution was so weak that the doctors sent him to Merano lest the cold winter harm him—and now he plays the piano as thunderously as a little Jupiter. In fact, he is *today* the only piano student at the Academy who may follow in Dohnányi's footsteps.[18]

In 1900 and 1901 Bartók's attention was directed towards his development as a pianist, and he did little in the way of composition.

I did not at the time grasp Liszt's true significance for the development of modern music and only saw the technical brilliance of his compositions. I did no independent work for two years, and at the Academy of Music was considered only a first-class pianist.[19]

It was during this time, Bartók later related to a pupil, that he received an accolade from his piano teacher. When Thomán was a pupil of Liszt, the latter kissed him on the forehead after Thomán had performed particularly well. In similar fashion, Thomán kissed the young Bartók, saying, "This kiss is handed down from Liszt!"[20] Bartók received his first fee, ten gold pieces, at his recital given at the Lipótváros Casino on 14 December 1901. He appeared as an accompanist in March 1902, and his next performance at the academy, in December of that year, resulted in his being hailed by a newspaper critic as "a new, extraordinarily strong talent, who is undoubtedly destined for a brilliant career."[21]

In January 1903, he went to Vienna for a recital at the Tonkünstlerverein, where he played his transcription of Richard Strauss's symphonic poem *Ein*

Heldenleben (A Hero's Life) that he had committed to memory in its entirety. A few months later he returned to his native town, Nagyszentmiklós, after an absence of fourteen years, to play the first formal recital given there.[22]

It was the custom at the Academy of Music for each student to undergo an examination in his area or areas of specialization in order to receive the diplomas attesting to his competency. According to Bartók's letter to his mother, dated 25 May 1903, after he left the Academy of Music: "To the greatest wonderment of my fellows I was not required to undergo even the smallest examination, all the authorities agreed there was no point to it."[23]

In a subsequent interchange of letters with his mother, Bartók vetoed her suggestion that he continue his piano studies with Emil Sauer in Vienna. His decision was to spend the summer of 1903 working on repertory with Dohnányi, whom he admired greatly as a pianist.

The Concert Artist: 1903–1943

Although Bartók played Beethoven's Fifth Piano Concerto at the Konzertverein in Vienna, on November 1903, he considered his December recital in the Berlin Bechstein-Saal of utmost importance in his quest for a concert career.

> The very significant Dec. 14 is over: my first real job of clearing accounts in the course of a concert. What I most feared—that my strength might not be equal to it—didn't happen; after the concert I was so little tired that I could have played another program from beginning to end. [My] Study for the Left Hand went splendidly; the greater part of the public was most impressed by this. The hall was quite 2/3 full. . . . Two 'celebrities' were in the audience, [Leopold] Godowsky and [Ferruccio] Busoni. The latter came to the artist's room after the third part, introduced himself, and congratulated me; . . . he expressed admiration that I, who have such a fine left hand technique—as he heard in the Study—still played the Chopin C-minor Etude so satisfyingly.[24]

Serge Moreux adds that Godowsky, "a pianist adored by two continents," exclaimed that the Study sounded as if it were played by three hands, and prophesied great things of Bartók.[25]

A favorable review of the concert was given by the critic of the *Vossische Zeitung*:

> Béla Bartók, a newly-discovered pianist . . . aroused interest; he stood out among his innumerable colleagues who year after year seek to win public attention. Bartók is a man who has his own ideas of God and the world; he is a strong personality in himself. His playing has a spiritual undercurrent without which a performance remains only a display. If he succeeds in making his tone production more varied and colorful, we will then be able to class him among the young pianists whose future holds great promise.[26]

On the other hand, a later description of Bartók's special qualities as a pianist states that:

> foremost among them was a transcendent sense of phrasing, comparable to that of the very greatest international artists. . . . Bartók's second quality as a pianist was a tone at once rich and precise—a range of shades of color so exactly differentiate that it might be compared to that of Alexander Borovsky.[27]

Bartók played a series of concerts in England in January 1904 and, after his return to Hungary, devoted himself to composition and made his first notations of Hungarian peasant music. In Paris during August 1905, he participated in the *Prix Rubinstein* competition as a pianist and composer but was unsuccessful in either category. His disappointment by the results of the piano competition was overshadowed by his resentment of the way the adjudicators unfairly politicized the composition award.[28]

Until 1904, Bartók's career objectives were composition and the piano. The next year he added musical folklore as third interest: "I felt an urge to go deeper into this question [of Hungarian folk songs] and set out in 1905 to collect and study Hungarian peasant music unknown until then."[29]

That year was also notable in terms of Bartók's development of his aptitude for linguistics. He had begun the study of English while he was a student at the Budapest Academy of Music (he already read, wrote, and spoke German and Hungarian fluently). He studied French during his stay in Paris for the *Prix Rubinstein* competition. In 1906, he took up Spanish when he accompanied the thirteen-year-old Hungarian violin prodigy, Ferenc Vecsey, to the Iberian Peninsula, and added the Slovak language during his first fieldwork in Slovak peasant villages. And he studied Romanian in 1908, following his collection of Transylvanian-Romanian instrumental and vocal folk music during 1907.[30] It was only the necessity of earning a living that kept Bartók at the piano in those early days of collecting folk music:

> I am to play for the writers' group there [Pressburg, now Bratislava, Slovakia] on Sunday, that is tomorrow. . . . It's a great nuisance. I have hardly touched the piano for six months, so for two weeks now, I've been forcing my fingers to play the nullities I know by heart. I had a piano sent to me in Gömör [Gemerská, Slovakia] county. . . . But to the devil with exercises! They are the last things I want to waste my time on. I should have preferred to collect as many songs as possible.[31]

When István Thomán resigned from the Budapest Academy of Music in 1907, Bartók accepted the appointment as his teacher's successor and take over the advanced piano class as professor of piano:

> When an appointment to the chair of piano teaching at the Academy of Music in Budapest was offered to me in 1907, I considered this a happy event, because it enabled me to settle in Hungary and to continue my studies in musical folklore."[32]

Beginning in 1909, the performance of Bartók's orchestral works were received in Budapest with animosity, because the obvious influence of peasant music—folk modes, pentatonic scales, and peculiarities of rhythm—offended the sensibilities of music critics as well as the audiences. Furthermore, neither orchestras nor conductors understood this new music, to the point where they were unable to perform it adequately. And when the New Hungarian Music Society—organized by Bartók, Kodály, and other young musicians to perform contemporary Hungarian music—collapsed for lack of support and interest, Bartók temporarily withdrew from public life in 1912. He continued collecting folk music until the advent of World War I and the ensuing political and economic breakdown brought an end to his fieldwork in 1918.[33]

It was not until 1920 that Bartók returned to public life as a concert pianist, both at home and abroad. A pupil of Bartók recalled that:

> In the years that I studied with him, from 1923 to 1929 in Budapest, Bartók was considered among the front rank of Hungarian pianists, even above Dohnányi. He played mostly Beethoven, few of his own compositions. His recitals were sellouts; tickets had to be procured weeks in advance for good seats."[34]

Bartók's international success as a virtuoso and composer began in 1922, when he played in England and France. In 1923 he had further successes in the same countries as well as in Czechoslovakia, Holland, and Germany. During the next two years, other tours of the continent, including Italy and Sicily, added to his renown.[35]

In 1927, after a visit to Russia, Bartók arrived in New York and played his Rhapsody for Piano and Orchestra with the New York Philharmonic Orchestra under Wilhelm Mengelberg. A few weeks prior to the concert, César Saerchinger, writing from London, stated that:

> Bartók's pianistic gifts would have made it easy for him to become a successful virtuoso . . . as a pianist Bartók is possessed of extraordinary technical powers placed at the service of an encyclopedic musical mind. In his own country he ranks close to Dohnányi as an interpreter.[36]

A review of the concert was laudatory in terms of the composer's pianistic skills:

> The piano part of the concert is difficult and original in its technique. Mr. Bartók played as the composer-pianist with a born instinct for the keyboard, with a poetry of conception and at times a fury of virtuosity and élan astonishing in a man of his modesty and unostentationess.[37]

The next year Bartók played his First Piano Concerto in Cincinnati, Fritz Reiner conducting. Tibor Serly, who played viola in the orchestra that afternoon reported that "absolute silence followed the performance; a few handclaps were heard when Bartók came out for one bow."[38]

Thereafter, an American tour sponsored by the Pro-Musica Society brought Bartók to San Francisco, Los Angeles, Portland, Seattle, Denver, Kansas City, Chicago, St. Paul, Philadelphia, and Boston. He prefaced certain recitals with a short lecture in English on the problems of the contemporary composer in relating his art music to folk music.[39] He returned to Europe by way of South America, where he met Heitor Villa-Lobos in Brazil, and he repeated the performance of the First Piano Concerto in Berlin. The audience response was similar to that in Cincinnati, according to Lajos Hernádi:

> I attended [the concert] and it was excellent . . . but the applause was cold and there were some boos. I talked to Bartók afterwards and told him of my anger. Bartók replied, "Why are you so angry? If someone buys a ticket to a concert he has the right to boo as well as applaud." After a while, Bartók added, "I myself would not boo if I did not like something.[40]

In 1929, Bartók gave concerts in the Soviet Union and in Switzerland, and the next year he played an hour-long recital on the Budapest radio station, including some two-piano works with Hernádi.

> I was his partner then, and he told me that he did not think it would be right for him to play the primo part always, so we changed seats alternatingly. Bartók said, smilingly: "The listeners now can guess who is playing the primo." I don't think the audience had to think too much about who was playing primo![41]

From 1929 to 1931, Bartók recorded some of his works as pianist and accompanist for Columbia Records and His Master's Voice. In 1932, he played his First Piano Concerto at the Salle Pleyel, with the Paris Orchestral Society Orchestra under the direction of Pierre Monteux, and the next year was soloist in his Second Piano Concerto in Amsterdam, Frankfurt, London, Vienna, Strassburg, Stockholm, Winterthur, and Zurich.[42]

Bartók was granted a leave of absence from his Academy of Music teaching duties in 1934 and devoted himself to the study of Hungarian folk music at the Budapest Academy of Sciences. He interrupted his research work in 1937 for another series of concerts and broadcasts in Holland, Belgium, France, England, and Switzerland, returning to Basel the next year for the premiere of his Sonata for Two Pianos and Percussion. Concerts in Luxembourg, Holland, Belgium, and England followed, and Paris was revisited in 1939 to audition a rehearsal of his Second Violin Concerto. When Bartók's mother died later that year, he decided to take up residence in the United States until the end of World War II. In October 1940, he arrived in New York with his wife, Ditta. A series of Town Hall concerts was followed by Bartók's receipt of the honorary degree of Doctor of Music from Columbia University on 25 November.[44]

At the beginning of the new year, the Bartóks played piano recitals in selected American cities, and in March he began the study of the Milman Parry
collection of Yugoslav folk music, under a grant from the Alice M. Ditson Fund
and a stipend from Columbia University. To augment his income, he sought
playing engagements for the season of 1941–1942. These were difficult to ob-
tain; Bartók had to be content with an orchestral concert, three duo-piano recitals, and four solo performances. At the close of 1942, his grant from Columbia
University terminated, and on 21 January 1943, he played his last public concert, with the New York Philharmonic Orchestra under Fritz Reiner. Bartók's
final public appearance was made on 2 July 1944, when he was interviewed at
the Brooklyn Museum for an "Ask the Composer" broadcast over Station WNYC.
Not quite fifteen months later, on 26 September 1945, Bartók died of leukemia
in the West Side Hospital in New York City.

The Piano Style

A characteristic of Bartók's piano playing throughout his lifetime was his
deportment while at the keyboard.[45] One of his colleagues recalls a concert he
gave at the Academy of Music in Budapest:

> This is where, as a little girl, I first heard him. . . . He played some Bach, Beethoven,
> Schumann's F-Sharp Minor Sonata, and a few of his own compositions. To be
> sure, I would not remember this program so distinctly if it were not for the strong
> impact that emanated both from his playing and his personality. . . . Indeed, he
> struck me as being utterly detached from anything that has to do with outward
> appearances.[46]

Another report offers a more detailed description of Bartók at the keyboard:

> His piano playing was concentrated and precise, without unnecessary flourishes.
> His posture and playing apparatus were as one with the piano. Every tone or note
> was concentrated essence. He had emotion but it never penetrated his concen-
> tration in performance. This resulted in his playing looking like it was made out of
> one piece of stone, with dimensions and purity characteristic and convincing only
> for him, no one else.[47]

Concerning Bartók's piano touch, the divergence of published opinion in-
vites examination of the available data. On the one hand, he is described as a
pianist whose special quality was the possession of a rich, precise tone with a
range of shades of color comparable to that of Walter Gieseking or Alexander
Borovsky.[48] One of Bartók's last pupils describes Bartók's touch as

> Dry and crisp when the music called for such tone, that is, in certain staccato
> passages. But Bartók could—and did—produce a warm, luscious tone when he
> wished to . . . he could produce more varieties of tone at the piano than any physi-
> cist would consider possible.[49]

In György Sandor's opinion, "Bartók played Debussy richly and variedly. His playing was plastic and he did not use the pedal to cover up. This would appear to refute statements to the effect that his sound was dry and percussive."[50] The tendency to classify Bartók's piano playing as percussive, in toto, may have been engendered by the composer's utilization of the touch as an innovation in his piano works, resulting in widespread published opinion by musicians concerned with the analysis of his style.[51]

Aaron Copland cites Bartók as a composer who found a valuable outlet in the new use of the piano as a nonvibrating instrument, turning it into "a kind or large xylophone."[52] William Murdoch concedes that Bartók "is one composer who is striking a new sound," but argues that "it is not the result of a new piano technique: Bartók's percussive style is just a higher development of another instrument—the cimbalom. To realize his self-expression he uses the cimbalom as the background of his writings—and naturally the piano is only thought of as an instrument to be hit."[53] Asked for his comment, Tibor Serly—whose friendship with the composer began in 1927—stated that:

> Bartók wanted to be known as a good pianist. People misunderstood what he was doing pianistically. He deplored the fact that the piano had become an arpeggio instrument. He evolved a new technique for the piano as he did for the strings, which served as a basis for his piano compositions: he saw in the piano a new art of playing the instrument as a percussion instrument as well as a musical one.[54]

2

Bartók as Teacher

For almost a half-century, from 1897 to 1945, Béla Bartók was a piano teacher, with more than twenty-five of those years as Professor of Piano at the Academy of Music in Budapest. His teaching experiences were many and varied; in fact, they also included the instruction of private piano students of different degrees of skill and advancement (including several beginners); the editing of a substantial amount of piano music that became standard pedagogical editions in Hungary; the composition of pedagogical works for the piano, including the writing of a piano school for beginners; and the presentation of lecture recitals on the teaching of contemporary music.

Bartók's pedagogical approach assigned greater value to musicianship than technique, for he conceived of the latter as the means rather than the end in piano playing. A second fundamental principle was the extension of his philosophy of performance to his teaching: to follow the intention of the composer as expressed in the written score. A third precept was preliminary preparation and subsequent demonstration of the pieces his pupils selected, a procedure he consistently followed with patience and seeming tirelessness until he was satisfied that his pupils understood the musical problems involved.

Tutorial and Editorial Activities

It appears that Bartók was already giving piano lessons at the age of seventeen and that he used the money earned to buy scores for study purposes.[1] A year later, in September 1899, he entered the Academy of Music in Budapest as a student of piano and composition and he gave private piano lessons in order to augment the funds he received from his mother for food and lodging. He soon discovered the financial problems that seem to befall the neophyte private piano teacher:

> The young lady has stopped her lessons for the present, because her piano needs tuning. After that she wants to go on—if it really comes to anything. In that case, I shall ask one and a half florins and give only two lessons. If that does not suit,

then she can do what she likes. The bore is that she has not paid what is owing. Last Friday I found I was without funds and decided I would not wait but demand. On Saturday I tried to get the money, so far no success. Here in my lodgings I drum my fingers; how monstrous of her not to send the money when I am without it. If two florins come today, perhaps the rest will follow in three days.[2]

When in 1907 Bartók joined the piano faculty of the Budapest Academy of Music, he gave individual as well as group instruction. In addition, he gave private lessons at his lodgings or, if it was more to his convenience, at the pupil's home.[3] Some pupils studied with Bartók privately in addition to the instruction they received from him at the academy.[4]

Bartók edited a substantial amount of keyboard music in the years following his academy appointment: Purcell, Couperin, J. S. Bach, D. Scarlatti, F. J. Haydn, Mozart, Beethoven, Chopin, Mendelssohn, Mozart, Schubert, Schumann, and transcriptions of Italian cembalo and organ works of the seventeenth and eighteenth centuries.[5] Most of this music became the standard pedagogical editions in Hungary and the basis for piano study within the Academy of Music.[6]

Pedagogical Works

Although Bartók's private and academy teaching was, according to first witness reports, limited to the instruction of advanced pianists who were preparing for concert or teaching careers, he was apparently much concerned with the musical and technical training of beginning pianists. Indeed, evidence of this concern is manifest in the number of works he composed with pedagogical purposes in mind.

In 1908 Bartók composed the first of such works, the Ten Easy Pieces for Piano.

The Ten Easy Pieces—with a *'Dedication'* as an eleventh—are a complement of the [Fourteen] Bagatelles. They were written with a pedagogical purpose, that is, to supply piano students with easy contemporary pieces. This accounts for the still more simplified means used in them.[7]

From 1908 to 1909 he worked on a collection of eighty-five piano pieces, titled *For Children*, which were based on Hungarian and Slovakian folk music. In his lecture notes, Bartók explains his purpose in composing this work:

Already at the very beginning of my career as a composer I had the idea to write some easy works for piano students. This idea originated in my experience as a piano teacher; I had always the feeling that the available material for beginners has no real musical value, with the exception of very few works—for instance, Bach's easiest pieces and Schumann's *Jugendalbum*. I thought these works to be insufficient, and so, more than thirty years ago, I myself tried to write some easy piano pieces. At that time the best thing to do would be to use folk tunes. Folk-

> melodies, in general, have great musical value; so, at least the thematical value would be secured.[8]

Bartók collaborated with an Academy colleague, Sándor Reschofsky, in the writing of *Zongora Iskola* (Piano School) in 1913. This work, a manual for teachers of beginning piano students, was written at the request of Rózsavölgyi, the Budapest publisher. The company wanted Bartók to write a series of methods from the beginning of piano study to the highest or virtuoso degree. Bartók's agreement was predicated on the condition that Reschofsky would serve as co-editor.

> The idea was to write first a School, then divide the material between us two and work separately under mutual supervision. So for the second year Bartók selected easy pieces by Bach,[9] whereas I wrote technical exercises and selected easy pieces by different composers.[10]

During the First World War, Reschofsky was in England and Bartók in Hungary, a circumstance which interrupted the work. After the war ended, the publishers were not interested in continuing the series nor were the collaborators inclined to complete them.[11] It should be noted, moreover, that Bartók as well as Reschofsky had planned the outline of *Zongora Iskola,* and that the objectives did not reach their final form until there had been a substantial number of discussions concerning methodology.[12] Thereafter, as a result of these conferences, Reschofsky wrote most of the exercises and Bartók composed those pieces illustrating technical problems.[13] In 1929, without informing his collaborator, Bartók selected eighteen of the pieces from the method and published them under the title of The First Term at the Piano.[14] Bartók's third and last pedagogical work for the piano was the *Mikrokosmos*, composed from 1926 to 1939.

In 1934, Bartók was granted a leave of absence from his teaching duties at the Academy of Music and became a working member of the Hungarian Academy of Sciences where he devoted full time to folk music studies.[15] He continued to give private lessons to a few students from 1934 to 1939 in Budapest and thereafter in the United States.

Beginning in December 1940, Bartók gave lecture-recitals on the teaching of contemporary piano music at a number of American colleges and universities, and he illustrated his talks with pieces from *For Children*, *Mikrokosmos,* and other Bartók works.[16]

Bartók's last piano lesson was given in 1945, the year of his death. It seems that Agnes Butcher[17] visited Bartók during Easter of that year, traveling from Canada to New York City with the intention of resuming her studies with him. She found him sick in bed and sad that he could not give her a lesson that day. Bartók happily accepted her suggestion that she would play some Bach and Mozart music on the piano in the next room and that if he wanted to make any

corrections he should signal for her to return to the sickroom by striking his
water glass with a spoon.

> I had the idea that I played like an angel but it was a good joke for him to hit the
> glass so that I ran back and forth. Finally, I became quite upset and unhappy, for it
> is not easy to stop, especially in the Mozart, and start it again, and in the meantime
> jump between the piano and the sickroom. Of course, Bartók knew it too. I took it
> very seriously, which is what he wanted, for he enjoyed the practical joke.[18]

Principles of Piano Teaching

It has been stated that Bartók was most effective in directing the musical
aims and ideals of his pupils due to the absolutely musical foundation he gave
them in that he taught music first and the instrument second.[19] Bartók believed
that musicianship preceded and formed the foundation for performance at the
piano. For example, when Peter Bartók began the study of the piano under his
father's tutelage, he was not permitted to touch the piano for about six months.[20]
He sang intervals and folk songs, practiced the writing of notes and transpositions, and studied the musical signs and their meanings. When he asked his
father why it had been necessary to undertake that preliminary musical instruction the elder Bartók replied, "one cannot be a pianist without being a musician."[21]

An early example of Bartók's emphasis on musicianship can be found in
Zongora Iskola, in which the teaching of pitch discrimination, rhythm, and other
aspects of notation through singing exercises precedes technical instruction.[22] It
is perhaps worthy of mention that Bartók's concept of "musicianship first and
the instrument second" is also one of Jaques-Dalcroze's theories which the latter advanced in an essay written about the time Bartók was working on *Zongora
Iskola* (hereafter cited as Piano School). Jaques-Dalcroze attacks the system of
instruction which emphasizes finger exercises as the basis for piano study and
states that such activity "makes a *pianist* not a musician—nothing is developed
except the fingers,"[23] and he recommends that ear training and rhythmic movement should precede piano lessons.[24]

As additional evidence of Bartók's concern with musicianship as a foundation for piano study, the recollection of Andor Földes is that Bartók insisted that
his students should thoroughly analyze their pieces from every point of view.[25]
Dorothy Parrish stressed that her major achievement as a Bartók pupil was the
acquisition of a concept of form and architecture in music.[26] During July 1944,
while Bartók was discussing the pedagogy of the *Mikrokosmos* with Ann Chenée,
he mentioned his belief that a background in harmony and musicianship was
essential to piano playing.[27] Another Bartók pupil stated that:

> No detail escaped notice, from mechanical matters of fingering to the most ex-
> quisite particulars of phrasing and tone color and, above all, rhythm. After study-

ing Bach with him and hearing him play the Suites and Partitas, all other Bach playing sounds dull and lifeless to me.[28]

Principles of Piano Technique

The Bartók-Reschofsky Piano School, Bartók's editions of Bach and Beethoven keyboard works, and the statements of Bartók's pupils provide most of the technical and theoretical description and instruction not incorporated in the *Mikrokosmos*. In fact, the above-mentioned publications, by their agreement in terms of symbolic representation of the various touch-forms of piano technique, provide the evidence concerning the basic way the piano is to be played: by finger-key striking—the so-called percussive touch. This keyboard approach, explored and illustrated below, is one of the essential guiding principles that govern the study and performance of the *Mikrokosmos*.

When István Thomán's illness forced his retirement from the Academy of Music in 1907, Bartók was appointed as his successor. Twenty years later he published an essay in honor of Thomán's fortieth jubilee celebration of his artistic career.[29]

> I must have been a real "savage" as a pianist when I first came to Thomán. My technique was good enough, but thoroughly crude. Thomán taught me the correct position of the hands and all the different "natural" and "summarizing" movements which the newer pedagogy has since made into a truly theoretical system and which, however, Liszt had already applied instinctively and Thomán, a former pupil of Liszt, could acquire directly from his great master. Thus, the most initiated hands imparted to me the mastery of poetically coloring the piano tone.[30]

At the turn of the century, when Bartók began his piano studies, the most famous pedagogue was the Viennese composer-pianist Theodor Leschetizky (1830–1915). His method of playing attracted an international group of outstanding pupils, including his teaching assistant, Edwin Hughes (1884–1965) who recalled that:

> One day [Leschetizky] suddenly struck the top of the piano with his fingers, at the same time moving his wrist flexibly up and down, and said, "You see? This is all there is to the so-called Leschetizky method!" The touch of his fingers on the wood sounded like a sharp little crack, while in the wrist and arm there was controlled resiliency. This use of the fingers, hands, and arms was, indeed, an important means of securing technical freedom, but it was by no means the only secret of his teaching.[31]

A different method, the so-called Matthay System, was promulgated in 1900 by the eminent English pianist and pedagogue, Tobias Matthay (1858–1945), at his internationally famous piano school in London, where the emphasis was on tone production by means of nonpercussive finger-key descent. It was not until

1903, however, that Matthay's first publication, *The Act of Touch*, appeared.[32]

The first scientific studies of the effect of touch on the piano key and the piano tone were the experiments of Otto Ortmann (1889–1979).[33] His measuring apparatus revealed that percussion and intensity are the only determinants of piano tone-quality: undesirable sound quality results from (a) excessive percussiveness (the presence of noise elements) and (b) a minimum of tonal value (failure to depress the key with sufficient speed to produce a tone of moderate intensity).[34] In other words, color in the piano tone complex results from the presence of tonal elements. Conversely, color is obscured by the predominance of noise elements: the impact of finger against key and its bed, hammer against string and its check, and (to a lesser degree) friction among action parts.[35]

Thus, by way of summary and in accordance with Ortmann's findings, it seems reasonable to conclude that the Leschetizky method reflects a percussive touch, the Matthay System a nonpercussive one, and Liszt's approach apparently was based on percussive touch but alternated with nonpercussive touchforms to "poetically color" the piano tone. And Bartók as a Lisztian adherent can be traced to his experimental First Bagatelle op 6, for Piano, written in May 1908 (Ex. 2.1).

In these [Bagatelles], a new piano style appears . . . stripped of all unessential elements, deliberately using only the most restricted technical means. As later developments show, the Bagatelles inaugurate a new trend of piano writing in my career, which is consistently followed in almost all of my successive piano works, with more or less modifications . . . accentuating the percussive character of the piano . . . especially in the *Mikrokosmos* pieces [which] appear as a synthesis of all technical and musical problems.[36]

Ex. 2.1. Bartók, First Bagatelle op 6, for Piano, mm. 1–4. Note the use of dotted-tenuto touch in the second and fourth bars of the L.H.

3

Background and Development of the *Mikrokosmos*

Bartók's resumption of his concert career in the 1920s, expanded to an international scale, apparently was the cause of his increased activity in the composition of piano music. In fact, 1926 was the year in which he wrote the Concerto No. 1 for Piano and Orchestra, Sonata for Piano, *Out of Doors* for Piano, Nine Little Piano Pieces, and began the collection of piano pieces eventually called *Mikrokosmos*.[1]

Verification of 1926 as the year in which the *Mikrokosmos* originated can be found in two documents containing Bartók's handwriting. One, an offprint from Denijs Dille's biography of the composer, has Bartók's additions and corrections to what is apparently the first published chronological catalogue of his works in which the *Mikrokosmos* is listed.[2] The other, titled "List of all noticed errors in piano score of Violin Concerto," is in part a request from Bartók to his publisher (Boosey and Hawkes, London) to change the entry concerning the *Mikrokosmos* (printed on the back cover page of the Concerto) as follows:

> piano solo . . . last item: omit (1940), or substitute (1926-1939) for it.[3]

Which one of the 153 pieces comprising the *Mikrokosmos* was composed first is a matter of conjecture; the evidence, however, indicates "Unison" (No. 137)—and this can be conclusively attributed to having been composed in 1926. Bartók catalogued most of his manuscripts numerically, assigning the number 32 (printed with green crayon on the title page) to a thirty-one page manuscript containing sketches and second (intermediary) drafts of Nine Little Piano Pieces, incomplete sketches of unidentified piano music, and one sketch each from *Out of Doors* for Piano, First Piano Concerto, and *Mikrokosmos*.[4] The original title on the cover page was written in pencil: *kis zongoradarabok* (little piano pieces) and above it, in bright blue ink, the following:

> 9 Kleine Klavierstücke (Skizzen) (einige Skizzen zu "Mikrokosmos" "Im Freien" I. Klavierkonzert)

The entire manuscript was neatly written first in blue-black ink with a narrow pen and later corrected in pencil. Page 25 contains a continuation of the

"Second Dialogue" (Nine Little Piano Pieces No. 2) on the first four staves. The remainder of the page consists of a sketch of "Unison" (*Mikrokosmos* No. 137) completed in two operations: first, an outline of the piece was written in the same color ink and the identical penmanship as that of the other pieces comprising the complete manuscript; then corrections, additions, and extensions were made in blue ink with a broad pen, and with an autography considerably less neat in appearance. In fact, the revisions of "Unison" are identical in terms of ink, pen, and handwriting to those sketches contained in Bartók's MS 49 (*Mikrokosmos Klavierstücke, Brouillon*), which represent the first drafts of *Mikrokosmos*.

It seems likely that Bartók composed the preliminary (then unfinished) sketch to "Unison" as part of a collection of piano pieces intended for publication in 1926. For one reason or another, perhaps because of his preoccupation with the composition of *Out of Doors* or the First Piano Concerto that same year, he decided to submit for publication under the title of Nine Little Piano Pieces those sketches he had completed,[5] and he returned to the manuscript at a later date to finish the sketch to "Unison." Incidentally, this piece is not included in Bartók's MS 49.

With regard to Bartók's conception of *Mikrokosmos* as a title, perhaps its origin resides in Goethe's *Faust*, where Mephistopheles (the devil) tells Dr. Faust (the erring seeker) that:

> If there were such a man, I'd like to meet him,
> As Herrn Mikrokosmus I would greet him.[6]

The idea of the *Mikrokosmos* as a collection of pieces with a pedagogical purpose may have been prompted by a somewhat similar compilation that appeared in the 1930s.

> I possess no letter from Bartók myself on the subject of "Mikrokosmos," but I feel myself connected with this work in a small way of which I am rather proud. In 1933 I wrote a series of short piano pieces which were published by Schott, Mainz, under the title "Rhythmic Studies." The pieces dealt with various rhythmical problems like "Syncopation," "Shifting of Accents," Cross-Rhythms," etc., and were mainly devised for teaching purposes. As usual, after publication I sent a copy of it to Bartók, together with my "Easy Dances," published shortly before. Years later when I met Bartók again (I think it must have been in London in 1938) I asked him what he thought of my Rhythmic Studies. He congratulated me warmly, saying what excellent teaching material they were, then continued: "In fact, I took up your idea and expanded it further: I am now working on a series of piano pieces which deal not only with the rhythmic, but also with melodic, harmonic and pianistic problems." This series was to become the *Mikrokosmos*.[7]

According to Peter Bartók, his father's first reference to the title *Mikrokosmos* and first assertion that the collection of pieces under that name constituted a piano method was made in 1936.

I served as a "guinea pig" in my father's experiments with the *Mikrokosmos* in 1936, the first year I began piano study; in fact, he wrote the pieces faster than I could learn them. Then he composed the *Mikrokosmos* independent of any consideration of its suitability for me . . . the ink hardly dried on some when I started practicing them.[8]

A former Bartók colleague on the piano faculty at the Budapest Academy of Music disclosed that the composer asked for her assistance in the preparation of certain volumes of the *Mikrokosmos.*

Since he had never taught beginners himself, the composer honored me repeatedly by asking for my suggestions concerning the musical and technical problems to be solved in the early grades. While we discussed sundry details of the pieces included in the first three volumes, what struck me most was not the systematic way in which he reached the solution of each problem, but his keen sense of responsibility towards the pupil whose progress he wanted to serve.[9]

On 9 February 1937, Bartók played the first performance of pieces from the *Mikrokosmos* at Cowdray Hall, London, and accompanied the violinist Zoltán Székely in the composer's Sonata No. 2 for Violin and Piano and the Rhapsody No. 2 for Violin and Piano.[10] He wrote to Székely less than a month before the concert: "A program loquacious enough! But at least these many flea-pieces are all 'manuscript'"[11]

A few days after the German occupation of Vienna in 1938, Ralph Hawkes flew to Budapest and met with Bartók.

There was certainly no reticence on Bartók's part in agreeing to publish all his future works with us (Boosey and Hawkes). He had several manuscripts in preparation, such as the Sonata for Two Pianos and Percussion and *Mikrokosmos,* which were partly done.[12]

The correspondence between Bartók and Boosey and Hawkes, Ltd., mainly postmarked Budapest and London, respectively, includes more than 200 letters and other documents related to the preparation of the *Mikrokosmos* for publication.[13] The interchange of letters begins with an invitation from Hawkes to Bartók for the latter to appear at one of "the intimate little Concerts we give in our Organ Studio here in London."[14] Bartók's reply states, "Of course I am with pleasure at your disposal and would play at your concert some of my piano pieces from 'Mikrokosmos'.[15] Less than a week later Bartók sent the following program to Hawkes:

From "Mikrokosmos" (piano pieces): Tale;/ Wrestling;/ Major seconds broken and together;/ Minor and Major;/ Theme and inversion;/ Boating;/ Burlesque rustique;/ Chords of the Fifth;/ From the Isle Bali;/ Merry Andrew;/ Five dances in "Bulgarian" rhythm. This takes approximately 20 minutes.[16]

The publisher's answer to the foregoing letter informs Bartók that the concert would be given at five o'clock in the afternoon on 20 June 1938.[17] In what seems to be an office memorandum, the following statement appears: "Among his new works, the Studies for Piano 'Microcosmos' would be the most important for us."[18]

No further reference to the *Mikrokosmos* is made in the correspondence until early in 1939, the year in which Universal-Edition released Bartók from his publishing agreement with them. On 6 March, Hawkes wrote to Bartók that he was ready to publish all the new works the composer had ready.

> Mrs. Hertzke, who called to see me the other day, tells me that you have a School for Piano in preparation. This work will, of course, be very interesting indeed but I do not recall that you told me anything about it when I had lunch with you.

Bartók's reply, sent from Basel on 9 March, states:

> That piano-school is nothing else than first part of the "Mikrokosmos"! In fact, it will be something like a school, with exercises, progressive order of the (very easy and easy) pieces. If you prefer to have it more similar to a School, I could add to it some changements.

The publisher then informed Bartók that "a strict Piano School in such a form" was not actually wanted, the former wished to go ahead with the publication and not wait for the "absolute completion" of the composer's idea, and individual pieces from the *Mikrokosmos* could be incorporated into a school at a later date.[19]

It seems likely that at this time Bartók discarded any ideas he might have had concerning the publication of the *Mikrokosmos* as piano pieces, per se, according to the following letter mailed from Budapest:

> Mikrokosmos. It is absolutely important to add still 20 or 30 very small and very easy pieces, to write them will not take much time. Besides, I want to transcribe most of the easier pieces for 4 hands, and to insert before some of the (easier) pieces presenting a new technical problem, a respective study (Fingerübung)—all that for pedagogical reasons.[20]

The letter continues with a suggestion that certain pieces could be published with pictures "only if the pictures are very good and original" (such as that of a web in No. 142, *From the Diary of a Fly*). Hawkes agreed with Bartók's proposals, particularly with reference to the use of sketches in illustration of the *Mikrokosmos,* voiced the opinion that publication might be possible in the early part of 1940, and suggested that if Bartók could not secure the services of an artist in Budapest he should come to London and confer with one there.[21]

The correspondence continues with Bartók's suggestion that the publisher should the choose the artist, since the composer would not be able to travel to

London until November or December. Then, on 17 June, he wrote that he was sending the *Mikrokosmos* pieces whose order was "more or less pêle-mêle (given by haphazard)."

> The definitive order will be according to difficulty. My idea is to have them published in three volumes (you must not forget, there will be some 30 or 40 more of them!): I. the easiest pieces (intended for the 1. and 2. year), II. the less easier pieces, III. the more difficult ones. The I. volume should be printed in bigger characters (this is better for beginners) than the II. and III.[22]

Following receipt of the shipment, Hawkes engaged the services of an artist and sent several sketches to Bartók for approval. But the composer found them to be unsuitable for children and suggested that they should be redrawn. In the same letter he adds, "As for a new work, you know I want to score some of the Mikrokosmos pieces. . . . I hope this will be ready perhaps end of Oct."[23] Hawkes assured Bartók that the sketches would be improved and suggested that there should be a preface of some kind in each of the four volumes planned for publication which would explain the various pieces and give an indication of the whole series. He enclosed the draft of an essay, intended as a pamphlet to be issued with the works when they are published, and asked for Bartók's approval.[24]

On 2 November 1939, Bartók informed Hawkes that the *Mikrokosmos,* consisting of 153 pieces, was ready except for the preface and the "foot-notes" to some of the pieces.[25] Three weeks later, Hawkes reported that he had received the complete *Mikrokosmos* manuscript and that he would write again within a few days concerning the progress made towards its publication. It was not until 9 December, however, that a rather lengthy letter was mailed to Bartók which suggested that the sketches planned as illustrations for certain pieces should be eliminated, and that sales factors might require division of the first volume— containing sixty-six pieces—into two parts, resulting in the publication of six volumes. It was also noted that the composer's preface did not give sufficient information or detail.

> and will be what we call "sales resisting," unless it is done in a much more simple and easy manner. . . . I am proposing to send you a revised preface at an early date which I think will meet this purpose." [26]

Bartók's letter of 18 December accepted Hawkes's proposals and included corrections to a number of pieces. Because of the publisher's decision to use English, French, and German designations for the title of each piece, Bartók was concerned about his insertion of Hungarian comments in the score of No. 142 ("From the Diary of a Fly").

> No.142: "jaj, pókháló!" means "Woe, a cobweb!" I wanted to depict the desperate sound of a fly's buzz when getting into a cobweb. Now, I don't know, if we use three languages for this explanation, the joke will be spoilt. Will you kindly decide, what to do here. We may leave out these words.[27]

In view of Ralph Hawkes' imminent visit to the United States for a stay of three or more months, he informed Bartók that future production problems concerning the *Mikrokosmos* publication would be assumed by Ernst Roth. The latter's first letter to Bartók, dated 2 January 1940, concerned the problem of a suitable subtitle for the cover page, such as:

> "Progressive Pieces for Piano" or, what sounds very good in English, "Progressive Piano Pieces in Modern Idiom" or something of this kind. As far as the Preface is concerned, we added a paragraph emphasizing that particular aim of your work. You might alter or rewrite it on similar lines.[28]

Bartók accepted the subtitle "Progressive Pieces for Piano" but voiced his disapproval in no uncertain terms concerning the use of the word "modernity" in the paragraph that had been written by the company and inserted in his original preface to the *Mikrokosmos*.

> 2. In the English and French Preface, I have some slight remarks. But as for those parts about the "modernity" inserted by you, that is quite impossible to publish it in a Preface, signed by my name, where I am speaking, and giving hints and winks in my own name. I would never do that: to make excuses for the "modernity" etc.; besides I don't like the word "modern" at all! Think of it: in 20, or let us say in 40 years this work will cease to be "modern." And what does it mean "modern"? This word has no definite sens [sic], can be misinterpreted, misunderstood![29]

Bartók's original plan to publish the first sixty-six pieces in one volume was rejected by the publisher. The reason: it would be more practical in terms of a lower selling price per volume if the pieces were assembled into two books. Bartók could not understand why the division had to be made, since the proofs of the sixth volume contained almost as many pages (fifty-five) as the sixty-six comprising the first two volumes (including exercises and explanatory notes).

> It is a pity, that this division has been made: now, the first book gives a very poor impression; besides, the contents of those 60 pages are a real unity; they are meant for the first year of piano-studying. Now, every student will have to buy—after a few month's studying, the second book! Could not be changed this disposition?[30]

Roth replied that the first three volumes were to be priced lower than the last three, and he asked Bartók to accept the division. In the meantime, additional proofs were mailed to Budapest as soon as they were engraved, in more or less haphazard order, together with urgent requests that he expedite correction and return of the proofs in the order of their receipt. Finally, production of the *Mikrokosmos* was completed and the work placed on sale during April.[31]

The Manuscripts

When in 1983 I began my tenure as curator of the New York Bartók Archive—an entity of the estate of Béla Bartók—my first task was the identification and assembly of the *Mikrokosmos* manuscripts, then sorting them into three classes: Sketches (abbr. S), Intermediary Drafts (ID), and Final Copies (FC). After similar processing of the other estate holdings, the *Mikrokosmos* materials were assigned the location subset number 59. Comparison of the autographs and publications as well as study of the related correspondence between Bartók and Boosey and Hawkes, including the New York office of the company, not only became an integral part of my doctoral dissertation[32] but disclosed the composer's procedure in the composition, revision, and correction of the *Mikrokosmos* for Piano and the Seven Pieces from *Mikrokosmos* for Two Pianos. Following below are selected data from my research as of 20 August 1956, which should be useful for readers interested in the *Mikrokosmos* primary source material for further investigation.[33]

Sketches. MS 59PS1 consists of eighty-six pages of various sizes and type of staves, written for the most part in faded blue ink, and with many corrections in pencil and red and green crayon.[34] Deletions and insertions, ranging from single notes to whole sections, appear in profusion throughout the manuscript. The scrawly autography seems to indicate a certain amount of feverish activity on the part of the composer to notate his musical ideas as rapidly as possible. Five pieces, all crossed out, and two exercises are contained in this manuscript which do not appear in the published volumes of the *Mikrokosmos*. And the sketch of "Unison" (No. 137) appears in the MS of Nine Little Piano Pieces.

Intermediary Drafts. MS 59PID1/ID2 has eighty-two pages of so-called transparencies (that is, translucent music MS paper) written in black ink, with some penciled additions. There are a considerable number of deletions and insertions but not to the extent that they appear in the Sketches. On the other hand, the notation here is neat and precise. Titles are in Hungarian and German for the most part (some are in English), and almost all of the pieces contain timings, expression marks, and metronomic indications. There are twenty-two pieces marked with the numeric designations assigned to them in the published copies. However, these numbers were probably added after the final copies had been drafted, since the designation of "Thumb Under" as No. 98 appears on a transparency but not on its proof (that is, photographic reproduction).

Although this manuscript seems to represent a second draft, several pieces appear in more than one version.[35] For example, a preliminary draft of No. 46 is notated with the melody beginning with the right hand instead of the left one; 51 and 88 appear also in transpositions down a minor third and up a perfect fifth, respectively; and there are additional, incomplete versions of 111 and 142. An interesting supplement to 145 consists of two variants which do not appear in the published version. The first variant is in retrograde motion and transposed down a major third. The second variant is a melodic inversion. No. 147 appears also in a simplified form, without octaves and hand crossings. And one of the cancelled pieces of the sketch draft also appears here but it, too, is crossed out.

Final Copies.[36] MS 59PFC1 has twenty-two pages of MS paper written in blue ink and fifty-six pages of transparency proofs with Bartók's corrections. MS 59PFC2 was assembled from Bartók's corrected copy of the third and sixth volumes of the publication. MS 59PFC3 consists of Bartók's corrected set of transparency proofs.[37] MS 59PFC4, prepared for the engraver, has a cover folio for each of the six volumes. Bartók, working with another set of transparency proofs, cut apart and then reassembled the individual melodies in their final order (Nos. 1–153). The MS also includes the Notes to the Melodies, Song Texts, and the typescript text of the Hungarian and German versions of the preface, all corrected by Bartók in blue ink.

Bartók's Recitals and Recordings

This section documents the frequency of occurrence and other details of specific *Mikrokosmos* pieces played by the composer. The data also should be useful for programming purposes.[38]

Beginning with Bartók's first performance of the work on 9 February 1937 in London, he played twenty-seven pieces which were divided into two groups and in the following order: Nos. 70, 81, 90, 78, 100, 62, 87, 84, 110, 91, 92, 73, 129, 131, 116, 124, and 122 (9 minutes and 39 seconds) and, after the intermission, 133, 126, 140, 142, 143, 147, 144, 145, 137, and 146 (10 minutes and 30 seconds).[39] Again in London, this time for a BBC broadcast on 20 January 1938, he played the following pieces in three groups: (1) Nos. 125, 88, 130, 138, 120, 109, and 139 (8 minutes and 30 seconds); (2) 53, 106, 94, 108, 132, 103, 114, and 123 (8 minutes and 15 seconds); and (3) 148–153 (8 minutes and 48 seconds). On 17 February he was in Zurich for a performance of Nos. 140, 142, 144, 137, and 146, and June he returned to London for a recital at the Boosey and Hawkes Organ Studio, where he played Nos. 94, 108, 132, 103, 114, 125, 130, 120, 109, 139, and 148–153 ("This takes about 20 minutes").[40]

The first American performance was given by Bartók on 16 April 1940, at Juniata College, Huntington, Pennsylvania. He played two groups of pieces: (1) Nos. 116, 129, 131, 68, 126, 102, 113, and 115; (2) 140, 142, 144, 137, 133, 138, 109, and 148–153. Bartók returned to Hungary on 18 May, to settle his affairs before establishing residence in the United States. His farewell concert in Budapest on 8 October included five pieces from the *Mikrokosmos*: Nos. 141, 128, 126, 102, and 148-153. After his return to New York on 30 October, his preparations for the 1940–1941 concert season also included a lecture-recital on "Contemporary Music and Piano Teaching."[41] The featured *Mikrokosmos* pieces were Nos. 40–42, 52–53, 62, 68–69, 73, 78, 82, 84, 87, 94, and 90–92.[42]

The regular concert programs, for the most part given at colleges and universities, included the following *Mikrokosmos* pieces: Nos. 122, 128, 126, 102, and 148–153.[43] or 140, 142, 144, 137, and 136,[44] and other recitals combined those groups.[45] In 1938, Bartók recorded *Mikrokosmos* Nos. 124 and 126 for

British Columbia; in 1941: Nos. 94, 97, 100, 108–109, 113–114, 116, 118, 120, 125–26, 128–131, 133, 136, 138–144, and 147–153 for Columbia (American) Records.[46]

PART TWO

Pedagogy

4

Technique and Musicianship

It has been stated by several sources that no music is liable to lose so much as Béla Bartók's at the hands of executants; indeed, that the performer, no matter how technically skilled, must be in sympathy with and have an insight into Bartók's intentions.

But what were Bartók's intentions, particularly with reference to his piano works? Among the published sources are his lecture notes on piano playing, edited piano works from the standard repertory, *Mikrokosmos* preface and notes, the Bartók-Reschofsky piano method, and the recollections of his piano students. These diverse source indicate that he was familiar with educational theory and trends in piano teaching, followed certain principles in his role as music educator, and had definite ideas about the way the piano should be played.

The Mikrokosmos *and General Educational Theory*

Bartók was quite aware of individual differences among piano pupils. For example, in the preface to *Mikrokosmos* he refers to "gifted" and "less gifted" pupils. In other sources he refers learners as "average," "unusual," and "the pupil who has great control." With regard to meeting individual needs in performing *Mikrokosmos* pieces, Bartók recommends the following procedures: (a) the order of pieces may be altered in accordance with the ability of the pupil, (b) certain pieces may be played faster or slower than indicated, (c) teacher and pupil have the opportunity of making choices, since there are a number of pieces that deal with the same problem, (d) the teacher should invent exercises for the pupil as well as "present pieces in any way that seems best to the student's needs."

An indication of the composer's desire to stimulate pupil interest in the *Mikrokosmos* can be seen in those pieces which contain attractive titles, such as: "Boating," "Dragons' Dance," "Wrestling," "From the Island of Bali," and so forth. Bartók believed that certain pieces were interesting because of their unusual rhythmic patterns, changes of time or of tempo, hand crossings, colorful tonality, use of the pedal, or irregularity of phrase structure.

The satisfaction that comes with success is of the great importance in arousing readiness toward piano playing. The first three volumes of the *Mikrokosmos* apparently have been compiled with that thought in mind, for they are comprised of short pieces (many of them sixteen measures or less), written within a five-finger range, that are arranged in graded order according to difficulty. And there are equally brief preparatory exercises to a third of the pieces.

The Mikrokosmos *and Trends in Piano Teaching*

In the *Mikrokosmos* preface, Bartók asserts that "Instrumental tuition should be developed from suitable singing exercises." This approach, one of the fundamental concepts of Jaques-Dalcroze, Zoltán Kodály, and elementary school music education, is developed by the inclusion of pieces for voice and piano to be sung and self-accompanied by the pupil.

Another important element in piano playing is the ability to play as freely in one key as in another. In accordance with this principle, Bartók recommends the transposition of the easier pieces and exercises into other keys. Furthermore, the *Mikrokosmos* pieces are written in a variety of keys which place greater emphasis on the folk modes and nondiatonic scales rather than the Western major-minor tonal system.

Bartók also understood the value of creative expression as a means of stimulating pupil interest and encouraging good practice habits. He suggests that the pupil should transcribe suitable pieces from the first three volumes for two pianos, and he states that many opportunities are given for original and inventive work in terms of simplification of accompaniments and "other developments."

Finally, the *Mikrokosmos* exemplifies the approach to music theory through keyboard practice. The fundamentals of musicianship are introduced one by one in the interesting materials at hand to such an extent that the use of the *Mikrokosmos* as part of the lesson plan may eliminate or supplement the need for separate elementary theory classes.

Bartók's Pedagogical Approach

Throughout his teaching career Béla Bartók believed that musicianship preceded and formed the foundation for performance at the piano. In fact, he said that "One cannot be a pianist without being a musician." It should not be inferred that Bartók was not concerned with technical development; indeed, in the preface to *Mikrokosmos* he suggests "the appropriate studies by Czerny, etc." But he assigned greater value to musicianship, for he conceived of technique as the means, rather than the end, in piano playing.

Bartók extended his philosophy of performance to his teaching: to follow the intention of the composer as expressed in the written score. His attention was directed also to the smallest of details, and he did not permit deviations unless they could be justified by the pupil.

A second fundamental principle was his personal preparation of each piece undertaken by the pupil, in order to demonstrate at the piano his suggested approach to solving particular problems. Moreover, with patience and seeming tirelessness, he would repeatedly play specific passages until the pupil clearly understood the needed corrections.

Bartók's Ideas Concerning Piano Playing

Bartók's conception of the piano was in terms of its being an instrument capable of producing sounds, ranging from the most to the least percussive in quality, and he specified key-striking, the so-called percussive touch as the basic way the piano is to be played. In fact, it is only in terms of percussive finger-stroke as the fundamental approach to key depression that the symbols Bartók uses in the *Mikrokosmos* take on their full meaning. For example, pianists usually interpret the tenuto sign (–) as a dynamic accent of weak intensity or as an indication that a note should be held for its full value. Bartók, however, adds a third meaning: "To such notes a certain color shading must be added by pressing the key instead of striking it."[1]

The various touch-forms used in the *Mikrokosmos* are illustrated in Example 4.1, and further explicated below as described by Bartók in his other pedagogical works and editions for the piano.

Ex. 4.1. Symbolic representations of touch-forms.

Percussive Touch-Forms[2]

Staccatissimo (▾▾) is an increased staccato in which the tone becomes the shortest possible.

Staccato (. . .) means that the sounding of the note ranges from the shortest in value to one-half the value of the note.

Non-legato is played when no other touch-form designations appear in the music, so that the gap between two tones is imperceptibly small.

Legato is indicated by the use of curved lines (slur marks) or the sign *legato*.

Legatissimo is an exaggerated legato, when every tone is held over a little into the beginning of the next one. It can be perfected by using the half-pedal and is used at the sign *legatissimo*.

Nonpercussive Touch-Forms[3]

Tenuto (– – –) indicates that its note is to be given full value, particularly when preceded by a staccato note, or it may signify a weak accent. In many other cases, however, it serves as a kind of warning that the note is more important and colorful. Thus, a certain color shading must be added by pressing the key instead of striking it. It is played with weight.

Dotted tenuto means that the notes are never less than one-half their value and that they are to be played with the tenuto touch. Also played with weight.

Portamento is in close connection with dotted tenuto. They have one difference: it is necessary to play portamento lightly (that is, without weight).

Espressivo (with expression) and dolce (with softness) cannot be learned by description. The student can acquire them only if the teacher demonstrates at the piano. The so-called espressivo touch is played with hand motion.

The playing of marcato (>) and sforzato (*sf*) should be carried out by the fingers and should not be perceivable in the hand. In this touch the position of the fingers does not change.

Bartók's Ideas Concerning Musicianship

The composer was careful to indicate in the *Mikrokosmos* exactly how he wanted the work played. In fact, almost all the pieces contain three tempo indications (tempo marks, metronome marks, and time of performance); dynamic markings; explanatory terms; and other symbols to the extent that the work can be considered as a kind of dictionary of music.

In the discussion of Bartók's teaching principles (above), it is indicated that he emphasized truth in interpretation. In accordance with this philosophy, listed below are a number of signs whose meaning may be obscure or open to more than one interpretation, together with Bartók's specific instructions as assembled from his other pedagogical works and editions for the piano.

Dynamics. A dynamic sign is effective until replaced by another. The signs *sf* (sforzato), ʌ (marcatissimo), and > (marcato) are listed in order of diminishing emphasis,[4] and accents within the frame of *p* are weaker than within *f*.

Syncopated notes should be played with some weight and emphasis, and a decrescendo takes place towards the second of two slurred notes.

Rhythm and Tempo. The first part of each measure receives the chief emphasis. Sostenuto indicates a sudden ritardando, and the pause sign ⌢ (fermata) about doubles the value of the note beneath it.

Phrasing. Curved lines (slur marks) are used to indicate legato, and they also mark the phrasing. Legato phrases are not to be separated where the curved lines meet unless they are marked with separating signs. Legato phrases can be emphasized, however, by beginning them with a slight dynamic shading. When two slurs meet at one note, the phrase begins and ends at that note.

The separating sign | (a superscript vertical line) indicates the interruption of legato between phrases. The last note of the phrase preceding this sign should be played staccato or otherwise shortened. The separating sign ' (a superscript comma) also indicates the interruption of legato. In this case, it means a slight, almost unnoticeable pause in which the time of separation is taken equally from the notes preceding and following the comma.

5

Format and Definitions[1]

Of the four major headings used in the description of the pieces, A. Technique and B. Musicianship represent the findings of the author and other analysts of the *Mikrokosmos*; C. Bartók's Comments contains extracts from the preface and notes to *Mikrokosmos* and Bartók's comments on pedagogy and contents of the individual pieces as recorded by Ann Chenée during their discussions in July 1944;[2] and D. Suggestions includes the experiences of the author and other teachers of the *Mikrokosmos*. The categories concerned with technique and musicianship are divided further into appropriate subheads as follows:

A. **Technique**.
1. TOUCH: the various legato touch-forms (legato, legatissimo, espressivo, dolce, and cantabile) and non-legato touch-forms (non-legato, tenuto, dotted tenuto, portamento [or portato], staccato, and staccatissimo).

2. HAND INDEPENDENCE: the dissociate movement or separate function of the hands.
   (a) Counterpoint: the simultaneous playing, between the hands, of two or more independent parts.
   (b) Combined Touch-Forms: playing legato in one hand as the other one plays staccato, etc.
   (c) Dynamic Contrast: playing marcato in one hand as the other one maintains a consistent dynamic level, etc.
   (d) Accompanying Figurations: the playing of ostinato patterns (motives, intervals, chords, or broken chords) in one hand as the other one plays a melody which may or may not require dynamic contrast.

3. FINGER INDEPENDENCE: the simultaneous playing, in one hand, of two independent parts. In the *Mikrokosmos*, this consists for the most part of sustained tones against a moving voice.

4. INTERVAL, CHORD, AND/OR BROKEN CHORD PLAYING: the *Mikrokosmos* contains harmonic intervals up to and including a tenth; triads and their inversions, various types of chords comprised of three or more tones; and arpeggios where none involve passing of the thumb.

5. POSITION: five-finger range; two or more changes of position; the hands one or more octaves apart; interlocking of the hands; and cross ing of the hands in which the right or the left hand crosses over (sopra) or under (sotto).

6. PEDALLING: use of the damper or solo sostenuto pedals as indicated in the *Mikrokosmos*. There is no specific indication in the work for use of the soft pedal.

7. PASSAGE-WORK: scalar-type passages, usually in quick tempo, which may or may not involve passing of the fingers.

8. EMBELLISHMENTS: grace notes, turns, the pralltriller (inverted mordent), fast or slow trills, and fast or slow tremolos (trills comprised of intervals greater than a second).

9. FINGERING PROBLEMS: black key playing (particularly with the first and fifth fingers), "discontinuous" fingerings, replacement of fingers, and so forth.

10. ENSEMBLE PLAYING: vocal or instrumental accompanying and the performance of pieces for two pianos (four hands).

B. **Musicianship**.
   1. NOTATION: note and rest values, clef changes, key signatures, accidentals, pitch names, and various characters used in music notation.
   2. RHYTHM: meter signatures, change of time, noncoinciding or overlapping meters, subdivision of the beat, cross-rhythm (polyrhythm), and syncopation.
   3. EXPRESSION: those fundamentals of musicianship concerned with
      (a) Tempo: metronome marks; tempo changes; and various signs indicating steady, accelerating, or slackening rate of speed.
      (b) Dynamics: accents; symbols (*pp* to *fff*); and various signs which maintain or change levels of intensity.
      (c) Phrasing: regularity or irregularity of phrase structure, certain cadences, and aspects of form (ternary, rondo, and theme and variations).
      (d) Terms: other directions (for example, Ia seconda volta), and character signs with more than one expressive meaning (stringendo).

6

Volume One[1]

Nos. 1–6. Six Unison Melodies.

  A. **Technique.**

    1. TOUCH. Legato.

    2. POSITION. One, the hands an octave or two octaves apart.

  B. **Musicianship.**

    1. NOTATION. Whole, half, and quarter notes. Half and quarter rests. The phrase mark.

    2. RHYTHM. 4/4.

    3. EXPRESSION.

    (a) Phrasing: regular and irregular structure.

  C. **Bartók's Comments.** Melodies are scalewise with consistent note values and five-finger range. Small staves above each piece indicate range of five-finger position. Nos. 1 and 2 are symmetrical or balanced in phrase structure. No. 3 is written in a sort of D minor, beginning on the dominant. No. 4 contains combinations of note values in shorter sentences, beginning on the seventh tone and ending on C. No. 5 is in the natural A minor; it contains a stepwise sequence of asymmetrical phrases. No. 6 begins and ends on the fifth tone, and it introduces the quarter rest.

  D. **Suggestions.** The melodies written two octaves apart should foster good elbow position (check this during the playing of No. 3). In bar 6 of No. 6, do not give the half note less than its full value in anticipation of the quarter rest. Try several transpositions according to Bartók's recommendation in the preface.

No. 7. Dotted Notes.

  A. **Technique.**

    1.TOUCH. Legato.

  B. **Musicianship.**

    1. NOTATION. The dotted half note.

  C. **Bartók's Comments.** This melody is also used in No. 28. Dotted notes in the Phrygian mode. No interruption of legato should take place between legato phrases.

  D. **Suggestions.** In his preface, Bartók refers to young or old beginners and gifted or less gifted pupils. In certain cases, therefore, the teacher may find it

useful to take up the structural similarity—in terms of half and whole steps—
between a C-major pentachord (Nos. 1–2a, 4) and its G-major transposition
(No. 6); between an A-minor pentachord (No. 2b) and its D-minor transposition, (No. 3); and the structural difference between a minor pentachord and a
Phrygian one (No. 7).[2]

No. 8. Repetition (1).

A. **Technique.**
1. TOUCH. Legato, non-legato.
2. FINGERING PROBLEMS. Black key playing.
3. POSITION. Five-note range in two positions.

B. **Musicianship**
1. NOTATION. Key of G.

C. **Bartók's Comments.** In the key signature it is more convenient to put the
sharp on the same space as the note. It is easier to see, too. Combination of rests.
Theme is inverted. Short phrases because of repeated notes.

D. **Suggestions.** First example of change of hand position. A Bartók-devised
key signature which the composer used in his folk music notations. The sharp
sign usually appears on the fifth line of the treble clef. The gap between the
repeated notes should be "hardly perceivable."

No. 9. Syncopation (1).

A. **Technique.**
1. TOUCH. Legato.

B. **Musicianship.**
1. NOTATION. The tie.
2. RHYTHM. Syncopation.

C. **Bartók's Comments.** The rhythmic feeling of the suspensions should be
emphasized by some energetic movement, such as tapping with the foot, nod-
ding the head, or using the voice in the respective places which are marked by
rhythm signatures between the staves. This melody is also used in No. 27.

D. **Suggestions.** Be sure that the half note is given its full value in bar 12, and
note that the phrase markings in bars 8–14 indicate that the third phrase ends
and the last phrase begins on the same tone (G).

No. 10. With Alternate Hands.

A. **Technique.**
1. TOUCH. Legato.
2. FINGERING PROBLEMS. Black key playing.

B. **Musicianship.**
1. NOTATION. Bartók-devised key signature.
2. RHYTHM. 3/4. Syncopation.

C. **Bartók's Comments.** The signature is A♭. Lowered fifth for special color.
Combines past experiences.

D. **Suggestions.** Accent slightly the half notes in bars 18 and 21.

No. 11. Parallel Motion.

A. **Technique.**
　1. TOUCH. Legato.
B. **Musicianship.**
　1. NOTATION. Reading of two voices which proceed in similar motion at the interval of a tenth.
C. **Bartók's Comments.** Mixolydian mode, begins on the second degree [A].
D. **Suggestions.** Do not overlook the contrary motion between bars 14 and 15. The G-Mixolydian mode is a major mode with lowered seventh degree (F♮).

No. 12. Reflection.

A. **Technique.**
　1. TOUCH. Legato.
　2. HAND INDEPENDENCE.
　　(a) Counterpoint.
B. **Musicianship.**
　1. RHYTHM. Change of time: 2/2 and 3/2. Subdivision of the beat into two parts, the half note as the pulse unit.
C. **Bartók's Comments.** Present the time signatures in any way that seems best to the student's needs. Bimodal—contrast of major (R.H.) and minor (L.H.) modes. The left hand reflects the right hand, and the voices move in opposite direction. The structure is more lively due to change of meter.
D. **Suggestions.** The voices move in parallel motion between bars 16 and 17.

No. 13. Change of Position.

A. **Technique.**
　1. TOUCH. Legato.
　2. POSITION. Five-note range in two positions.
B. **Musicianship.**
　1. EXPRESSION.
　　(a) Phrasing: symmetrical phrases in ternary form.
C. **Bartók's Comments.** The same melody is used in No. 17.
D. **Suggestions.** The first and last phrases are identical, and the second phrase is similar (five tones higher) to the first phrase. Mark the phrases A A⁵ B A. Such analysis is valuable in determining identical portions of a composition, thus making for its quicker mastery or easier memorization.

No. 14. Question and Answer.

A. **Technique.**
　1. TOUCH. Legato.
　2. POSITION. Five-note range in three positions.
　3. ENSEMBLE PLAYING. Accompanying techniques.

B. **Musicianship.**
    1. NOTATION. Simultaneous reading of piano score and song text.
C. **Bartók's Comments.** Sing and play the piece. Compare it to speech. In order to emphasize the ability of expression of music—contrary to the opinion of postwar years—interrogatory and answering verses have been put to the respective sections of the melody. It is recommended that the piece be sung by two pupils (or two groups of pupils) alternatively before practicing it.
    D. **Suggestions.** The piece can be performed in a variety of ways: self-accompanied, pupil and teacher can alternate the singing of its phrases, and the teacher can accompany the pupil's singing.

No. 15. Village Song.

A. **Technique.**
    1. TOUCH. Legato.
    2. POSITION. Five-note range in four positions.
    3. FINGERING PROBLEMS. Black key playing.
B. **Musicianship.**
    1. NOTATION. Bartók-devised key signature. Accidentals.
    2. EXPRESSION.
        (a) Phrasing: ternary form.
C. **Bartók's Comments.** First study with a title. It is a sort of G major with altered fourth. A parallel can be found in the "Sarabande" from the First Partita of J. S. Bach. Asymmetrical phrase structure.
    D. **Suggestions.** Note the metronome mark. Compare the form and phrase structure of this piece with that of no.13.

No. 16. Parallel Motion with Change of Position.

A. **Technique.**
    1. TOUCH. Legato.
    2. POSITION. Five-note range in two positions.
B. **Musicianship.**
    1. NOTATION. Reading of two voices which proceed in the same direction at the interval of a tenth.
    2. RHYTHM. Syncopation.
C. **Bartók's Comments.** Irregularity and variety of structure. Key of C.
    D. **Suggestions.** Accent slightly the half notes in bar 20, and note the contrary motion between bars 21 and 22.

No. 17. Contrary Motion (1).

A. **Technique.**
    1. TOUCH. Legato.
    2. HAND INDEPENDENCE.
        (a) Counterpoint.
    3. FINGERING PROBLEMS. Black key playing L.H. only.

B. **Musicianship.**
   1. NOTATION. Accidentals.
   2. RHYTHM. Syncopation.
   3. EXPRESSION.
     (a) Phrasing: symmetrical phrases in ternary form.
C. **Bartók's Comments.** Same dissonance can be observed in Bach. This melody is used in No. 13.
D. **Suggestions.** Accent slightly the half notes in bars 3, 7, and 15.

Nos. 18–21. Four Unison Melodies.

A. **Technique.**
   1. TOUCH. Legato.
   2. FINGERING PROBLEMS. Extension of the hand in playing of various melodic intervals.
B. **Musicianship.**
   1. NOTATION. The whole rest. The separating sign I indicates the interruption of legato between phrases.
   2. EXPRESSION.
     (a) Dynamics: the marcato (>) accent.
C. **Bartók's Comments.** The melodies stress interval playing. Use the exercises to explain them. No. 20 combines intervals and change of direction. No. 21 is in A minor; it introduces accents.
D. **Suggestions.** Play Nos. 18–20 as one unit, and Exercises 1a–c. No. 21 is concerned with the playing of accents. Practice Exercises 1d–f with No. 21. In No. 20, the second phrase is extended by the addition of a bar of rest, and the fourth phrase is extended by the addition of the tied whole note. The use of these contrasting types of additions serves to extend asymmetrical phrases into balanced structures. The accents appearing in No. 21 call for slight intensification of the notes they modify, and they should be played without hand motion (that is, with the fingers only). In bar 8, the separating signs also serve as a warning that the following bars require alternate motion of the hands. The pupil, because of preoccupation with the playing of accents, may overlook the ties and rests in the last three bars.

No. 22. Imitation and Counterpoint.

A. **Technique**.
   1. TOUCH. Legato.
   2. HAND INDEPENDENCE.
     (a) Counterpoint.
B. **Musicianship.**
   1. NOTATION. Reading of treble clef notation in L.H.
   2. EXPRESSION.
     (a) Dynamics: *f*.
C. **Bartók's Comments.** Similar voices in contrapuntal style. Imitation: the

second voice commences later and is similar to the first voice. G tonality.

D. **Suggestions.** This piece is more difficult to play than No. 23. It may be advisable, therefore, to reverse the order of pieces and perform No. 23, then practice Example 2 as an introduction to polyphonic playing. Be sure that all rests are observed and that the reentry of one voice does not interrupt the flow of legato in the other voice. Observe also that f = forte = loud, and that counterpoint is the simultaneous playing of two or more independent melodic lines.

No. 23. Imitation and Inversion (1).

A. **Technique.**
1. TOUCH. Legato.
2. HAND INDEPENDENCE.
   (a) Counterpoint.

B. **Musicianship.**
1. NOTATION. Reading of individual melodic lines with bass clef notation in L.H.
2. EXPRESSION.
   (a) Dynamics: f.

C. **Bartók's Comments.** One voice imitates the other and then inverts. Inversion: the position of the (two) voices is so changed that the upper voice becomes the lower and vice versa (bars 1–3 and 7–9 show the original position, the remaining bars show the inversion).

D. **Suggestions.** See No. 22 above.

No. 24. Pastorale.

A. **Technique.**
1. TOUCH. Legato.
2. FINGERING PROBLEMS. Black key playing.

B. **Musicianship.**
1. NOTATION. Whole rest in 3/4 time. A (F♯, C♯, G♯) key signature.
2. RHYTHM. Syncopation.
   (a) Dynamics: p = piano = soft.
   (b) Phrasing: the last bar is added for structural balance. Ternary form.

C. **Bartók's Comments.** Key of D with G♯ added for practical purposes.

D. **Suggestions.** In the Lydian mode—a major mode with augmented fourth degree—built from D as principal tone. Built from C: C-D-E-F♯-G-A-B.

No. 25. Imitation and Inversion (2).

A. **Technique.**
1. TOUCH. Legato.
2. HAND INDEPENDENCE.
   (a) Counterpoint.

B. **Musicianship.**
1. NOTATION. Bartók-devised key signature. The whole rest in 2/4 time. Repeat signs ‖: and :‖.

2. RHYTHM. 2/4.

3. EXPRESSION.

   (a) Tempo: M.M. = 150 (!).

   (b) Dynamics: *sf* = sforzato (or sforzando) = loud accent.

C. **Bartók's Comments.** B minor feeling with lowered fifth. Asymmetrical in form. The signature is C♯. See notes.

D. **Suggestions.** The tempo may be too rapid for certain pupils. In such cases, the composer advises a reduction in speed (see the preface).

No. 26. Repetition (2).

A. **Technique.**

   1. TOUCH. Legato and non-legato.

   2. HAND INDEPENDENCE.

      (a) Counterpoint.

      (b) Combined Touch-Forms: legato vs. non-legato.

B. **Musicianship.**

   1. NOTATION. D key signature.

C. **Bartók's Comments.** Second voice repeats first voice in sequence in rhythmic form beginning on the dominant. Has the character of D major, ending on the fifth degree in the L.H. and the second degree in the R.H. This is called a half-cadence, frequently used in Yugoslav music.

D. **Suggestions.** There may be some difficulty in playing this piece at the indicated tempo. The repeated notes played in one hand must not interrupt the legato playing in the other hand. Play Exercise 3 as a preparation for No. 27.

No. 27. Syncopation (2).

A. **Technique.**

   1. TOUCH. Legato.

   2. HAND INDEPENDENCE.

      (a) Counterpoint.

   3. FINGERING PROBLEMS. Black key playing.

B. **Musicianship.**

   1. RHYTHM. Syncopation.

C. **Bartók's Comments.** Asymmetrical phrase structure. Tied-over syncopation. Same melody used in No. 9.

D. **Suggestions.** Review the meaning of counterpoint by comparing Nos. 9 and 27.

No. 28. Canon at the Octave.

A. **Technique.**

   1. TOUCH. Legato.

   2. HAND INDEPENDENCE.

      (a) Counterpoint.

B. **Musicianship.**

   1. RHYTHM. Syncopation.

2. EXPRESSION.
   (a) Dynamics: *p*.
   (b) Phrasing: in canonic form.

C. **Bartók's Comments.** Canon: two equal voices are introduced so that one commences later than the other. There can be any interval between the voices. In No. 28 it is an octave, hence the title "Canon at the Octave." E minor with altered second. Same melody used in No. 7.

D. **Suggestions.** Compare this piece with No. 7 to illustrate the explanation of canonic form. Syncopated notes should be accented slightly. Note the dynamic level. Practice Exercise 4 as a preparation for No. 29.

No. 29. Imitation Reflected.

A. **Technique.**
   1. TOUCH. Legato.
   2. HAND INDEPENDENCE.
      (a) Counterpoint.
   3. FINGERING PROBLEMS. Black key playing in R.H.

B. **Musicianship.**
   1. NOTATION. Accidentals.

C. **Bartók's Comments.** Seven-bar sections. Direct mirror-like reflection of the first voice. Imitation reflected: the melodic line of the imitating (lower) voice runs in contrary direction to that of the upper voice.

D. **Suggestions.** The flow of legato between phrases must not be interrupted.

No. 30. Canon at the Lower Fifth.

A. **Technique.**
   1. TOUCH. Legato and non-legato.
   2. HAND INDEPENDENCE.
      (a) Counterpoint.
      (b) Combined Touch-Forms: Legato vs. non-legato.

B. **Musicianship.**
   1. RHYTHM. Syncopation.
   2. EXPRESSION.
      (a) Tempo: moderato = at a moderate rate of speed.
      (b) Phrasing: in canonic form.

C. **Bartók's Comments.** Intervals and direction of the two voices are the same, but the interval between them is different. See the note to No. 28. The interval of the two voices is here a fifth.

D. **Suggestions.** The repeated notes in one hand must not interrupt the legato playing in the other hand. First tempo indication.

No. 31. Dance in Canon Form.

A. **Technique.**
   1. TOUCH. Legato and non-legato.
   2. HAND INDEPENDENCE.

(a) Counterpoint.
(b) Combined Touch-Forms: legato vs. non-legato.
(c) Dynamic Contrast: > vs. f.

B. **Musicianship.**
1. NOTATION. The repeat sign.
2. EXPRESSION.
(a) Tempo: allegro = quick, brisk. M.M. = 160.
(b) Dynamics: marcato accents in each hand.
(c) Phrasing: in canonic form.

C. **Bartók's Comments.** An identical canon in pitch and interval.

D. **Suggestions.** First example in which the voices are contrasted dynamically. It is more important to acquire control of accents than to attempt the playing of this piece at the indicated tempo.

No. 32. In Dorian Mode.

A. **Technique.**
1. TOUCH. Legato.
2. HAND INDEPENDENCE.
(a) Counterpoint.
3. INTERVAL AND BROKEN CHORD PLAYING. L.H. only.
4. FINGERING PROBLEMS.

B. **Musicianship.**
1. NOTATION. Dotted whole note in 3/2 time. The dotted line between staves.
2. RHYTHM. Subdivision of the beat into two parts, the half note as the pulse unit.
3. EXPRESSION.
(a) Tempo: lento = slow.
(b) Terms: legato = in a smooth and connected manner, with no break between the tones.

C. **Bartók's Comments.** Dorian mode: One of the so-called ecclesiastical modes. Beginning on D as principal tone the degrees of this scale have no accidentals (there are white keys only). Built from C as principal tone the scale should read as follows: C-D-E♭-G-A-B♭-C. Therefore, it is a minor (minor third) scale with a major sixth and a minor seventh. This and the following ecclesiastical modes were used in the middle ages until about the seventeenth century but, since J. S. Bach, they have been replaced in art music by the major and minor scales. However, besides many other unnamed scales, they are still flourishing in the folk music of Eastern Europe (Hungary, Romania, Yugoslavia, etc.) and Asia and are not at all antiquated. This piece has a major chord ending as in Bach.

D. **Suggestions.** In bars 7 and 12, G is played with the first finger of each hand. In bar 6, the dotted line indicates that F (played by the L.H.) is a continuation of the melody in the R.H. A solid line would indicate the playing of that note with the R.H. Take notice of the metronome mark: it indicates rate of speed of the quarter note and does not affect conception of the half note as the pulse unit (count *one and two and three and* in each bar). See **Suggestions** in No. 33, below.

No. 33. Slow Dance.

A.**Technique.**
   1. TOUCH. Legato.
   2. HAND INDEPENDENCE.
      (a) Counterpoint.
   3. FINGERING PROBLEMS. Black key playing in L.H. only.
B. **Musicianship.**
   1. NOTATION. The dotted whole note in 6/4 time. Bass clef leger-line notes above the staff.
   2. RHYTHM. 6/4. Syncopation.
   3. EXPRESSION.
      (a) Tempo: andante = moving, walking.
      (b) Dynamics: *mf* = mezzo forte = softer than forte (half-loud), hairpin = crescendo = increasing gradually in loudness.
   C. **Bartók's Comments.** G tonality, C♯ gives color in contemporary music. Ends on a half-cadence.
   D. **Suggestions.** 3/2 is a simple triple meter and 6/4 is a compound duple meter: Note the difference between these time signatures in terms of accentuation and their similarity with reference to notation. It is recommended that the pupil demonstrate his or her understanding by playing No. 32 in 6/4 and No. 33 in 3/2.

No. 34. In Phrygian Mode.

A. **Technique.**
   1. TOUCH. Legato.
   2. HAND INDEPENDENCE.
      (a) Counterpoint.
      (b) Dynamic Contrast: *sf* vs. *f*.
B. **Musicianship.**
   1. RHYTHM. Subdivision of the beat into two parts : the half note as the pulse unit. Syncopation.
   2. EXPRESSION.
      (a) Tempo: calmo = moderate.
      (b) Dynamics: cresc. = crescendo; dim. = diminuendo = becoming gradually softer.
   C. **Bartók's Comments.** Phrygian mode: One of the ecclesiastical modes. Beginning on E as principal tone, the degrees of this scale have no accidentals (there are white keys only). Built from C as principal tone, the scale should read as follows: C-D♭-E♭-F-G-A♭-B♭. Therefore, it is a minor scale with a minor

second, sixth, and seventh). Tonal and rhythmic variety within a short range. 2/
2 meter. This modal style used in Hungary for the last 150 years.

No. 35. Chorale.

  A. **Technique.**
    1. TOUCH. Legato.
    2. HAND INDEPENDENCE.
      (a) Counterpoint.
  B. **Musicianship.**
    1. **EXPRESSION.**
      (a) Tempo: largamente = slow (broadly, largely).
  C. **Bartók's Comments.** Voices resemble free canon writing.

  D. **Suggestions.** Chorale = a hymn tune of the German Protestant Church.
There seems to be a certain similarity between this piece and a chorale, particularly in terms of construction.

No. 36. Free Canon.

  A. **Technique.**
    1. TOUCH. Legato.
    2. INDEPENDENCE.
      (a) Counterpoint.
  B. **Musicianship.**
    1. EXPRESSION.
      (a) Tempo: teneramente = (tenderly, delicately) moderate in speed.

  C. **Bartók's Comments.** See the note for No. 28. The canon is "free" if the
second voice deviates inconsiderably from the first. Natural A minor.

  D. **Suggestions.** The "Natural A minor" = the Aeolian mode built on A as
principal tone: A-B-C-D-E-F-G. Do not overlook the quarter rests in bars 3–10.
Péteré (printed parallel to the double bar) indicates that Bartók has dedicated
Volume I of the *Mikrokosmos* to his second son, Peter.

7

Volume Two

Nos. 37–66 and Exercises 5–18

No. 37. In Lydian Mode.
  A. **Technique.**
   1. TOUCH. Legato, non-legato, and tenuto.
   2. HAND INDEPENDENCE.
      (a) Counterpoint.
  B. **Musicianship.**
   1. NOTATION. The eighth note and rest in 2/4. ⌢ = fermata = pause or hold.
   2. RHYTHM. Subdivision of the beat into two parts: the quarter note as the pulse unit.
   3. EXPRESSION.
      (a) Tempo: allegretto = slower than allegro, moderately fast.
  C. **Bartók's Comments.** Lydian mode: Another ecclesiastical mode, beginning on F as principal tone with seven degrees without accidentals, a major scale with augmented fourth (F♮). This interval is so characteristic in this scale that a melody based on the first five degrees only (as No. 37) may be called "Lydian." Direct imitation in voices. Ends on the dominant (C).
  D. **Suggestions.** Tenuto touch: the key is pressed rather than struck down. The fermata "about doubles the value of the note beneath it." Prepare Exercise 5.

No. 38. Staccato and Legato.
  A. **Technique.**
   1. TOUCH. Legato and staccato.
   2. HAND INDEPENDENCE.
      (a) Counterpoint.
      (b) Combined Touch-Forms: legato vs. staccato.
  B. **Musicianship.**
   1. NOTATION. D key signature. Staccato signs.
   2. RHYTHM. Subdivision of the beat into two parts: the quarter note as the pulse unit in 3/4.
  C. **Bartók's Comments.** The signature is not conventional. Develops ability to play staccato and legato. Voices are reflected. See exercise in appendix.

D. **Suggestions.** Note the hand independence required in bar 7. Staccato tones should be sounded for "one-half the value of the note (or less)."

No. 39. Staccato and Legato.

A. **Technique.**
1. TOUCH. Legato and staccato.
2. HAND INDEPENDENCE.
    (a) Counterpoint.
    (b) Combined Touch-Forms: legato vs. staccato.

B. **Musicianship.**
1. NOTATION. F key signature.
2. RHYTHM. Subdivision of the beat into two parts: the quarter note as the pulse unit in 4/4.
3. EXPRESSION.
    (a) Tempo: comodo = at a convenient pace, leisurely.
    (b) Phrasing: in canonic form.

C. **Bartók's Comments.** Contrast of staccato and legato in each hand in contrapuntal style. Might be good to talk about different types of staccato—the shorter and longer types.[1]

D. **Suggestions.** The playing of legato vs. staccato may prove difficult. Slow practice is recommended. If Bartók's comment concerning the teaching of staccato types is followed, demonstrate how the piece would sound if played staccatissimo.

No. 40. In Yugoslav Mode.

A. **Technique.**
1. TOUCH. Legato.
2. HAND INDEPENDENCE.
    (a) Accompanying Figurations: in L.H.

B. **Musicianship.**
1. NOTATION. A key signature.
2. EXPRESSION.
    (a) Dynamics: ^ = marcatissimo accent = moderately strong accent.
    (b) Phrasing: in ternary form.
    (c) Terms: la seconda volta = the second time.

C. **Bartók's Comments.** E-Mixolydian mode. Ends on half-cadence. Imitation of Yugoslav bagpipes: the piece is written for two pipes although the instrument has three. The Scotch bagpipe has only a chanter and a drone. The Yugoslav bagpipe has a chanter, tonic-dominant pipe, and drone (a tonic pipe). A bagpipe melody can be found in the main theme of Beethoven's Sixth Symphony.

D. **Suggestions.** Mixolydian mode: An ecclesiastical mode beginning on G as principal tone, with seven degrees without accidentals. Built from E as principal tone, the scale should read: E F♯-G♯-A-B-C♯-D♮-E. Ending on the dominant

(B) has the same effect for the Yugoslav peasant as the ending on the tonic (E) has for those exposed to Western (Europe) art music. Practice Exercises 6–8.

No. 41. Melody with Accompaniment.

A. **Technique.**
   1. TOUCH. Legato.
   2. HAND INDEPENDENCE.
      (a) Dynamic Contrast: *mf* vs. *p.*
      (b) Accompanying Figurations: in L.H.
   3. BROKEN CHORD PLAYING. In L.H.
   4. FINGER INDEPENDENCE. First example of part-playing in L.H.

B. **Musicianship.**
   1. NOTATION. Bartók-devised key signature. The whole rest in 6/8.
   2. RHYTHM. Change of meter. Subdivision of the beat into three parts: the dotted quarter as the pulse unit in 6/8 and 9/8.
   3. EXPRESSION.
      (a) Tempo: adagio = slow.
      (b) Terms: sempre legato = always legato. The use of this instruction eliminates the necessity of inserting legato slurs in the L.H.

C. **Bartók's Comments.** Changes in meter and rhythmic patterns. Cs for key signature. Broken chords up and in reverse direction. G major with an augmented fourth and a minor seventh.

D. **Suggestions.** First example of Bartók's use of a polymode, consisting of the G-Mixolydian mode (n7 degree) with the Lydian s4 degree: G-A-B-Cs-D-E-Fn-G. Observe the tied notes in the last two bars.

No. 42. Accompaniment in Broken Triads.

A. **Technique.**
   1. TOUCH. Legato and staccato.
   2. HAND INDEPENDENCE.
      (a) Dynamic Contrast: *p* vs. *mf.*
      (b) Accompanying Figurations: in each hand.
   3. BROKEN CHORD PLAYING. In each hand.

B. **Musicianship.**
   1. NOTATION. Leger-line notes below staff in the treble clef.
   2. EXPRESSION.
      (a) Tempo: andante tranquillo = moving tranquilly, at a moderate rate of speed.

C. **Bartók's Comments.** Sustained theme in R.H., broken chords in L.H., then reversed. Chords are all practically the same but with a few altered or foreign tones.

D. **Suggestions.** In bar 14, the C in the R.H. is natural, as is the L.H. in bar 34. The effect is polymodal: major vs. minor with A as principal tone. The basically pentatonic melody, A-C-D-E-G, ends on the dominant (E). Practice Exercise 9.

No. 43. In Hungarian Style.

A. **Technique.**
   1. TOUCH. Legato and staccato.
   2. HAND INDEPENDENCE.
      (a) Counterpoint.
   3. FINGERING PROBLEMS. Black key playing in Piano II.
   4. ENSEMBLE PLAYING. For two pianos, four hands.

B. **Musicianship.**
   1. NOTATION. Mixed accidentals and dotted notes. Bass clef notation in each hand.
   2. RHYTHM. The dotted quarter in 4/4.
   3. EXPRESSSION.
      (a) Terms: più = more.

C. **Bartók's Comments.** First example of an arrangement for two pianos. Piano I plays broken thirds in parallel motion. See exercises in appendix. After the solo version "a" has been played, the second piano part of the same grade of difficulty which is provided may be added. Version "b" shows the melody written in conventional style. The theme is the same but the thirds are in contrary motion. G minor with augmented sixth.

D. **Suggestions.** Alternate the playing of both parts. If only one piano is available, transpose the primo (Piano I) part two octaves higher and play with another pianist as a duet for four hands. Hungarian style: the A A⁵ B A form of this piece is typical of Hungarian folk song structure. G-Dorian mode: G-A-B♭-C-D-E♮-F G.

No. 44. Contrary Motion.

A. **Technique.**
   1. TOUCH. Legato, staccato, and tenuto.
   2. HAND INDEPENDENCE.
      (a) Counterpoint.
      (b) Combined Touch-Forms: legato vs. staccato.
   3. ENSEMBLE PLAYING. For two pianos, four hands.

B. **Musicianship.**
   1. NOTATION. Devised two-sharp signature (F♯-G♯) in Piano I and E key signature (F♯-C♯–G♯-D♯) in Piano II.
   2. EXPRESSION.
      (a) Terms: vivace = lively.

C. **Bartók's Comments.** Note the signature in Piano I: key of E but additional sharps not added because they are not used. Ends with an augmented third (G♯-B♯) in doubled notes. Can be played without the second piano part.

D. **Suggestions.** See **Suggestions** in No. 43 above.

No. 45. Méditation.

A. **Technique.**

1. TOUCH. Legato, staccato, and tenuto.
2. HAND INDEPENDENCE.
 (a) Combined Touch-Forms: legato vs. staccato and tenuto.
 (b) Dynamic Contrast: *p* vs. *mf.*
 (c) Accompanying Figurations: in each hand.
3. BROKEN CHORD PLAYING. In each hand.
4. FINGERING PROBLEMS. Black key playing in each hand.
B. **Musicianship.**
1. NOTATION. E♭ key signature.
2. EXPRESSION.
 (a) Dynamics: *mp* = mezzo piano = half-soft, louder than *p*.
 (b) Terms: subito = suddenly.
C. **Bartók's Comments.** Although signature of piece is C minor, the composition is in F minor with a major sixth. Abstract in theme and rhythm. Returns to former Dorian mode (bar 16). Can be played on two pianos, the second player executing the same piece on the higher octave.
D. **Suggestions.** Check fingering in bars 11–12. The D is natural in bars 14–16.

No. 46. Increasing-Diminishing.

A. **Technique.**
1. TOUCH. Legato.
2. HAND INDEPENDENCE.
 (a) Counterpoint.
 (b) Dynamic Contrasts: *mf* vs. *p*, *f* vs. *mf*, *pp* vs. *p*.
B. **Musicianship.**
1. RHYTHM. Syncopation.
2. EXPRESSION.
 (a) Dynamics: *pp* = pianissimo = softer than *p*.
C. **Bartók's Comments.** Tone control. Not for the average pupil.
D. **Suggestions.** Phrygian mode, E-F(♮)-G-A-B-C-D, ending on the dominant. Double bar in bar 14 not only indicates the midpoint of this piece in terms of dynamic level but also a transition to F Lydian (bars 15–18). A second transition to G major ensues, ending on the third degree, B. Key attack is the determining factor in achieving dynamic levels: fast key descent will produce a loud tone and slow key descent will result in a soft tone. Prepare Exercises 10–11.

No. 47. Big Fair.

A. **Technique.**
1. TOUCH. Non-legato.
2. HAND INDEPENDENCE.
 (a) Counterpoint.
 (b) Dynamic Contrasts: *sf* and ^ vs. *f*.
 (c) Accompanying Figurations: L.H. only.

3. PEDALLING. Use of the damper pedal.

4. FINGERING PROBLEMS. "Discontinuous" fingerings.

B. **Musicianship.**

1. NOTATION. G key signature.

2. RHYTHM. Subdivision of the beat into two parts: the half note as the pulse unit in 2/2.

3. EXPRESSION.

(a) Tempo: con brio = with spirit. M.M. = 132.

(b) Phrasing: in ternary form.

(c) Terms: strepitoso = noisily; sempre simile = in like manner throughout; senza = without; Ped. = depress the damper pedal; meno = less; ✳ = release the damper pedal.

C. **Bartók's Comments.** Voices moving in broken thirds and fourths in contrary motion which creates an atmosphere of excitement. Use of the pedal and shading very important.

D. **Suggestions.** One of the difficult pieces in this volume; in fact, the combination of pedalling, accentuation, and discontinuity of fingering may be beyond the ability of some students at the indicated tempo.

No. 48. In Mixolydian Mode.

A. **Technique.**

1. TOUCH. Legato.

2. HAND INDEPENDENCE.

(a) Counterpoint.

(b) Dynamic Contrast: *mf* vs. *f.*

(c) Accompanying Figurations: in each hand.

3. BROKEN CHORD PLAYING. In each hand.

B. **Musicianship.**

1. RHYTHM. 5/4. Syncopation.

2. EXPRESSION.

(a) Tempo: allegro non troppo = not too fast.

C. **Bartók's Comments.** Key of G with no accidentals. Mixolydian Mode: an ecclesiastical mode with G as principal tone and seven degrees without accidentals. Ends on dominant. L.H. figures in broken chords or chord of G with foreign notes. Chord in E minor. R.H. melody in contrary motion. Very good for individual finger control. I checked all the *Mikrokosmos* pieces against the metronome.

D. **Suggestions.** Accent slightly the first beat of each measure of accompanying figurations as well as the syncopated notes. Observe the dynamic changes in the last five bars.

No. 49. Crescendo-Diminuendo.

A. **Technique.**

1. TOUCH. Legato and staccato.

2. HAND INDEPENDENCE.

   (a) Counterpoint.

   (b) Combined Touch-Forms: legato vs. staccato.

B. **Musicianship.**

  1. NOTATION. Mixed accidentals.

  2. EXPRESSION.

   (a) Dynamics: as indicated by the title.

C. **Bartók's Comments.** Quick change from legato to staccato. Key of C with accidentals. Crescendo and diminuendo.

D. **Suggestions.** Practice first without dynamics at M.M. $\flat$ = 96–160. Then play at indicated tempo and intensities.

No. 50. Minuetto.

A. **Technique.**

  1. TOUCH. Legato and staccato.

  2. HAND INDEPENDENCE.

   (a) Counterpoint.

   (b) Combined Touch-Forms: legato vs. staccato.

B. **Musicianship.**

  1. NOTATION. Devised one-sharp key signature.

  2. EXPRESSION.

   (a) Tempo: tempo di Menuetto = at the speed of a minuet. The minuet—a slow, stately dance in triple meter—dates from about the end of the seventeenth century.

   (b) Phrasing: in ternary form.

   (c) Dynamics: > = gradually get softer.

C. **Bartók's Comments.** Application of staccato and legato playing. Key of A major with altered tones.

D. **Suggestions.** Polymodal pentachords: A Lydian ascending, A-B-C♯-D♯-E; A major descending, E-D♮-C♯-B-A. Check the playing of legato (R.H.) vs. staccato (L.H.) in the last two bars.

No. 51. Waves.

A. **Technique.**

  1. TOUCH. Legato and espressivo.

  2. HAND INDEPENDENCE.

   (a) Counterpoint.

  3. FINGERING PROBLEMS. Black key playing.

B. **Musicianship.**

  1. NOTATION. D♭ key signature.

  2. RHYTHM. The upbeat and syncopation in 6/8.

  3. EXPRESSION.

   (a) Tempo: poco ritard. = growing a little slower.

   (b) Dynamics: *p* subito = suddenly soft.

C. **Bartók's Comments.** Good demonstration of the tie on different beats in one voice while the other voice proceeds. Key of D♭ ending on dominant. Imitation of voices: one in the tonic and one in the dominant. Can be played on two pianos, the second player executing the same piece in the higher octave.

D. **Suggestions.** To play dolce, use pressure touch (tenuto) combined with flexible wrist action (without weight) so that percussiveness is reduced to a minimum. Note the decrescendo marks above the slurred notes in R.H. of bars 14–15.

No. 52. Unison Divided.

A. **Technique.**
   1. TOUCH. Legato, non-legato, and tenuto: from hand to hand.
B. **Musicianship.**
   1. EXPRESSION.
      (a) Dynamics: cresc. and >.
C. **Bartók's Comments.** Melody is divided between the hands. Key of G with altered fourths.

D. **Suggestions.** G-Mixolydian (seventh degree = F♮)/Lydian (fourth degree = C♯) polymodal hexachord (E is excluded). There may be a tendency to play legatissimo when changing from hand to hand, or to play legato in the second and last bars. Notes in bass and treble clefs are to be played with L.H. and R.H., respectively.

No. 53. In Transylvanian Style.

A. **Technique.**
   1. TOUCH. Legato, non-legato, and tenuto: from hand to hand.
   2. HAND INDEPENDENCE.
   (a) Counterpoint.
B. **Musicianship.**
   1. NOTATION. Clef changes.
   2. RHYTHM. Subdivision of the beat into two and four parts: the half note as the pulse unit in 2/2. Syncopation.
   3. EXPRESSION.
      (a) Tempo: risoluto = energetic, with decision.
C. **Bartók's Comments.** Imitation of R.H. in L.H. Continuity from one hand to the other expresses one idea. Note changes in clef signs and hand positions. Key of D.

D. **Suggestions.** Subdivision of the beat (♩) into two or four parts through use of the quarter or eighth note in 2/2 meter. Dotted lines indicate the melody is taken up by the L.H. Note the separating sign in the L.H. of bar 24. Transylvania is an area formerly part of Hungary, comprised mainly of Romanian peasantry, lying to the east of Hungary and north of Romania. Bartók collected folk music in Transylvania in the decade prior to its assignment to Romania in 1920 by the Treaty of Trianon. This piece is built on the rhythm patterns 2/2 ♫♩, ♩♫ and

♪♪♪♩, which Bartók discovered to be typical of Transylvanian-Romanian bag-pipe melodies.

No. 54. Chromatic.

A. **Technique.**
    1. TOUCH. Legato and staccato.
    2. HAND INDEPENDENCE.
      (a) Counterpoint.
    3. FINGERING PROBLEMS. Chromatics.
B. **Musicianship.**
    1. NOTATION. Accidentals.
    2. EXPRESSION.
      (a) Dynamics: *p—f—p* hairpins, *sf*.

C. **Bartók's Comments.** Chromatic study with quick, forceful, and sudden staccato. Definite shading and accents. Good place to take up the chromatic scale if the pupil hasn't had it.

D. **Suggestions.** Be sure to observe the rests on the first beat of bars 3, 6, and 11. Contrary motion between the hands in bars 9-10 may call for extra practice. Bartók's original title ("Crescendo-Diminuendo") indicates the importance of perfecting dynamic shadings. Prepare Exercises 12–13.

No. 55. Triplets in Lydian Mode.

A. **Technique.**
    1. TOUCH. Legato and staccato.
    2. HAND INDEPENDENCE.
      (a) Counterpoint.
      (b) Dynamic Contrast: in relievo = bring out, in relief.
      (c) Accompanying Figurations: staccato intervals in each hand.
    3. INTERVAL PLAYING. Fifths.
    4. ENSEMBLE PLAYING. For two pianos, four hands.
B. **Musicianship.**
    1. NOTATION. Clef changes (secondo only).
    2. RHYTHM. Subdivision of the beat into three parts: the quarter note as pulse unit in 3/4. Polyrhythm: the simultaneous combination of two to the beat (in one part) vs. three to the beat (in the other part). Change of time.
    3. EXPRESSION.
      (a) Tempo: tempo di marcia = in march time.

C. **Bartók's Comments.** Consult exercises in appendix before playing this piece. Consecutive fifths used: avoided yesterday, used today. See notes for Nos. 37 and 44. The accidentals are used for color, although this mode has none. L.H. is the metronome, since it keeps the beat steady.

D. **Suggestions.** Bring out the melody in L.H. of bars 9–15 (in Piano I) as indicated. In the same part, because of the change from 2/4 to 3/4 at bar 17, the pianist may interpolate a quarter rest between bars 17 and 18. Play both parts. If only one piano is available, another performer can play the secondo part transposed an octave down (bars 10–15 transposed two octaves down). Practice Exercise 14 as preparation for the part-playing to be encountered in No. 56, making sure that the ties are observed when repeating each two-bar section or when proceeding from one section to another.

No. 56. Melody in Tenths.

A. **Technique**.
   1. TOUCH. Legato.
   2. FINGER INDEPENDENCE. Part-playing in each hand.
B. **Musicianship**.
   1. NOTATION. Treble clef in each hand.
   2. EXPRESSION.
     (a) Dynamics.
  C. **Bartók's Comments**. Two voices are sustained while others move. Ends on a consonant chord. In old music, a chord built of consecutive thirds, even with the seventh degree added, was called a consonant chord. At first the chord contained a major third, but later one with a minor third was also considered to be consonant. Can be played on two pianos, the second player executing the piece in the higher octave.
  D. **Suggestions**. As a preparation for part-playing, Bartók recommends use of both hands in playing the individual line systems of one staff. If this is done, the fingerings should be rearranged to avoid awkward juxtaposition of the hands. When the piece is played as written, be sure the held tones are maintained throughout each phrase. Note the alternation of modes: Aeolian (A-B-C-D-E-F-G-A) to Dorian (A-B-C-D-E-F♯-G-A) to Phrygian (A-B♭-C-D-E-F-G-A), each with A as the principal tone.

No. 57. Accents.

A. **Technique**.
   1. TOUCH. Non-legato.
   2. HAND INDEPENDENCE.
     (a) Counterpoint.
     (b) Dynamic Contrasts: > vs. *p*, *mf* and *f*. ^ vs. *f* and *ff*.
   3. POSITION. Hand crossings: L.H. over, R.H. under.
   4. FINGER INDEPENDENCE. Part-playing in each hand.
B. **Musicianship.**
   1. NOTATION. Change of signature: key of C, A, and E. Change of clef.
   2. RHYTHM. Subdivision of the beat into two and four parts: the half note as the pulse unit in 2/2. Syncopation.
   3. EXPRESSION.
     (a) Tempo: non troppo vivo = not too lively.
     (b) Dynamics: molto marcato = very marked, accented.

(c) Phrasing: canonic writing in variation form.

C. **Bartók's Comments**. Accents on upbeats. Notice changes of keys and positions. Feeling is key of A in which the piece begins and ends, but the tonality is indefinite. Requires very good control for the accentuation.

D. **Suggestions**. In the L.H. of bars 6 and 12, the separating sign indicates the end of the phrase and that the half note preceding the sign can be shortened to allow for the quick change of position in bars 7 and 13. Another of the more difficult pieces in this volume. Play Exercise 15.

No. 58. In Oriental Style.

A. **Technique**.
   1. TOUCH. Espressivo.
   2. HAND INDEPENDENCE.
      (a) Counterpoint.
B. **Musicianship**.
   1. NOTATION. Change of clef (L.H. only).
   2. EXPRESSION.
      (a) Tempo: assai lento = very slow, but not as slow as molto lento.
      (b) Phrasing: the comma. In ternary form.

C. **Bartók's Comments**. G -minor tonality typical of Oriental style contains a minor third and an augmented fourth. Ends on a half-cadence. See exercise in appendix.

D. **Suggestions**. To be played with espressivo touch (see **Suggestions** of No. 51 above). The comma in the treble clef of bar 7 indicates a slight, almost unnoticeable pause. In this case, the time for separation should be taken from the note preceding the comma. Thus, bar 7 can be thought as consisting of a half note and a quarter rest. In this case, the time for separation should be taken from the note preceding the comma.

In 1913, Bartók collected Arab folk music in North Africa. Characteristics of this music, he found, are melodies formed of continuously repeated motives of relatively few neighboring tones which include the interval of the augmented second, e.g. G♭-A♯, and 6/8 meter.

No. 59. Major and Minor.

A. **Technique**.
   1. TOUCH. Legato.
   2. HAND INDEPENDENCE.
      (a) Counterpoint.
      (b) Dynamic Contrasts: ^, >, and *sf* vs. *f*.
B. **Musicianship**.
   1. NOTATION. The reading of accidentals involved in the simultaneous performance of F minor and F-Lydian modes.

C. **Bartók's Comments**. Contrasting minor in one part and major with alterations in the other. Could discuss here varieties of minor modes.

D. **Suggestions**. Play the Aeolian mode, A-B-C-D-E-F-G, and convert it to the A-Phrygian mode by lowering the second degree a half-step (B to B♭), then to the A-Dorian mode by raising the sixth degree a half-step (F to F♯). Note that the characteristic degree of the three A-minor modes is the lowered third, C.

No. 60. Canon with Sustained Notes.

A. **Technique**.
1. TOUCH. Legato and non-legato.
2. FINGER INDEPENDENCE. Part-playing in each hand.

B. **Musicianship**.
1. NOTATION. E key signature.
2. RHYTHM. 1/2 meter sign. Change of time.
3. EXPRESSION.
  (a) Tempo: grave = slow, serious, heavy.
  (b) Phrasing: in canonic form.

C. **Bartók's Comments**. Play carefully so that the sustained notes are heard. Four-voice canon in 2/2 and 1/2 meter. In E.

D. **Suggestions**. The separating signs here also indicate phrase endings. 1/2 meter = one beat in the measure, the half note receives one beat.

No. 61. Pentatonic Melody.

A. **Technique**.
1. TOUCH. Legato.
2. HAND INDEPENDENCE.
  (a) Dynamic Contrast: in relievo.
  (b) Accompanying Figurations: in each hand.

B. **Musicianship**.
1. NOTATION. Change of clef in L.H.

C. **Bartók's Comments**. Pentatonic: The scientific name is "anhemitone-pentatonic," which means a scale of five degrees without any semitone, or a minor scale where the second and sixth degrees are missing. It was used frequently in the old Christian monodic ecclesiastical music and is still living in three centers: with the American Indians, with the African Negroes, and in Central Asia—which is the most important one. Each of these centers built different types upon the same basis. The Central Asian center spread its influence as far west as the Hungarians, eastwards to the Chinese and southwards to the Turks. The character of No. 61 resembles the Central Asian type. There are many kinds of pentatonic scales, some are in major. This is in the key of A minor although it ends on tonic and dominant fifths of C, a common ending in old music.

D. **Suggestions**. Prepare Exercise 16.

No. 62. Minor Sixths in Parallel Motion.

A. **Technique**.
1. TOUCH. Legato, staccato, and tenuto.

2. HAND INDEPENDENCE.
   (a) Counterpoint.
   (b) Dynamic Contrasts: > vs. *f*.
3. FINGER INDEPENDENCE. Part-playing in L.H. (bar 40).
B. **Musicianship.**
  1. NOTATION. Mixed accidentals. Clef changes in L.H.
  2. EXPRESSION.
   (a) Tempo: vivace, ma non troppo, risoluto = resolutely but not too lively.
   (b) Dynamics: marcato.
C. **Bartók's Comments.** Gives impression of duo- or bitonality. Oriental feelings. Can be harmonized—see exercise in appendix.
D. **Suggestions.** Note juxtaposition of hands in bar 23. Strict observance of eighth rests also will contribute to accuracy in terms of providing time needed to make the quick leaps in bars 24, 26, and 38. Note the separating signs in bar 6, where the second quarter note is to be played staccato.

No. 63. Buzzing.

A. **Technique.**
  1. TOUCH. Legato.
  2. HAND INDEPENDENCE.
   (a) Counterpoint.
  3. FINGER INDEPENDENCE. Part-playing in L.H. (bars 1–2).
  4. EMBELLISHMENTS. Slow trills in each hand.
B. **Musicianship.**
  1. RHYTHM. Syncopation.
  2. EXPRESSION.
   (a) Tempo: con moto = with animation, energetic movement.
   (b) Dynamics: sempre pianissimo = always very soft.
C. **Bartók's Comments.** Could be practiced as a trill exercise. However, when played as intended, requires conspicuous finger control because it must be played softly. Not intended for the average pupil.
D. **Suggestions.** Begin practicing at medium intensities. Be sure that all rests are observed and that syncopated notes are accented slightly.

No. 64. Line against Point.

A. **Technique.**
  1. TOUCH. Legato and non-legato.
  2. FINGER INDEPENDENCE. Part-playing in each hand.
  3. PEDALLING. Use of the damper.
B. **Musicianship.**
  1. NOTATION. Mixed accidentals.
  2. RHYTHM. 2/2.
  3. EXPRESSION.

(a) Dynamics: marcato

C. Bartók's Comments. 64a: From a sustained interval of a second, voices proceed in opposite directions. It is not considered difficult. Good illustration of bimodality and 2/2 meter. 64b: Chromatic figures proceeding from the same point an octave apart. Version "b" is a chromatic compression of version "a." This is the first example of compression from diatonic into chromatic.

D. Suggestions. Note the use of leger-line half and whole rests in bars 12 and 16, respectively, of No. 64a. Practice Exercise 17.

No. 65. Dialogue.[2]

A. **Technique**.
  1. TOUCH. Staccato.
  2. INTERVAL PLAYING. Fifths in each hand.
  3. ENSEMBLE PLAYING. Vocal accompaniment.
B. **Musicianship**.
  1. NOTATION. The vocal score.
  2. EXPRESSION.
     (a) Dynamics: >.

C. Bartók's Comments. Song appearing in Volume I (cf. no.14) is here played with accompaniment. Suggestions for playing are in appendix. Referring to the notes in the preface, the piece can be played without voice as follows: (a) on one piano—the left hand plays the lower line of the accompaniment, the right hand plays the melody. In the last four bars, the right hand continues to play the upper line of the accompaniment. (b) on two pianos: one player plays the accompaniment in its original form, the other one plays the melody by doubling the upper octave. Exercises in different types of fifths would be of help. In D minor with altered sixth.

D. Suggestions. D-Aeolian mode: D-E-F-G-A-Bb-C-D. If the piece is sung and self-accompanied, check for accuracy of pitch during the singing of the melody in bars 15 and 19. Practice Exercise 18.

No. 66. Melody Divided.

A. **Technique**.
  1. TOUCH. Legato and espressivo.
  2. HAND INDEPENDENCE.
     (a) Combined Touch-Forms: legato vs. espressivo.
     (b) Dynamic Contrasts: *p* vs. più *p.*
     (c) Accompanying Figurations: in each hand.
  3. INTERVAL PLAYING.
  4. EMBELLISHMENTS. Slow double-stop tremolos.
B. **Musicianship**.
  1. NOTATION. Change of clef in R.H. D key signature.
  2. EXPRESSION.
     (a) Dynamics.

C. **Bartók's Comments**. Study in double notes in pentatonic melody, transposed. In E or mixed keys.

D. **Suggestions**. Exercise 18 explores Bartókian polymodality by way of diatonic and chromatic configurations. The interesting sequences in Exercise 18b result from the whole-tone progression of the bass voice: C-D-E-G♭-A♭-B♭. This volume is also dedicated to Peter Bartók.

8

Volume Three

Nos. 67–96 and Exercises 19–31

No. 67. Thirds against a Single Voice.

A. **Technique**.
  1. TOUCH. Legato and non-legato.
  2. HAND INDEPENDENCE.
    (a) Counterpoint: as indicated in the title.
    (b) Dynamic Contrasts: > in R.H.
  3. INTERVAL PLAYING. Thirds in each hand.
B. **Musicianship**.
  1. RHYTHM. Syncopation.
  2. EXPRESSION.
    (a) Dynamics: seven-bar crescendo.
C. **Bartók's Comments**. Nothing special to consider. Consult exercises in appendix.
  D. **Suggestions**. Be sure that all tied notes are held for their full value and that there is evenness of articulation when playing the legato thirds in each hand. See **Suggestions** in No.103 regarding Exercise 20.

No. 68. Hungarian Dance.

A. **Technique**.
  1. TOUCH. Legato, staccato, and tenuto.
  2. HAND INDEPENDENCE.
    (a) Counterpoint.
    (b) Combined Touch-Forms: legato vs. staccato and tenuto, staccato vs. tenuto.
  3. INTERVAL PLAYING.
  4. ACCOMPANYING FIGURATIONS. In each hand.
  5. ENSEMBLE PLAYING. Two pianos, four hands.
B. **Musicianship**.
  1. NOTATION. D key signature.
  2. EXPRESSION.
    (a) Tempo: con spirito = with spirit.
C. **Bartók's Comments**. Can be played without the second piano part. A colorful piece for two pianos. Key of D.

D. **Suggestions**. If only one piano is available, the teacher or another pianist can play the upper staff of the secondo part an octave higher than written. Practice both parts. Prepare Exercise 21 which is the first example of staccato chord playing in the *Mikrokosmos*. This piece is representative of the "new style" of Hungarian peasant music which, according to Bartók's estimate, began to develop during the 1850s (the "old style" is over a thousand years old!). Characteristics are the eleven-syllable tune line (the first two bars contain eleven notes), use of the major scale rather than a pentatonic scale, the rounded (A A^5 B A) structure, and the possible use of the tune for singing as well as dancing.

No. 69. Chord Study.

A. **Technique**.
  1. TOUCH. Staccato, tenuto, and espressivo.
  2. HAND INDEPENDENCE.
      (a) Combined Touch-Forms: staccato and tenuto vs. espressivo.
      (b) Dynamic Contrast: *p* vs. *mf*.
      (c) Accompanying Figurations: in each hand.
  3. CHORD PLAYING. Triads in each hand.
  4. PASSAGE-WORK. Chordal, R.H. only.
B. **Musicianship**.
  1. EXPRESSION.
      (a) Terms: cantabile = in a singing style (that is, with espressivo touch).
C. **Bartók's Comments**. See exercise in appendix. Simple basic triads good for hand position in grasping chords and playing crisp staccato. (Be sure to read the preface to Volume 3 for Bartók's suggestions regarding simplification of the accompaniment and "some slight difficulties" in the listed bars.)

D. **Suggestions**. Bartók transcribed this piece for two pianos under the title, "Chord and Trill Study" (No. 2 in Seven Pieces from *Mikrokosmos*, published by Boosey and Hawkes). In this transcription, No. 69 appears as the secondo part in which the melody and some chords contain octave doublings. The transcription is suitable for performance by certain pianists and it may be used effectively as a recital piece in which the teacher or an advanced pianist plays the primo part. Béla and Ditta Bartók can be heard in the definitive performance of the transcription: see REMINGTON R19994.

No. 70. Melody against Double Notes.

A. **Technique**.
  1. TOUCH. Legato and espressivo.
  2. HAND INDEPENDENCE.
      (a) Combined Touch-Form: legato vs. espressivo.
      (b) Dynamic Contrast: *p* vs. *f*.
      (c) Accompanying Figurations: in each hand.
  3. INTERVAL PLAYING. In each hand.
  4. POSITION. Crossed hands: R.H. over, L.H. under.

B. **Musicianship**.

1. NOTATION. B key signature in R.H., C key signature in L.H. Bass clef in each hand.

2. EXPRESSION.

(a) Terms: calando = decreasing in intensity and speed.

C. **Bartók's Comments**. Bimodal. R.H. is in F♯ minor with raised sixth [F♯ Dorian mode]. The signature is actually B major but the piece is written in dominant [F♯] minor. L.H. is in D minor.

D. **Suggestions**. Practice first for mastery of touch and then work for control of dynamic contrast. Review Exercises 19–20 in preparation for No. 71.

No. 71. Thirds.

A. **Technique**.

1. TOUCH. Legato and tenuto.

2. HAND INDEPENDENCE.

(a) Counterpoint in thirds.

3. FINGER INDEPENDENCE. Part-playing in L.H. only.

B. **Musicianship**.

1. RHYTHM. Change of time: 2/2, 3/2.

2. EXPRESSION.

(a) Tempo: un poco più mosso = a little faster. Tempo I = at the tempo indicated by the first tempo mark (M.M. = 66).

C. **Bartók's Comments**. Note changes of meter and tempo, also F major R.H. vs. D minor L.H. Key of D minor ending on a major triad. Dignified, quiet atmosphere. Note how theme comes to rest on a major chord.

D. **Suggestions**. Begin Exercises 23a and b here in advance preparation for No. 73. Practice hands separately at first, working for evenness of finger articulation of the legato thirds.

No. 72. Dragon's Dance.

A. **Technique**.

1. TOUCH. Legato, non-legato, tenuto, and staccato.

2. HAND INDEPENDENCE.

(a) Combined Touch-Form: legato vs. tenuto and non-legato.

(b) Dynamic Contrast: marcatissimo vs. tenuto.

3. FINGER INDEPENDENCE. Part-playing in each hand.

B. **Musicianship**.

1. NOTATION. Change of clef in L.H. Mixed accidentals.

2. EXPRESSION.

(a) Tempo: molto pesante = very ponderously, heavily.

C. **Bartók's Comments**. Tonality and intervals lend a bizarre effect. Pay attention to phrasing of second voice. Key may be G or it may be called a hovering or uncertain tonality.

D. **Suggestions**. Begin by playing hands separately, then together, at slow tempi. Attend with care all legato-staccato markings. Prepare Exercises 22 and 23c–d.

No. 73. Sixths and Triads.

A. **Technique**.
  1. TOUCH. Non-legato.
  2. HAND INDEPENDENCE.
    (a) Counterpoint.
  3. INTERVAL AND CHORD PLAYING. As indicated by title.
B. **Musicianship**.
  1. EXPRESSION.
    (a) Dynamics: f subito.
C. **Bartók's Comments**. Again the major against minor in triads and their inversions. Key of C ending on dominant chord. Could be practiced in various ways and speeds. Plagal ending.
D. **Suggestions**. Can be played in the style of Exercise 23a: play all eighth notes staccato and all quarter and half notes tenuto, M.M. $\bullet$ = 96-144. Plagal ending: a cadence in which the final Tonic (I) chord is preceded by a Subdominant (IV) harmony. In this piece, the Dominant (G-B-D) replaces the Tonic (C-E-G) as the final chord and it is preceded by a Subdominant seventh chord (F-A-C-E).

No. 74. Hungarian Matchmaking Song.[1]

A. **Technique**.
  1. TOUCH. Legato, non-legato, and tenuto.
  2. HAND INDEPENDENCE.
    (a) Combined Touch-Forms: legato vs. non-legato and tenuto.
    (b) Dynamic Contrasts: *mf* and *sf* vs. *f*.
    (c) Accompanying Figurations: in each hand.
  3. FINGER INDEPENDENCE. Part-playing in each hand.
  4. ENSEMBLE PLAYING. Accompanied song.
B. **Musicianship**.
  1. NOTATION. Reading of vocal score.
  2. RHYTHM. Syncopation.
C. **Bartók's Comments**. Written first as a piano solo, then as song with accompaniment. Valuable for learning how to accompany. Pupil and/or teacher should sing the melody. See the related notes in the preface.
D. **Suggestions**. Observe the interruption of legato as indicated by the separating sign in L.H., bar 32 of parts "a" and "b." The Hungarian title of this piece indicates that it is a teasing song to pair off a courting couple.

No. 75. Triplets.

A. **Technique**.
  1. TOUCH. Legato.

2. HAND INDEPENDENCE.
   (a) Counterpoint.
3. FINGER INDEPENDENCE. Part-playing in each hand.
4. BROKEN CHORD PLAYING. In each hand.
B. **Musicianship**.
1. RHYTHM. Subdivision of the beat into two and three parts: the quarter note as the pulse unit in 2/4 and 3/4.
2. EXPRESSION.
   (a) Tempo: poco allarg. = growing a little slower.
C. **Bartók's Comments**. Interesting rhythmic patterns. Key of D. Notice change of meter and accents.
D. **Suggestions**. It is recommended that Exercise 24 should be played here in preparation for No. 76 (the exercise seems to have little pertinency to No. 77).

No. 76. In Three Parts.

A. **Technique**.
1. TOUCH. Legato and staccatissimo.
2. HAND INDEPENDENCE.
   (a) Combined Touch-Forms: legato vs. staccatissimo.
   (b) Dynamic Contrast: ^ vs. *f*.
3. FINGER INDEPENDENCE. Part-playing in each hand.
B. **Musicianship**.
1. NOTATION. Devised G key signature.
2. RHYTHM. 2/2.
3. EXPRESSION.
   (a) Tempo: allegro molto = very fast.
   (b) Dynamics: marcato = marked, accented.
C. **Bartók's Comments**. Note placement of the sharp in the key signature. Tied notes over moving voice require good finger control. Key of G ending on dominant chord.
D. **Suggestions**. Staccatissimo is the most percussive touch-form employed by Bartók, who specifies that the sound is to be "almost sharp." The key should be released as quickly as possible after depression. Prepare Exercise 25.

No. 77. Little Study.[2]

A. **Technique**.
1. TOUCH. Legato, staccato, and tenuto.
2. HAND INDEPENDENCE.
   (a) Counterpoint.
   (b) Combined Touch-Forms: legato vs. staccato.
3. BROKEN CHORD PLAYING. In each hand. Some intervals in L.H.
4. PASSAGE-WORK. Scalar passages in each hand.
B. **Musicianship**.
1. NOTATION. F key signature.

2. RHYTHM. Subdivision of the beat into four parts: the quarter note as the unit of pulse in 2/4 and 3/4.

C. **Bartók's Comments**. Good for finger facility and parallel direction. G minor, ending on G-major chord. Good example in appendix.

D. **Suggestions**. Note the diverse rhythm patterns: ♫♫, ♫♩, ♩♫ and the cadential triplet schema ♫♫ ♩.

No. 78. Pentatonic Scale.

A. **Technique**.
   1. TOUCH. Legato.
   2. HAND INDEPENDENCE.
      (a) Counterpoint.
      (b) Dynamic Contrast: > vs. *f*.
      (c) Accompanying Figurations: in R.H. only.
   3. BROKEN CHORD PLAYING. In each hand.
   4. EMBELLISHMENTS. Slow trill in R.H.
B. **Musicianship**.
   1. RHYTHM. Syncopation. Ben ritmato = rhythmically.
   2. EXPRESSION.
      (a) Dynamics.

C. **Bartók's Comments**. Voices are in five-note ranges in changing position. In E minor. Consonant chords.

D. **Suggestions**. Note the tied notes in the last two bars. Play Exercises 26–28 and be sure the accents are observed in 27 and 28.

No. 79. Hommage à J. S. B.

A. **Technique**.
   1. TOUCH. Legato.
   2. HAND INDEPENDENCE.
      (a) Counterpoint.
      (b) Dynamic Contrast: > vs. *p*, *mp*, and *mf*
   3. BROKEN CHORD PLAYING. In each hand.
   4. EMBELLISHMENTS. Slow tremolo in each hand (bar 17).
B. **Musicianship**.
   1. NOTATION. G key signature. Mixed accidentals. The sixteenth rest.
   2. RHYTHM. Subdivision of the beat into four parts: the quarter note as the pulse unit in 3/4. The dotted eighth-sixteenth rhythm. Syncopation.
   3. EXPRESSION.
      (a) Tempo: calmo = tranquilly, calmly; poco rit. = gradually a little slower; ritard. = growing slower; a tempo = return to the original tempo.

C. **Bartók's Comments**. Signature looks like E minor but the piece is written in E major. In no fixed key. Left hand imitates right hand figures in inversion. Minor intervals are superimposed over major ones. Requires well-balanced playing. See exercises: variety of intervals from a set note. Also irregular accents.

D. **Suggestions**. Check carefully the playing of bar 16: there may be a tendency to play bars 17–29 as dotted rhythms throughout.

No. 80. Hommage à R. Sch.

A. **Technique**.
   1. TOUCH. Legato and staccatissimo.
   2. HAND INDEPENDENCE.
      (a) Counterpoint.
      (b) Dynamic Contrast: in relievo.
      (c) Combined Touch-Forms: legato vs. staccatissimo.
      (d) Accompanying Figurations: in each hand.
B. **Musicianship**.
   1. NOTATION. E♭ key signature. Mixed accidentals.
   2. RHYTHM. The dotted eighth-sixteenth rhythm.
   3. EXPRESSION.
      (a) Tempo: andantino, piacevole = faster than andante, played in a smooth nonaccented manner.
C. **Bartók's Comments**. Employs the more complex and richer harmonies of the early Romantic Period. Atmosphere like Schumann's music.
D. **Suggestions**. There may be a tendency to play bars 17–20 (particularly bars 17 and 18) as dotted rhythms throughout. Referring to **Bartók's Comments** above, note in this piece the chromaticism, mellifluous parallel sixths, and diminished chords, all popular with certain Romantic (nineteenth-century) composers.

No. 81. Wandering.

A. **Technique**.
   1. TOUCH. Legato.
   2. HAND INDEPENDENCE.
      (a) Counterpoint.
      (b) Dynamic Contrast: *mp* vs. *p*.
B. **Musicianship**.
   1. NOTATION. Change of clef in L.H.
   2. RHYTHM. Change of time: 2/4, 3/4.
   3. EXPRESSION.
      (a) Tempo: non troppo lento = not too slow.
      (b) Dynamics.
C. **Bartók's Comments**. Melodic figures repeated a tone higher or lower. Contrasting major and minor thirds. No fixed key. Abstract music.
D. **Suggestions**. Abstract music = absolute music = music representative of nothing but musical ideas. In contradistinction to this is Program music with which is associated nonmusical ideas such as a story or a picture. Program music almost always bears a descriptive title. In this piece, in view of Bartók's comment above, the title "Wandering" apparently refers to the meandering of

the motive through the keys as if in search of a tonality. In actuality, a kind of Bartókian "neutral" tonality is achieved through (a) use of a major pentachord imitated in stretto* by a parallel minor pentachord in bars 1–14 and, (b) use of the same contrapuntal device, this time in inversion, whose bimodal materials consist of major pentachords a perfect fifth apart in bars 15ff. Prepare Exercise 29 (see **Bartók's Comments** in No. 82 below).

*Stretto = a fugal device in which a musical idea (such as the pentachord illustrated above) is imitated or overlapped by the entry of another musical idea prior to the conclusion of the first idea.

No. 82. Scherzo.

A. **Technique**.
　　1. TOUCH. Legato, non-legato, staccato, and tenuto.
　　2. HAND INDEPENDENCE.
　　　　(a) Counterpoint.
　　　　(b) Combined Touch-Forms: tenuto vs. staccato.
　　　　(c) Dynamic Contrast: < vs. *mf*.
　　3. INTERVAL PLAYING. In each hand.
B. **Musicianship**.
　　1. NOTATION. G key signature.
　　2. RHYTHM. Change of time: 7/8, 3/8, 3/4, 2/4. Syncopation.
　　3. EXPRESSION.
　　　　(a) Tempo: allegretto scherzando = slower than allegro and in a playful, joking manner.
　　　　(b) Dynamics: accents.
C. **Bartók's Comments**. Should be played crisply with *strong* accents, especially left hand. Appendix exercise demonstrates accented beats in 7/8 time.
D. **Suggestions**. Accent beats 1 and 5 in the first four bars. Scherzo = joke, jest. This title can be given to an instrumental piece of a humorous character, whose leading features are animated movement, accentuation, and contrast.

No. 83. Melody with Interruptions.

A. **Technique**.
　　1. TOUCH. Legato, non-legato, and tenuto.
　　2. INTERVAL AND CHORD PLAYING. In each hand.
　　3. EMBELLISHMENTS. Slow double-stop tremolos in each hand.
　　4. PEDALLING. Use of the damper.
B. **Musicianship**.
　　1. EXPRESSION.
　　　　(a) Dynamics: marcato
C. **Bartók's Comments**. Hungarian folk tune: genuine, not made up. Double notes in trill form with repeated, strongly accented notes which interrupt. Similar to a theme in [Stravinsky's] *Petrouchka*.
D. **Suggestions**. Observe the syncopated pedalling. Every R.H. G is G♮.

No. 84. Merriment.

A. **Technique**.
    1. TOUCH. Legato, non-legato, tenuto, and espressivo (dolce).
    2. HAND INDEPENDENCE.
      (a) Counterpoint.
    3. FINGERING INDEPENDENCE. Part-playing in each hand.
    4. CHORD PLAYING. In R.H. only.
    5. PEDALLING. Use of the damper.

B. **Musicianship**.
    1. NOTATION. A key signature. Treble clef in each hand.
    2. RHYTHM. Syncopation.
    3. EXPRESSION.
      (a) Tempo: tranquillo = slower.
      (b) Dynamics: accents.

C. **Bartók's Comments**. Good study in syncopated rhythm. In Mixolydian mode in E with minor seventh: E-F♯-G♯-A-B-C♯-D♮-E.

D. **Suggestions**. Take notice of the part-writing in bar 7 (R.H.) and 11 (L.H.). Prepare Exercises 30–31. In bar 15 (beat 3), place the first finger of each hand on A.

No. 85. Broken Chords.

A. **Technique**.
    1. TOUCH. Legato and tenuto.
    2. FINGER INDEPENDENCE. Part-playing in R.H.
    3. BROKEN CHORD PLAYING. In each hand.
    4. POSITION. Hand crossings: R.H. under (sotto), L.H. over (sopra).

B. **Musicianship**.
    1. NOTATION. Change of clef in L.H.
    2. RHYTHM. The eighth-note duplet in 6/8.
    3. EXPRESSION.
      (a) Tempo: change of tempo.
      (b) Dynamics: accents, eight-bar crescendo.

C. **Bartók's Comments**. Broken chord pattern in continuation from right hand to left hand and vice versa. Note the changes in rhythmic patterns. Scorrevole means fluently. Key is not very certain but it seems to be in G. Appendix exercises are based on all chords of the scale, with the seventh added, and their resolution. Very good to introduce here.

D. **Suggestions**. The duplet rhythm pattern in bars 3, 27, and 59–60 can be interpreted as 2/4 M.M. ♩ = 88.

No. 86. Two Major Pentachords.

A. **Technique**.
    1. TOUCH. Legato.
    2. HAND INDEPENDENCE.

(a) Counterpoint.
(b) Dynamic Contrast: *sf* vs. *pp* (crescendo).
3. FINGER INDEPENDENCE. Part-playing in each hand.
B. **Musicianship**.
1. NOTATION. Reading of sharps in L.H. only.
2. RHYTHM. Syncopation.
3. EXPRESSION.
(a) Tempo: change of tempo.
(b) Dynamics: from *pp* to *ff*.
C. **Bartók's Comments**. Pentachord means the first five degrees of a scale of seven degrees. One voice in C, the other in F♯ in juxtaposition. Often employed in modern music and when understood would solve many of its mysteries. Not for average pupils.
D. **Suggestions**. The first phrase begins in the L.H. and proceeds from bass to treble clef in the first four bars. The second phrase (bars 5–8) begins with the retrograde form of bar 1. Retrograde = crab motion or cancrizans (that is, the repetition of a musical idea in reverse order so that the last note begins the repetition and the first note ends it). Take note of the tie in the L.H. of the last two bars.

No. 87. Variations.

A. **Technique**.
1. TOUCH. Legato, tenuto, dotted tenuto, and espressivo (cantabile, dolce).
2. HAND INDEPENDENCE.
(a) Combined Touch-Forms: legato vs. dotted tenuto.
(b) Dynamic Contrasts: ^ and *sf* vs. *f, p* vs. *pp*.
3. FINGER INDEPENDENCE. Part-playing in each hand.
4. INTERVAL AND CHORD PLAYING. In each hand.
5. POSITION. Hand crossings: R.H. over.
B. **Musicianship**.
1. NOTATION. Clef changes in each hand.
2. RHYTHM. Change of time. Syncopation.
3. EXPRESSION.
(a) Tempo: lo stesso tempo = the same tempo.
(b) Dynamics: accented voice parts, bars 34 and 36!
(c) Phrasing: theme and two variations.
C. **Bartók's Comments**. Use of more involved chords against melody in right hand and then reversed to left hand. Note changes in tempos and rhythms. In D minor feeling but ending on 6/4 chord of D major.
D. **Suggestions**. Dotted tenuto is an agogic variation of tenuto touch: the key is pressed rather than struck down and the tone is sounded usually for half the value of the note, never less. Cantabile and dolce are to be played with espressivo touch; in fact, the difference between them is one of dynamics (as indicated in the score). A 6/4 chord is a triad or chord in the position of the second inversion.

No. 88. Duet for Pipes.

A. Technique.

    1. TOUCH. Espressivo (cantabile) and staccato.

    2. HAND INDEPENDENCE.

       (a) Counterpoint.

    3. FINGER INDEPENDENCE. Last bar only.

    4. EMBELLISHMENTS. Slow trills in each hand.

B. Musicianship.

    1. NOTATION. The double flat. Treble clef in each hand.

    2. RHYTHM. Subdivision of the beat into two and three parts: the quarter note as the pulse unit in 2/4.

    3. EXPRESSION.

       (a) Tempo: change of tempo.

       (b) Phrasing: the separating sign.

C. Bartók's Comments.
Two pipes or flutes play chromatic melodies with skips and in triplets with various combinations.

D. Suggestions.
Play bar 4 non-legato. Take notice of the interruption of legato between bars 22 and 23. The accented, staccato sixteenths in the last measure require almost the equivalent of staccatissimo touch. Bartók's preliminary title, "Triplets," indicates the fundamental purpose of this piece.

No. 89. In Four Parts.

A. Technique.

    1. TOUCH. Legato, non-legato, and tenuto.

    2. FINGER INDEPENDENCE. Part-playing in each hand.

B. Musicianship.

    1. NOTATION. Devised two-sharp key signature.

    2. EXPRESSION.

       (a) Tempo: change of tempo.

       (b) Phrasing: separating signs.

C. Bartók's Comments.
Four voices: sometimes in chord form, sometimes in contrapuntal style. Preclassical.

D. Suggestions.
Observe the non-legato and the separating signs in the last two bars.

No. 90. In Russian Style.

A. Technique.

    1. TOUCH. Legato.

    2. FINGER INDEPENDENCE. Part-playing in each hand.

    3. INTERVAL PLAYING. As accompanying figurations in each hand (minor seconds, major sevenths).

B. Musicianship.

    1. NOTATION. Change of clef in L.H. Mixed accidentals.

    2. RHYTHM. Subdivision of the beat into two and four parts: the half note

as the pulse unit in 2/2.
3. EXPRESSION.
   (a) Dynamics: marcato e pesante.
   (b) Phrasing: separating signs.
   (c) Terms: Ossia = alternative passage.

C. **Bartók's Comments**. Voice in left hand against a minor second in right hand resolved to a minor third. Major third resolved to an augmented fourth. Not an original Russian tune but in the style: short themes and sentences, repetition. Good time for explanation of augmented and diminished intervals in key of C, etc.

D. **Suggestions**. Referring to the last four bars in L.H., compare the intervals with their inversions in the Ossia: major seventh-minor second, major sixth-minor third, perfect fifth-perfect fourth, and diminished fifth-augmented fourth. Inverting an augmented fourth results in a diminished fifth and vice versa. Alternate playing of Ossia and original versions.

The Russian aspect of this piece also probably lies in the use of the tonal components F-E♭-C. Other, more specific characteristics might be the use of duple meter, recurring rhythmic motives comprised of equal notes (quarter notes), and a kind of rhythmic solemnity arising from the use of short slurs which appear on each strong beat of the measure.

No. 91. Chromatic Invention [1].

A. **Technique**.
   1. TOUCH. Espressivo.
   2. HAND INDEPENDENCE.
      (a) Counterpoint.
   3. FINGERING PROBLEMS. Chromatics.
B. **Musicianship**.
   1. NOTATION. Mixed accidentals. Clef change in L.H.
   2. EXPRESSION.
      (a) Dynamics: smorzando = fading away.

C. **Bartók's Comments**. Patterned after the form of Bach, written in the chromatic idiom. Two-voice inventions, simple and clear. Voices in direct imitation and inversion. Teaching of it can be delayed if pupil is not ready.

D. **Suggestions**. Introduction (or review) of the chromatic scale can be undertaken with this piece.

No. 92. Chromatic Invention [2].

A. **Technique**.
   1. TOUCH. Legato and non-legato.
   2. HAND INDEPENDENCE.
      (a) Counterpoint.
      (b) Combined Touch-Forms: legato vs. non-legato.
      (c) Dynamic Contrasts: ^ and f vs. mf, f vs. ff.

(d) Accompanying Figurations: in each hand.

3. POSITION. Hand crossings: R.H. over. Unison playing with the hands two and five octaves apart. One- and two-octave leaps with the R.H. within a four-octave range.

4. EMBELLISHMENTS. Slow trills in each hand.

5. FINGERING PROBLEMS. Chromatics.

B. **Musicianship.**

1. NOTATION. Clef changes in R.H. Leger-line notes in L.H. The *ottava alta* sign *8* ⋯ .

2. RHYTHM. Syncopation.

3. EXPRESSION.

(a) Tempo: allegro robusto = fast, firm, and bold.

C. **Bartók's Comments.** Voices begin in unison. More freely written than the first invention and has entirely different character and spirit. Written within the limits of a pentachord with chromatic tones.

D. **Suggestions.** In bar 14, beat 1, the A remains sharp.

No. 93. In Four Parts [1].

A. **Technique.**

1. TOUCH. Legato.

2. FINGER INDEPENDENCE. Part-playing in each hand.

B. **Musicianship.**

1. NOTATION. G key signature (devised).

2. RHYTHM. Change of time: 2/4, 3/4, 5/8.

3. EXPRESSION.

(a) Phrasing: separating signs.

(b) Terms: sonoro = with a sonorous, ringing tone.

C. **Bartók's Comments.** Well-knit, four-voice study with an interesting and consistent rhythmic pattern. Note changes in meter. Key of G.

D. **Suggestions.** The legato should be interrupted between bars 10 and 11 (be careful not to interpolate an eighth rest here!). In bars 13–14, the tied, dotted half notes in each hand must be held down.

No. 94. Once Upon a Time . . .

A. **Technique.**

1. TOUCH. Espressivo, tenuto, and dotted tenuto.

2. HAND INDEPENDENCE.

(a) Counterpoint.

3. FINGER INDEPENDENCE. Part-playing in each hand.

B. **Musicianship.**

1. NOTATION. E♭ key signature. Clef changes in each hand. Mixed accidentals.

2. RHYTHM. Change of time.

3. EXPRESSION.

(a) Dynamics.

(b) Phrasing: the comma (bar 10).

C. **Bartók's Comments**. Descriptive little piece in contrapuntal form, alternating between 2/4 and 3/4 meters. Some polymodality. Key of C minor. Form is definite and very expressive.

D. **Suggestions**. The comma (bar 10) is a separating sign which means a slight, almost unnoticeable pause in which the time of separation is taken equally from the notes preceding and following the comma. The use of *Tale* as the title in the 1940 and 1948 printed editions does not appear in the MS drafts.

No. 95. Fox-Song.

A. **Technique**.

1. TOUCH. Legato, non-legato, staccato, tenuto, and portamento (portato).

2. HAND INDEPENDENCE.

(a) Counterpoint.

(b) Combined Touch-Forms: legato vs. non-legato and portamento, non-legato vs. staccato and portamento, and tenuto vs. portamento.

3. FINGER INDEPENDENCE. Part-playing in L.H. only.

4. INTERVAL AND CHORD PLAYING. In each band.

5. ENSEMBLE PLAYING. Vocal accompaniment.

B. **Musicianship**.

1. NOTATION. The vocal score. D key signature. Change of clef (R.H., part "b").

2. RHYTHM. Syncopation.

3. EXPRESSION.

(a) Phrasing: the separating signs | and '.

(b) Terms: poco a poco più tranquillo e rallentando al = little by little growing quieter and slower until. Ca. = about.

C. **Bartók's Comments**. Good study in syncopated rhythm. Simple melody made interesting by variety in harmony and changes in tempo. When in song form, the accompaniment is simple but interestingly done. See the related notes in the preface.

D. **Suggestions**. Portamento (portato) is a detached touch which combines key pressure (tenuto touch) with hand motion (flexible wrist action) so that the tone receives one-half the value of the note and is played without weight. Take notice of the separating signs in bars 4, 8, and 15 (comma!) of part "a" and bars 10 and 17 of part "b." This piece can be played as a self-accompanied vocal solo, a two-piano transcription, and/or an instrumental or vocal solo with piano accompaniment.

No. 96. Jolts.

A. **Technique**.

1. TOUCH. Espressivo and staccato.

2. HAND INDEPENDENCE.

(a) Counterpoint.
3. BROKEN CHORD PLAYING. In each hand.
4. FINGERING PROBLEMS.
B. **Musicianship.**
1. NOTATION. G key signature. Leger-line notes above the staff in the bass clef.
2. EXPRESSION.
(a) Dynamics.
C. **Bartók's Comments**. Good study for finger work in parallel motion. Good material for stressing arm coordination combined with fingers. Key of G.
D. **Suggestions**. The arrangement of the notes in bars 1–2 is suggestive of 6/8 time and, therefore, the pupil should be cautioned against interpolating accents anywhere except the first beat of a measure.

9

Volume Four

Nos. 97–121 and Exercises 32–33

No. 97. Notturno.

A. **Technique**.
  1. TOUCH. Legato, staccato, and espressivo.
  2. HAND INDEPENDENCE.
      (a) Combined Touch-Forms: legato vs. espressivo and staccato.
      (b) Accompanying Figurations: in each hand.
  3. BROKEN CHORD PLAYING. In each hand.
  4. PEDALLING. Use of the damper.

B. **Musicianship**.
  1. NOTATION. G key signature.
  2. RHYTHM. Subdivision of the beat into six parts: the dotted quarter as
      the pulse unit in 6/8. Polyrhythm (cross-rhythm): two (L.H.) vs. three
      (R.H.), bar 35.
  3. EXPRESSION.
      (a) Phrasing: in ternary form.

C. **Bartók's Comments.** Nostalgic piece in E minor reminiscent of Chopin or
Scriabin. Note left hand theme at end of piece. The fourth volume should be
combined with, e.g., the easy pieces from J. S. Bach's "Notebook for Anna
Magdalena Bach," the appropriate studies by Czerny, etc.

D. **Suggestions.** Prepare Exercise 32, a study in passing of the thumb, as preparation for No. 98, and take notice of the legato vs. staccato and marcato accents
in 7/8 time. As far as No. 97 is concerned, notturno = nocturne = a piano piece
of romantic or sentimental character usually lacking a distinct form.

No. 98. Thumbs Under.

A. **Technique**.
  1. TOUCH. Legato.
  2. FINGERING PROBLEMS. Passing of the thumb.

B. **Musicianship**.
  1. NOTATION. F key signature.
  2. EXPRESSION.
      (a) Phrasing: separating signs.
      (b) Dynamics: accents.

C. **Bartók's Comments.** Not difficult but good for thumb crossing. Refer to exercise in appendix. In F, ending on the second tone [G].

D. **Suggestions.** Note interruption of legato between bars 17 and 18.

No. 99. Hands Crossing.

A. **Technique**.
1. TOUCH. Legato and tenuto.
2. HAND INDEPENDENCE.
   (a) Dynamic Contrasts: > , *p* and *f* vs. *mf*.
3. POSITION. Hand crossings: L.H. over.

B. **Musicianship**.
1. NOTATION. Devised flat (E♭ only) and sharp (F♯ and G♯) key signatures in R.H. and L.H., respectively. Clef changes in L.H.

C. **Bartók's Comments.** Difficult for some pupils because of different key signatures for each hand. Show combination of parts to make scale or diminished seventh chord. Key is uncertain.

D. **Suggestions.** According to Bartók's comment above, the parts can be combined to form the following scale and diminished chords.

No. 100. In Folk Song Style.

A. **Technique**.
1. TOUCH. Espressivo.
2. HAND INDEPENDENCE.
   (a) Counterpoint.

B. **Musicianship**.
1. RHYTHM. Subdivision of the beat into two parts: the eighth note as the pulse unit in 5/8. The dotted eighth-sixteenth rhythm. Change of time: 5/8, 3/8.
2. EXPRESSION.
   (a) Terms: tutte le due voci con molta espressione = both parts or voices with much expression.

C. **Bartók's Comments.** This [L.H. bars 1–10, R.H. 11ff.] resembles the "Magic Fire" theme from Wagner's *Die Walküre*. Melody is long, written in two different positions. A Balkan melody, not my own invention.

D. **Suggestions.** Attend to the tied notes in the R.H. of the last two lines.

No. 101. Diminished Fifth.

A. **Technique**.
1. TOUCH. Legato.
2. HAND INDEPENDENCE.
   (a) Counterpoint.

B. **Musicianship**.
1. EXPRESSION.
   (a) Tempo: con moto = with animation.

C. **Bartók's Comments.** Two voices beginning at the interval of a diminished fifth and proceeding in various directions and patterns. Phrases are short and concise. Probably in the key of D minor, ending on diminished fifth.

D. **Suggestions.** Juxtaposition of the hands may cause some difficulty at first. Be sure to observe the eighth rests in bar 5 in order to avoid collision of the hands when proceeding to m. 6.

No. 102. Harmonics.

A. **Technique**.
1. TOUCH. Legato, non-legato, staccato, staccatissimo, tenuto, portamento, and espressivo (dolce).
2. CHORD PLAYING. In each hand.
3. POSITION. Hand crossing: R.H. over.
4. EMBELLISHMENTS. Grace notes in R.H.
5. PASSAGE-WORK. Scalar passages in R.H.
6. PEDALLING. Use of the damper.

B. **Musicianship**.
1. NOTATION. Use of diamond-shaped quarter, half, and dotted half notes. Use of treble clef in L.H. and clef change in R.H. The double sharp.
2. RHYTHM. Subdivision of the beat into two, three, and four parts: the quarter note as the pulse unit. Change of time: 2/4, 3/4.
3. EXPRESSION.
   (a) Tempo: un poco rubato = "robbed" a little in tempo. This direction means that the strict rhythmical flow can be modified by prolonging prominent melody notes or chords if there is an equivalent acceleration of less prominent tones. Changes of tempo.
   (b) Dynamics: *sff* = sforzato. This is the strongest accent sign used in the *Mikrokosmos*.

C. **Bartók's Comments.** Interesting effects produced from vibrations of overtones or harmonics when keys are silently pressed down and the same notes are sounded in a different range. Schoenberg was the first to use harmonics in three atonal pieces, op. 11. Henry Cowell uses these and many other devices such as plucking the strings in various ways at long or short distances to produce unusual sound effects or colors.

D. **Suggestions.** This piece can be considered as a summary of technical and musical problems encountered heretofore in the *Mikrokosmos*. Concerning the playing of harmonics, slow key descent (use tenuto touch) will permit key depression without sounding of tones.

No. 103. Minor and Major.

A. **Technique**.
1. TOUCH. Legato, non-legato, and espressivo.
2. HAND INDEPENDENCE.
   (a) Counterpoint.

3. BROKEN CHORD PLAYING. In each hand.

4. POSITION. Hand crossings: R.H. over (L.H. under).

B. **Musicianship**.

1. NOTATION. Change of clef in R.H. Dotted bar lines.

2. RHYTHM. Change of time: 5/8, 6/8, 7/8, 8/8, 9/8, 3x2/8. 9/8 appears as an additive (4+5/8) rhythm and as a divisive (compound time) rhythm. The dotted bar lines in bars 5–6 indicate additive rhythms of 2+3+2/8 and 3+2+3/8. The sign 3x2/8 is another way of indicating 3/4 so that the eighth note continues to serve as the pulse unit. Note also that 5/8 is considered as 3+2/8 and 2+3/8.

3. EXPRESSION.

   (a) Tempo: change of tempo. Presto = faster than allegro and slower than prestissimo. Accelerando = gradually growing faster.

   (b) Dynamics: *sff*, 15-bar crescendo.

   (c) Terms: rep. ad libitum = the performer is free to repeat these bars (bars 37–38).

C. **Bartók's Comments.** This is a minor pentachord superimposed against a major in an interesting variety of meters. 3x2/8 instead of 3/4 so as not to change speed notes.

D. **Suggestions.** 9/8 meter is used here as divisive (bars 19–24) and additive (bars 1–4) rhythms. A divisive rhythm is one in which the measure is divided into equal parts (in 9/8: four dotted quarter notes). An additive rhythm, on the other hand, is one in which the measure is composed of unequal groups added together (in 9/8, a group of four plus a group of five eighth notes). The basic difference between the two types of rhythm is one of accentuation. Review the additive rhythm in Exercise 20 (3+3+2/8).

No. 104. Wandering through the Keys.

A. **Technique**.

1. TOUCH. Legato.

2. FINGERING PROBLEMS. Passing of the fingers.

B. **Musicianship**.

1. NOTATION. D, E♭, E, A, and B♭ key signatures. Change of clef in L.H.

2. RHYTHM.

C. **Bartók's Comments.** Study in change of key without modulation. Same theme in unison and in similar motion.

D. **Suggestions.** Also serves as a study in extension and contraction of the hands. Emphasize slightly the syncopated notes in bars 14, 16, and 21 (and in part "b"). The Hungarian title means "Wandering from one key to another."

No. 105. Game Song (with two pentatonic scales).

A. **Technique**.

1. TOUCH. Legato, non-legato, and tenuto.

2. HAND INDEPENDENCE.

(a) Counterpoint.

(b) Dynamic Contrast: > vs. *f*.

3. FINGER INDEPENDENCE. Part-playing in each hand.

4. POSITION. Crossed hands: L.H. over, R.H. under.

5. FINGERING PROBLEMS. Black key playing in L.H. and white key playing in R.H.

B. **Musicianship**.

1. NOTATION. E key signature in L.H., C key signature in R.H. Treble clef in each hand.

2. RHYTHM. Change of time. Syncopation.

3. EXPRESSION.

(a) Tempo: change of tempo.

(b) Dynamics: marcato.

C. **Bartók's Comments.** Two pentatonic scales: a five-note scale in D minor in the right hand, D-E-G-A-B, and C♯ minor in the left hand, C♯-D♯-F♯-G♯-B. Similar to a theme in [Stravinsky's] *Le sacre du printemps*. Ends on dominant.

D. **Suggestions.** The separating signs in bars 12, 16, and 18 indicate phrase endings. Note the marcato (accents) in the alto and bass voices of bars 42–44.

No. 106. Children's Song.

A. **Technique**.

1. TOUCH. Legato.

2. HAND INDEPENDENCE.

(a) Counterpoint.

(b) Dynamic Contrasts: *p* vs. *mf* and *p* vs. *p in rilievo*.

3. FINGER INDEPENDENCE. Part-playing in L.H.

B. **Musicianship**.

1. NOTATION. The tie sign between staves (bars 35–36). Change of clef in L.H.

2. EXPRESSION.

(a) Tempo: change of tempo.

(b) Dynamics.

C. **Bartók's Comments.** A repetition of things done before.

D. **Suggestions.** Note the phrasing of bars 1-9 and the separating sign in the L.H. of bar 26. Bring out the L.H slightly in bars 27–34.

No. 107. Melody in the Mist.

A. **Technique**.

1. TOUCH. Legato, non-legato, and tenuto.

2. CHORD PLAYING. In each hand.

3. POSITION. Interlocked hands.

4. PEDALLING. Use of the damper (or solo sostenuto) pedal.

B. **Musicianship**.

1. NOTATION. Mixed accidentals; m.d. = right hand, m.s. = left hand.

2. RHYTHM. Syncopation.

C. **Bartók's Comments.** Dissonant chords played a half-tone apart create a vague, misty impression. To understand range and tonality of chords, play them in continuity broken from left hand to right hand. The melody emerges from the mist to complete the phrase. This is built to a climax and disappears in the mist. Key of C.

D. **Suggestions.** Depress the damper pedal exactly as marked in the score. The pedal should be used also on b. 3 of bars 34 and 38 (release the damper on beat 1 of bars 35 and 39). Finger the chords in bars 41–44 as before. In bars 40–45, the pedal tones (g in each hand) can be sustained by depressing the middle or solo sostenuto (sustaining) pedal on beat 2 of bar 40, or by depressing the damper pedal as indicated. If the damper is used, replace the fingers silently on the pedal tones, beat 2 of bar 44, and (keeping the keys held down) release the damper as marked in bar 45 (the last bar).

No. 108. Wrestling.

A. **Technique.**
   1. TOUCH. Non-legato.
   2. FINGER INDEPENDENCE. Part-playing in each hand.
   3. FINGERING PROBLEMS. Passing of the fingers.
B. **Musicianship.**
   1. NOTATION. Mixed accidentals.
   2. RHYTHM. Syncopation.
   3. EXPRESSION.
      (a) Dynamics: sempre marcatissimo = always very marked or accented.
C. **Bartók's Comments.** Picturesque struggle between tones of a minor second. Both hands in unison. One voice is tied while the other continues within the small range of a pentachord with chromatic tones. There are superimposed major and minor thirds. The voices finally resolve to the major triad of D.

D. **Suggestions.** The final chord is "neutral" because of the simultaneous use of the major (F♯) and minor (F♮) third. The effect, however, is a kind of "hovering" major tonality.

No. 109. From the Island of Bali.

A. **Technique.**
   1. TOUCH. Legato, non-legato, staccato, tenuto, espressivo (dolce), and dotted tenuto.
   2. HAND INDEPENDENCE.
      (a) Counterpoint.
   3. PEDALLING. Use of the solo sostenuto (sustaining) pedal, or the damper.
B. **Musicianship.**
   1. NOTATION. Change of clef in L.H.
   2. RHYTHM. Change of time: 6/8, 4/4.
   3. EXPRESSION.

(a) Tempo: change of tempo.

(b) Phrasing: in ternary form.

(c) Terms: (prol. Ped.) = pedale prolungato = (optional) use of the solo sostenuto pedal.

C. **Bartók's Comments.** Impressionistic composition possibly describing a tropical scene. Then, some action or dance takes place in the Risoluto section, finally returning to the original tempo and mood. Sostenuto pedal could be used if you have one. Tonality uncertain but it ends on D minor and F minor.

D. **Suggestions.** If the piano is not equipped with a solo sostenuto pedal, the half-depressed damper can be tried as a substitute (bars 30–38).

No. 110. And the Sounds Clash and Clang . . .[1]

A. **Technique.**

1. TOUCH. Legato, non-legato, and tenuto.

2. FINGER INDEPENDENCE. Part-playing in each hand.

3. INTERVAL PLAYING. In each hand.

4. POSITION. Interlocked hands.

5. PEDALLING. Use of the half-depressed damper.

6. EMBELLISHMENTS. Slow double-stop tremolos in each hand.

B. **Musicianship.**

1. NOTATION. Treble clef in each hand.

2. RHYTHM. Syncopation.

3. EXPRESSION.

(a) Tempo: assai allegro = very rapid, but not as fast as molto allegro. Tempo I, II. Un poco sostenuto = a little slower.

(b) Dynamics: mezza voce, ma marcato = half-voice (mezzo forte) but marked or accented.

(c) Terms: come sopra = as above (that is, marcato).

C. **Bartók's Comments.** Fifths in C and D♭, one against the other, beginning mezza voce with slower note values. The pattern is worked up to a frenzy of rhythmic sounds. This changes gradually to a sostenuto movement where the upper and lower voices of the chords proceed in unison. Tempo II returns, finally ending as it began with a common resolution to F♭ and E. The pedal is held down for many bars, only it is put halfway down.

D. **Suggestions.** Bartók does not use the term *sostenuto* to indicate a gradual decrease in speed and, therefore, bars 21–29 should be played at M.M. $\sard = 140$. The Hungarian title means "And the tones sound and pound."

No. 111. Intermezzo.

A. **Technique.**

1. TOUCH. Legato, tenuto, and espressivo.

2. HAND INDEPENDENCE.

(a) Dynamic Contrasts: *mp* vs. *p* (bar 22), *mf* vs. *p* (bar 25).

(b) Combined Touch-Forms: non-legato vs. legato and tenuto.

3. FINGER INDEPENDENCE. Part-playing in each hand.
4. INTERVAL PLAYING. In the L.H. only.
5. PEDALLING. Use of the damper.

B. **Musicianship.**
1. NOTATION. A key signature. Mixed accidentals. Clef change in L.H.
2. RHYTHM. Change of time: 5/4, 3/4.

C. **Bartók's Comments.** Melody in melancholy mood in 3/4 and 5/4 in characteristic Hungarian style: it is a common device to repeat the melody a fifth higher. In F♯ minor ending on the dominant.

D. **Suggestions.** The intervals in the L.H. of bars 48–49 are to be played non-legato and, in the same hand, F is natural in bars 38–40.

No. 112. Variations on a Folk Tune.

A. **Technique.**
1. TOUCH. Legato, non-legato, and staccato.
2. HAND INDEPENDENCE.
    (a) Counterpoint.
3. FINGER INDEPENDENCE. Part-playing in each hand.
4. INTERVAL PLAYING. In each hand.
5. PASSAGE-WORK. Scalar double sixths in each hand.
6. FINGERING PROBLEMS.

B. **Musicianship.**
1. RHYTHM. Change of time.
2. EXPRESSION.
    (a) Dynamics.

C. **Bartók's Comments.** This is an original Hungarian song. Everybody knows this tune, even the Russians, Poles, and Slovaks. Theme is announced in single tones, repeated in double sixths, and then in four-voice form in slower tempo. Then the theme is repeated in sixths, vivace. Diatonic is compressed into chromatic tonality.

D. **Suggestions.** Note fingering in the first lines and in bar 45. Observe crescendo marks. Prepare Exercise 33: here the L.H. brings out the additive rhythm of 4+3 and the R.H. plays legato and without accentuation (leggero). Cf. the chromatic compression in No. 64.

No. 113. Bulgarian Rhythm (1).[2]

A. **Technique.**
1. TOUCH. Legato and staccato.
2. HAND INDEPENDENCE.
    (a) Combined Touch-Forms: legato vs. staccato.
    (b) Dynamic Contrast: *mf* vs. *f* and *mp*, *mp* vs. *p*.
    (c) Accompanying Figurations: L.H. only.
3. POSITION. Interlocked hands.

B. **Musicianship.**

1. RHYTHM. 7/8 meter. Syncopation.
2. EXPRESSION.
    (a) Dynamics: leggero = lightly, without accentuation.
C. **Bartók's Comments.** The repetition can be played this way: with octaves throughout. In this case, the "seconda volta" shall be played louder than the "prima volta." In order to develop the sense of rhythm. it is recommended to play the piece as follows: two players (the exercise is useful even for more advanced players) who are able to play the piece perfectly shall play it as a piano duet, the second player playing the three introductory and the six closing bars and the accompaniment doubled in the lower octave (with both hands), the first player playing the melody doubled in the upper octave. Both parts should be studied by each. The theme is Hungarian and the rhythm is Bulgarian. Bulgarian rhythm has short units. 7/8 meter. The melody is syncopated and not symmetrical. 7/8 and 5/8 time are very common in Bulgarian music. Metronome time means to play 49 bars in one minute (including the repetition).
D. **Suggestions.** Play the L.H. without accentuation (leggero). See the two-piano transcription (No. 1) in Seven Pieces from *Mikrokosmos*.

No. 114. Theme and Inversion.

A. **Technique**.
    1. TOUCH. Legato and tenuto.
    2. HAND INDEPENDENCE.
        (a) Counterpoint.
        (b) Combined Touch-Forms: legato vs. tenuto.
B. **Musicianship**.
    1. NOTATION. D key signature. Clef changes in each hand. Mixed accidentals.
    2. RHYTHM. Change of time.
    3. EXPRESSION.
        (a) Dynamics.
C. **Bartók's Comments.** Theme must be clearly outlined and presented to the pupil. Explain its arrangement. It is a combination of B minor and E minor.
D. **Suggestions.** The first two bars contain an introductory phrase which is repeated in varied form in bars 9–10, 17–18. The theme itself begins in bar 3 and is repeated in inverted form in bar 11.

No. 115. Bulgarian Rhythm (2).

A. **Technique**.
    1. TOUCH. Legato.
    2. HAND INDEPENDENCE.
        (a) Counterpoint.
    3. FINGER INDEPENDENCE. Part-playing in L.H.
    4. INTERVAL AND BROKEN CHORD PLAYING.
        (a) Minor sevenths in L.H. and arpeggios in each hand.

5. FINGERING PROBLEMS.

B. **Musicianship.**
　1. NOTATION. Clef change in L.H. Mixed accidentals.
　2. RHYTHM. 5/8 as 3+2/8 and 2+3/8.
　3. EXPRESSION.
　　(a) Phrasing: in ternary form.
　　(b) Terms: scorrevole (fluently).

C. **Bartók's Comments.** This is an original Bulgarian theme. Altered key of G.

D. **Suggestions.** Check the hand-to-hand legato in bars 9–16 for steady dynamic level and clarity in articulation (there may be a tendency here to play legatissimo).

No. 116. Song.

A. **Technique.**
　1. TOUCH. Legato, non-legato, staccato, tenuto, dotted tenuto, portamento, and espressivo (cantabile).
　2. HAND INDEPENDENCE.
　　(a) Counterpoint.
　　(b) Combined Touch-Forms: legato and espressivo vs. tenuto, dotted tenuto, and portamento.
　　(c) Dynamic Contrast: > vs. *p*.
　3. CHORD PLAYING. In each hand.
　4. PEDALLING. Use of the damper.
　5. PASSAGE-WORK. Scalar passages in each hand.

B. **Musicianship.**
　1. NOTATION. The double-dotted half note. Clef changes in each hand.
　2. EXPRESSION.
　　(a) Tempo: Tempo di Marcia = march time. Change of tempo.
　　(b) Dynamics.

C. **Bartók's Comments.** Same framework at introduction and at end. In Hungarian structure. Key of G.

D. **Suggestions.** A difficult piece in terms of variety of touch; in fact, all the nonpercussive touch-forms are to be found here in various combinations. The second dot of a double-dotted note inturn adds half the value of the preceding dot to the note.

No. 117. Bourrée

A. **Technique.**
　1. TOUCH. Legato and dotted tenuto.
　2. HAND INDEPENDENCE.
　　(a) Counterpoint.
　　(b) Combined Touch-Forms: legato vs. dotted tenuto.
　　(c) Dynamic Contrasts: *sf* vs. *p*, > vs. *mf*.

3. BROKEN CHORD PLAYING. In the L.H.
4. POSITION. Hand crossing: R.H. over.
5. PASSAGE-WORK. Scalar passages in each hand.

B. **Musicianship**.
1. NOTATION. Clef changes in each hand. Mixed accidentals.
2. RHYTHM. Change of time: 4/4, 5/4, 3/2.
3. EXPRESSION.
(a) Dynamics.

C. **Bartók's Comments.** Name of piece derived from the rhythm, similar to Couperin.

D. **Suggestions.** Bourrée = an old dance of French or Spanish origin. The tempo does not change in bars 23 and 26, since the quarter note remains the unit of pulse.

No. 118. Triplets in 9/8 Time.

A. **Technique**.
1. TOUCH. Legato.
2. HAND INDEPENDENCE.
(a) Counterpoint.
(b) Dynamic Contrast: > vs. *p* and *mf*.
3. PASSAGE-WORK. Scalar passages in each hand.

B. **Musicianship**.
1. NOTATION. Clef changes in R.H.
2. RHYTHM. 9/8 as a compound triple meter.
3. EXPRESSION.
(a) Dynamics: accents.

C. **Bartók's Comments.** None.

D. **Suggestions.** A study also in accentuation.

No. 119. Dance in 3/4 Time.[3]

A. **Technique**.
1. TOUCH. Legato, staccato, and tenuto.
2. HAND INDEPENDENCE.
(a) Counterpoint.
(b) Combined Touch-Forms: legato vs. staccato.
3. POSITION. Hand crossing: L.H. under.
4. PEDALLING. Use of the damper.
5. PASSAGE-WORK. Scalar passages in each hand.
6. FINGERING PROBLEMS.

B. **Musicianship**.
1. NOTATION. E key signature.
2. EXPRESSION.
(a) Tempo: allegretto grazioso = moderately fast and gracefully. Pochiss.
allarg. = "a very little" gradual decrease in speed.

(b) Dynamics.

C. **Bartók's Comments.** Key of E—kind of a Mixolydian tonality.

D. **Suggestions.** Note the fermata between bars 27–28. Pause here slightly (one or two beats).

No. 120. Triads.

A. **Technique**.
    1. TOUCH. Legato, non-legato, staccato, and tenuto.
    2. FINGER INDEPENDENCE. Part-playing in each hand.
    3. CHORD PLAYING. Triads in each hand.
    4. POSITION. Interlocked hands.

B. **Musicianship.**
    1. NOTATION. Change of clef in each hand.
    2. RHYTHM. Change of time: 5/4, 3/2, 4/4, 3/4.
    3. EXPRESSION.
        (a) Tempo: accelerando from M.M. $\downarrow$ = 160 to $\downarrow$ = 108.
        (b) Dynamics.

C. **Bartók's Comments.** Device of blocked small chords. Altered C major. Has great technical value. Must be played with a very pointed touch and accentuation.

D. **Suggestions.** Bars 1–9 are in the C-Mixolydian mode, C-D-E-F-G-A-B♭.

No. 121. Two-Part Study.

A. **Technique**.
    1. TOUCH. Legato and non-legato.
    2. HAND INDEPENDENCE.
        (a) Counterpoint.
        (b) Combined Touch-Forms: legato vs. non-legato.
    3. PASSAGE-WORK. Scalar passages in each hand.
    4. FINGERING PROBLEMS.

B. **Musicianship.**
    1. NOTATION. A key signature. Mixed accidentals.
    2. RHYTHM. Change of time: 3/2, 4/4, 5/4, 3/4, 6/4. Syncopation.

C. **Bartók's Comments.** Different tonalities and scales. Mixed major and minor. Unusual procedure at end of piece.

D. **Suggestions.** Note separating signs which indicate interruption of legato in L.H. of bars 15 and 16. Be sure to observe the R.H. tie in the last two bars, so that the leading tone (Cs in L.H.) resolves properly to the tonic (D in R.H.). Emphatic rendition of the so-called Hungarian dotted-rhythm: ♪♩. ♩.

10

VOLUME FIVE

Nos. 122–139

No. 122. Chords Together and in Oppositon.

A. **Technique**.
    1. TOUCH. Non-legato and tenuto.
    2. HAND INDEPENDENCE.
        (a) Counterpoint.
        (b) Combined Touch-Forms: legato vs. tenuto.
        (c) Dynamic Contrast: ^ vs. *f*.
    3. INTERVAL AND CHORD PLAYING. In each hand.
    4. PEDALLING. Use of the damper.
B. **Musicianship**.
    1. NOTATION. Clef changes in each hand. G key signature.
    2. RHYTHM. Syncopation.
    3. EXPRESSION.
        (a) Dynamics: accents.
C. **Bartók's Comments.** Key of G. Tonic and dominant chords superimposed or against each other. Chords have foreign tones or they could be called eleventh or thirteenth chords. Framework of the chord is often the same with inner voices moving up or down the scale. Ends on chords of G and C with consecutive fifths added to each. Good for strengthening fingers in inner voices and for fast repetition. Foreign tones add color.
D. **Suggestions**. Note the key change in bar 49 and the fingering in bar 60. This piece, listed on the back jacket, does not appear in Bartók's recording (Columbia ML4419) of the *Mikrokosmos*.

No. 123. Staccato and Legato (2).[1]

A. **Technique**.
    1. TOUCH. Staccato, legato, and tenuto.
    2. HAND INDEPENDENCE.
        (a) Counterpoint.
        (b) Combined Touch-Forms: legato vs. staccato and tenuto.
B. **Musicianship**.
    1. NOTATION. Mixed accidentals.

2. EXPRESSION.
(a) Phrasing: canon at the fifth (part "b") and lower fifth (part "a").
C. **Bartók's Comments.** Key of C with much chromaticism. Requires keen observation and good control of fingers to make quick changes in touch.
D. **Suggestions.** Bartók's original English title was "Staccato versus Legato." His arrangement for two pianos appears in Seven Pieces from *Mikrokosmos*, and it is recommended that the pianist should alternate playing the primo and secondo parts with the teacher or another performer.[2]

No. 124. Staccato.

A. **Technique.**
1. TOUCH. Staccato.
2. HAND INDEPENDENCE.
(a) Counterpoint.
(b) Dynamic Contrasts: *sf* and *f* vs. *p*.
3. FINGERING PROBLEMS.
B. **Musicianship.**
1. NOTATION. Mixed accidentals. Changes of clef in R.H.
2. EXPRESSION.
(a) Tempo: allegretto mosso = rapidly but not as fast as allegro.
(b) Dynamics.
(c) Terms: secco quasi pizz. = dry as if plucked.
C. **Bartók's Comments.** Repeated notes in crisp, rapid staccato touch. Requires light, fast movements, strong accentuations, and variety of shading. Can be very effective if played with vitality.
D. **Suggestions.** To be played with percussive finger-stroke. The sforzato accents can be considered as designations of staccatissimo touch.

No. 125. Boating.

A. **Technique.**
1. TOUCH. Legato, staccato, and espressivo (cantabile).
2. HAND INDEPENDENCE.
(a) Combined Touch-Forms: legato vs. staccato and espressivo.
(b) Dynamic Contrast: *p* vs. *mf* and più *p*.
(c) Accompanying Figurations: in each hand.
3. BROKEN CHORD PLAYING. In each hand.
4. POSITION. Hand crossing: L.H. over.
B. **Musicianship.**
1. NOTATION. Clef changes in L.H.
2. RHYTHM. Change of time.
3. EXPRESSION.
(a) Tempo: pochett. rit. = "a very little" ritardando.
(b) Phrasing: in ternary form.
C. **Bartók's Comments.** Descriptive piece in a very unusual tonality. Repeti-

tion gives feeling of monotonous motion of the water.

D. **Suggestions**. In bar 46, the R.H. replaces the L.H. Bn on the third beat.

No. 126. Change of Time.

A. **Technique**.

    1. TOUCH. Non-legato.

    2. INTERVAL AND CHORD PLAYING. In each hand.

    3. PEDALLING. Use of the damper.

B. **Musicianship**.

    1. NOTATION. F key signature.

    2. RHYTHM. Change of time: 2/4, 3/4, 3/8, 5/8, 6/8.

    3. EXPRESSION.

        (a) Dynamics: *sf* accents.

C. **Bartók's Comments**. Unusual changes of time and construction. This is similar to Romanian style. The phrase structure is made up of one measure each of 2/4, 3/4, 3/8, and 5/8. This is consistently followed through more than one-half of the composition. The signature looks like F but the piece ends on the dominant of C. Count with the eighth note as the unit.

D. **Suggestions**. Be sure to observe the L.H. sforzato accent on the last beat of the 5/8 bars.

No. 127. New Hungarian Folk Song.

A. **Technique**.

    1. TOUCH. Legato, non-legato, staccato, tenuto, dotted tenuto, and portamento.

    2. HAND INDEPENDENCE.

        (a) Combined Touch-Forms: legato vs. staccato, tenuto, and dotted tenuto.

    3. FINGER INDEPENDENCE. Part-playing in R.H.

    4. INTERVAL PLAYING. Broken octaves in L.H.

    5. CHORD PLAYING. In each hand.

    6. EMBELLISHMENTS. Notated turn in L.H. (bar 23, beat 2).

    7. ENSEMBLE PLAYING. Vocal accompaniment.

B. **Musicianship**.

    1. NOTATION. D key signature. Clef changes in each hand.

    2. RHYTHM. Change of time. Syncopation.

    3. EXPRESSION.

        (a) Tempo: pochiss. allarg. = "a very little" gradual decrease in speed.

C. **Bartók's Comments**. This piece can be performed as follows: (a) the same performer singing and accompanying himself; (b) on two pianos, the first player playing the melody by doubling the octave, the second player by playing the original accompaniment; (c) for violin and piano. The violinist plays the first verse in the original position, the second in the higher octave. Pentatonic melody [B-D-E-F♯-A]. Valuable practice in accompanying. Pupil could sight read vocal part while teacher plays, and vice versa. Good ear training. Changes in rhythm make the pupil alert. In B minor, ending on D major. This Hungarian "new" tune is 100 years old—"old" tunes are older!

D. **Suggestions**. In the "new" style of Hungarian folk song, melodies are rounded in structure (that is, architectonic in form: AABA, ABBA, etc.). No. 127 is in ABBv (v = varied) A form. "Old" songs are nonrounded (ABCD, ABBC, and so forth). It is recommended that the pianist should play the primo and secondo parts of this piece in its transcribed form (see No. 5, Seven Pieces from *Mikrokosmos*). See also REMINGTON R19994.

No. 128. Stamping Dance.

A. **Technique**.
　　1. TOUCH. Legato, non-legato, staccato, and tenuto.
　　2. HAND INDEPENDENCE.
　　　　(a) Counterpoint.
　　　　(b) Combined Touch-Forms: legato vs. non-legato, staccato, and tenuto.
　　　　(c) Accompanying Figurations: in L.H.
　　3. INTERVAL PLAYING. In each hand. Broken octaves in L.H.
　　4. PASSAGE-WORK. Scalar passages in each hand.
　　5. EMBELLISHMENTS. Grace notes in R.H.
B. **Musicianship**.
　　1. NOTATION. Clef changes in L.H.
　　2. RHYTHM. Change of time. Syncopation.
　　3. EXPRESSION.
　　　　(a) Tempo: change of tempo.
　　　　(b) Dynamics: accents (>, ^, *sf*, *sff*).
　　　　(c) Phrasing: in ternary form.
C. **Bartók's Comments**. An original [Bartók] theme but in old Hungarian modal style. Interesting changes in rhythm and tempo. In the second section, one voice imitates the other. This is symmetrical in form. The ending is a Phrygian cadence. Altered key of G.

D. **Suggestions**. The characteristic interval of the Phrygian mode is the minor second between the first and second degrees. Transposed to G as principal tone: G-Ab-Bb-C-D Eb-F-G. Insofar as the Phrygian cadence is concerned, characteristics are the downward resolution of the minor second and the upward resolution of the seventh, both to the first degree (Tonic). The first edition title "Peasant Dance" is a mistranslation of Bartók's Hungarian and German titles.

No. 129. Alternating Thirds.

A. **Technique**.
　　1. TOUCH. Non-legato, staccato, dotted tenuto, and tenuto.
　　2. HAND INDEPENDENCE.
　　　　(a) Counterpoint.
　　　　(b) Dynamic Contrast: > vs. *p*.

3. INTERVAL PLAYING. In each hand.

4. PASSAGE-WORK. Double thirds.

B. **Musicianship**.

1. RHYTHM. Subdivision of the beat into two parts: the quarter note as the pulse unit. The quarter note triplet in 2/4 and the half note triplet in 2/

2. Change of time. Syncopation.

3. NOTATION. Clef change in L.H.

4. EXPRESSION.

(a) Tempo: quasi a tempo = nearly up to tempo, tornando al tempo I = returning to the first speed.

(b) Dynamics: leggero = lightly, without accent.

C. **Bartók's Comments**. This is in Phrygian mode. Most of the thirds are on white keys. Crisp, but stay very close to keys. Work very carefully on the rhythm at the ending—it must be exact.

D. **Suggestions**. The 2/4 and 2/2 triplets at the end can be counted by using eighth note and quarter note triplets, respectively, as frames of reference: Observe the diminuendo in the last seven bars. Bartók's original title was "Scherzo."

No. 130. Village Joke.

A. **Technique**.

1. TOUCH. legato and staccato.

2. HAND INDEPENDENCE.

(a) Combined Touch-Forms: legato vs. staccato.

(b) Dynamic Contrasts: ^ vs. *f*, > vs. *p*.

(c) Accompanying Figurations: in each hand.

3. INTERVAL AND CHORD PLAYING. Broken octaves and tenths in L.H. Chords in R.H.

4. PASSAGE-WORK. Scalar passages in each hand.

5. EMBELLISHMENTS. Five-note turns in each hand.

6. FINGERING PROBLEMS. The playing of black key major seconds with R.H. first finger. Chordal and intervallic leaps.

B. **Musicianship**.

1. NOTATION. Leger-line notes below the staff in the bass clef. Cluster-chord notation in the treble clef of bar 27. Mixed accidentals. Change of clef in R.H.

2. RHYTHM. Subdivision of the beat into five parts: the sixteenth note quintuplet in 2/4. Polyrhythm: five vs. two to the beat.

3. EXPRESSION.

(a) Dynamics: pesante and leggero

C. **Bartók's Comments**. Lydian mode. In playing it, make it droll and witty. Upward scales with augmented fourths add to the colorful effect. Also the rhythmic scheme. Note the alterations in the downward scales. Also that the process is reversed from R.H. to L.H. Should be a good concert number or encore.

D. **Suggestions**. Beginning seven bars from the end, be sure to observe all

L.H. accents.

No. 131. Fourths.

A. **Technique**.
   1. TOUCH. legato, non-legato, staccato, and tenuto.
   2. HAND INDEPENDENCE.
      (a) Combined Touch-Forms: legato vs. staccato.
   3. FINGER INDEPENDENCE. Part-playing in each hand.
   4. INTERVAL PLAYING. In each hand. Chord playing in the Ossia.
   5. EMBELLISHMENTS. Slow tremolos in each hand.

B. **Musicianship**.
   1. NOTATION. G♭ key signature. Mixed accidentals. Clef changes in each hand.
   2. EXPRESSION.
      (a) Dynamics.

C. **Bartók's Comments.** Contrasts of fourths in G♭ major and E♭ minor. Good example of bimodality. Has pentatonic feeling. Accentuation very positive and must be played clearly. Take your choice at the end—whichever preferable.

D. **Suggestions**. Check the part-playing in bars 35–40. The Ossia (which should be played) contains chords built of fourths. Termed *quartal harmony*—in contrast to the common tertian system in which chords are built of thirds—earlier (1908) examples of fourth chords can be found in No. 11 of Bartók's Fourteen Bagatelles op. 6, for Piano.

No. 132. Major Seconds Broken and Together.

A. **Technique**.
   1. TOUCH. Legato and espressivo.
   2. HAND INDEPENDENCE.
      (a) Counterpoint.
      (b) Combined Touch-Forms: legato vs. espressivo.
   3. FINGER INDEPENDENCE. Part-playing in each hand.
   4. FINGERING PROBLEMS. First finger R.H. on two keys.
   5. INTERVAL AND CHORD PLAYING. In each hand.

B. **Musicianship**.
   1. NOTATION. Treble clef in each hand. Mixed accidentals. The solid line (between staves) which indicates that the R.H. plays the melody note in the lower staff.
   2. RHYTHM. Change of time: 9/8 and 6/8 as compound meters.
   3. EXPRESSION.
      (a) Dynamics: smorzando = growing slower and softer.

C. **Bartók's Comments.** Study of chromaticism with a feeling of G major. Hovering tonality. An exotic effect can be produced.

D. **Suggestions**. The hand contractions required may prove awkward at first, but use the composer's fingerings to ensure a smooth legato. Review the chromatic scale in quick tempo (M.M. $\downarrow$ = 120–160).

No. 133. Syncopation (3).

A. **Technique.**
1. TOUCH. legato and non-legato.
2. CHORD PLAYING. In each hand.
3. POSITION. Hand crossings: each hand over and under.
4. PEDALLING. Use of the damper.
5. FINGERING PROBLEMS.

B. **Musicianship.**
1. NOTATION. Clef changes in each hand. Bass clef leger line notes below the staff. Mixed accidentals. $8 \cdots\cdots$ = *ottava bassa* = an octave lower in L.H.
2. RHYTHM. Change of time: 5/4, 3/4, 4/4. Syncopation.
3. EXPRESSION.
(a) Dynamics: pesante, accents, *pp* to *ff*.

C. **Bartók's Comments.** Difficult rhythmic patterns require close study. Not for average pupil. Key of G. Good preparation for Prokofiev.

D. **Suggestions.** Note the tied A♯ in bars 14–18 (R.H.).

No. 134. Studies in Double Notes.

A. **Technique.**
1. TOUCH. Legato and staccato.
2. HAND INDEPENDENCE.
(a) Dynamic Contrast: crescendo vs. diminuendo.
3. INTERVAL PLAYING. In each hand.
4. EMBELLISHMENTS. Double-note tremolos and grace notes in each hand.
5. FINGERING PROBLEMS.

B. **Musicianship.**
1. NOTATION. Mixed accidentals. Clef changes in each hand.
2. EXPRESSION.
(a) Dynamics.

C. **Bartók's Comments.** Excellent preparation for all fast double-note playing. Could be practiced in different rhythms, staccato, etc. Very valuable to develop a firm hold upon the keys.

D. **Suggestions.** The third study is useful for practice of hand independence: legato vs. staccato and dotted eighth-sixteenth patterns vs. eighths as written. According to the Hungarian title, a better heading for this piece would be "Studies in Double Stops."

No. 135. Perpetuum Mobile.

A. **Technique.**
1. TOUCH. Legato.
2. INTERVAL PLAYING. In each hand.

3. POSITION. Hand crossing: L.H. over.
4. EMBELLISHMENTS. Double-note tremolos in each hand.
5. FINGERING PROBLEMS.
B. **Musicianship.**
  1. NOTATION. Clef changes in L.H. Mixed accidentals.
  2. EXPRESSION.
    (a) Terms: repet. ad infinitum = repeat indefinitely.
C. **Bartók's Comments.** Excellent technical work in chromatic double notes in repetition. Altered key of F.
D. **Suggestions.** Perpetuum Mobile = perpetual motion = a piece which proceeds from beginning to end in the same rapid motion. A two-piano transcription of this piece appears as No. 3 in Seven Pieces from *Mikrokosmos*.

No. 136. Whole-Tone Scales.

A. **Technique.**
  1. TOUCH. Legato and espressivo (dolce, cantabile).
  2. HAND INDEPENDENCE.
    (a) Counterpoint.
  3. FINGER INDEPENDENCE. Part-playing in each hand.
  4. CHORD PLAYING. In each hand.
  5. POSITION. Hand crossings: R.H. and L.H. over and under.
  6. EMBELLISHMENTS. Five-note turn in L.H.
B. **Musicianship.**
  1. NOTATION. Mixed accidentals. Clef changes in each hand.
  2. RHYTHM. The eighth note quintuplet in 2/4. Change of time.
  3. EXPRESSION.
    (a) Tempo: change of tempo. Marcato.
    (b) Dynamics.
    (c) Phrasing: separating signs. Canonic rondo-variation form.
    (d) Terms: stringendo = growing faster and louder.
C. **Bartók's Comments.** Whole-tone scales: C-D-E-F♯-G♯-A♯ and A-B-C♯-D♯-E♯ in juxtaposition, worked out in many other keys, in changed rhythms and tempos. These devices are used to produce color.
D. **Suggestions.** Note the separating signs which interrupt the legato in bars 34, 40, and 49. Observe that the quintuplet in bar 79 is to be played sempre più lento.

No. 137. Unison.

A. **Technique.**
  1. TOUCH. Legato, legatissimo, tenuto, and espressivo.
  2. HAND INDEPENDENCE.
    (a) Combined Touch-Forms: legato vs. espressivo.
  3. FINGERING PROBLEMS.
  4. POSITION. The hands two, three, and four octaves apart. Playing in

extreme ranges of the keyboard.

B. **Musicianship**.

    1. NOTATION. Leger-line notes in each clef. Clef changes in each hand. D key signature.

    2. RHYTHM. Change of time: 2/4, 3/4, 5/8, 6/8, 7/8.

    3. EXPRESSION.

        (a) Tempo: lunga = long = the tone should be held (here) for at least double the value of the note. Change of tempo.

        (b) Dynamics: *pp* to *ff*.

        (c) Terms: ma sonoro = but with a sonorous or ringing tone.

        (d) Phrasing: in ternary form.

  C. **Bartók's Comments.** Excellent practice for reading, making quick changes of position, meter changes, clef signs, and style (dynamics and touch). Key of D.

  D. **Suggestions**. Legatissimo (bars 50–54) is an exaggerated legato: when every tone is held over a little into the beginning of the next one. It can be perfected by using the half pedal.

No. 138. Bagpipe Music.

A. **Technique**.

    1. TOUCH. Legato, non-legato, staccato, and tenuto.

    2. HAND INDEPENDENCE.

        (a) Combined Touch-Forms: non-legato vs. legato, staccato, and tenuto.

        (b) Dynamic Contrast: *p* vs. *mf*.

        (c) Accompanying Figurations: in L.H.

    3. FINGER INDEPENDENCE. Part-playing in each hand.

    4. PEDALLING. Optional use of the damper.

    5. PASSAGE-WORK. Scalar passages in R.H.

    6. EMBELLISHMENTS. Triplet and quintuplet trills in rapid tempo (R.H. only).

B. **Musicianship**.

    1. NOTATION. Clef changes in L.H.

    2. RHYTHM. Subdivision of the beat into five and six parts: the quarter note as the pulse unit in 2/4 and 3/4. The sixteenth-note triplet, quintuplet, sextuplet, and septuplet. Polyrhythm: five vs. two.

    3. EXPRESSION.

        (a) Tempo: change of tempo.

        (b) Dynamics.

        (c) Phrasing: in ternary form.

  C. **Bartók's Comments**. Use of all three pipes: chanter, tonic, and dominant, and the drone. Interesting division of the pipes. Squeaky effects are typical. It never ends normally because the air is going out of the pipes. Accent first beat of the five-note groupings.

  D. **Suggestions**. Bars 1–27 exemplify Bartók's use of noncoinciding meters:

the L.H. is in 3/8 and the R.H. is in 2/4 meter: The pipes are divided as follows: soprano voice = chanter, alto voice = drone pipe, and the bass and tenor voices = the tonic-dominant pipe. Be sure that A is held down in the last two bars (R.H.).

No. 139. Merry-Andrew.

A. **Technique**.

1. TOUCH. Legato, non-legato, staccato, tenuto, and dotted tenuto.

2. HAND INDEPENDENCE.

(a) Counterpoint.

(b) Combined Touch-Forms: legato vs. staccato, non-legato, tenuto, and dotted tenuto; non-legato and tenuto vs. staccato.

(c) Dynamic Contrast: ∧ vs. *f*.

3. FINGER INDEPENDENCE. Part-playing in L.H.

4. INTERVAL, CHORD, AND BROKEN CHORD PLAYING. In each hand.

5. POSITION. Interlocked hands. Hand crossings: R.H. and L.H. over.

6. PASSAGE-WORK. Scalar passages in R.H.

7. FINGERING PROBLEMS.

B. **Musicianship**.

1. NOTATION. Clef changes in R.H., treble clef in L.H.

2. EXPRESSION.

(a) Dynamics.

C. **Bartók's Comments**. Changes in key and tonality create a gay, droll effect. Major against minor in certain places. Key of C.

D. **Suggestions**. *Paprikajancsi* (Hung.) = Jack-Pudding or harlequin: a buffoon or clownish fellow.

11

VOLUME SIX

Nos. 140–153

No. 140. Free Variations.

A. **Technique**.

1. TOUCH. Legato, non-legato, staccato, and tenuto.
2. HAND INDEPENDENCE.
   (a) Counterpoint.
   (b) Combined Touch-Forms: non-legato vs. tenuto and staccato, legato vs. tenuto.
   (c) Dynamic Contrasts: p vs. mf, $\wedge$ vs. f.
   (d) Accompanying Figurations: in each hand.
3. INTERVAL, CHORD, AND BROKEN CHORD PLAYING. In each hand.
4. FINGER INDEPENDENCE. Part-playing in L.H.
5. PEDALLING. Use of the half-depressed damper.
6. PASSAGE-WORK. Rapid scalar passage in R.H.
7. FINGERING PROBLEMS.

B. **Musicianship**.

1. NOTATION. Clef changes in each hand.
2. RHYTHM. Subdivision of the beat into eight parts: the quarter note as the pulse unit in 2/4. Change of time: 3/8, 4/8, 5/8, 6/8, 7/8, 8/8, and 9/8. 9/8 as compound triple meter and as additive rhythm (4+3+2)/8. 7/8 as 4+3/8 and 8/8 as 3+3+2/8. Syncopation.
3. EXPRESSION.
   (a) Tempo: change of tempo. Il doppio più leuto = twice as slow. Stretto = quicker.
   (b) Dynamics: intenso = with intensity, stress.
   (c) Terms: lugubre = mournfully. Strepitoso = noisily.
   (d) Phrasing: in rondo-variation form.

C. **Bartók's Comments**. Ingenious variety of treatment. Change of mood, change of tempo and style. Excellent technical and rhythmic materials.

D. **Suggestions**. Observe the separating sign (comma) in bar 12. Begin bar 44 at M.M. $\quad\downarrow$ = 80.

No. 141. Subject and Reflection.[1]

A. **Technique**.
1. TOUCH. Legato, non-legato, staccato, and tenuto.
2. HAND INDEPENDENCE.
   (a) Combined Touch-Forms: legato vs. tenuto.
3. FINGER INDEPENDENCE. Part-playing in each hand.
4. POSITION. Crossing of the hands: R.H. under.

B. **Musicianship**.
1. NOTATION. Clef changes in each hand. Leger-line notes above the staff in the treble and below the staff in the bass clef. Mixed accidentals.
2. RHYTHM. Change of time: 2/4, 3/4, 3/8, 5/8, 7/8. Syncopation.
3. EXPRESSION.
   (a) Tempo: change of tempo: vivacissimo = very quick.
   (b) Phrasing: in rondo-variation form.
   (c) Dynamics: accents.

C. **Bartók's Comments**. Subject clearly defined and arranged in changing meters, keys, and styles of tonality. Tonality is B. I think of this as being mirrored in water: as the water becomes disturbed the reflection becomes distorted.

D. **Suggestions**. Observe the slight pause indicated by the separating sign in bar 22.

No. 142. From the Diary of a Fly.

A. **Technique**.
1. TOUCH. Legato, non-legato, staccato, and tenuto.
2. HAND INDEPENDENCE.
   (a) Counterpoint.
   (b) Combined Touch-Forms: legato, non-legato, and tenuto vs. staccato.
   (c) Dynamic Contrast: *sf* vs. *mf*.
3. FINGER INDEPENDENCE. Part-playing in each hand, where the individual voices reflect combined touch-forms as well as dynamic contrast.
4. POSITION. Interlocked hands. Hand crossings: R.H. and L.H. over and under.
5. CHORD PLAYING. In each hand.
6. EMBELLISHMENTS. Trills and tremolos in each hand.

B. **Musicianship**.
1. NOTATION. Mixed accidentals. Treble clef in each hand.
2. RHYTHM. Change of time. Syncopation.
3. EXPRESSION.
   (a) Tempo: change of tempo. Agitato = agitated. Poco stringendo = a little acceleration and increase in intensity.
   (b) Dynamics: *sff*, *sf*, ^, > . Leggero.
   (c) Terms: lamentoso = in a melancholy, sad style. Con gioia = joyfully.
   (d) Phrasing: in ternary form.

C. **Bartók's Comments**. I wanted to depict the desperate sound of a fly's buzz, when getting into a cobweb. The fly is telling the story as he writes in his diary. He was buzzing about and didn't see the spider web. Then he is caught in the web (Agitato: "Woe, a cobweb!"), but he manages to get himself free before he is eaten, and he escapes. A happy ending (con gioia). Play it delicately, close to the keys. Slight use of wrist in staccato, it must be flexible.

D. **Suggestions**. Take notice of the slight pause in bar 59 and the replacement of fingers in L.H. of bars 72–73. Note also the ties in bars 75–87 and 98–102.

No. 143. Divided Arpeggios.[2]

A. **Technique**.
    1. TOUCH. Legato, non-legato, staccato, tenuto, and espressivo.
    2. HAND INDEPENDENCE.
        (a) Counterpoint.
    3. FINGER INDEPENDENCE. Part-playing in each hand.
    4. CHORD AND BROKEN CHORD PLAYING. In each hand.
    5. POSITION. Hand crossings: L.H. and R.H. over and under.
    6. PEDALLING. Use of the damper.
    7. PASSAGE-WORK. Rapid arpeggios (without passing of the fingers) in each hand.

B. **Musicianship**.
    1. NOTATION. Clef changes in each hand. Mixed accidentals. Treble clef leger-line notes above and below the staff.
    2. RHYTHM. Change of time: 2/4, 1/4. Syncopation.
    3. EXPRESSION.
        (a) Tempo: change of tempo. Un poco stentato = retarding a little.
        (b) Dynamics: mezza voce = *mf* .

C. **Bartók's Comments**. This is very difficult for average pupils to play and understand. The themes must be introduced clearly and with great care for rhythmic accuracy. Only for unusual pupils.

D. **Suggestions**. Use espressivo touch in bars 27–28 only. The arpeggios are broken chords in five finger positions which do not require passing of the fingers.

No. 144. Minor Seconds, Major Sevenths.

A. **Technique**.
    1. TOUCH. Legato, non-legato, staccato, tenuto, and portamento (portato).
    2. HAND INDEPENDENCE.
        (a) Counterpoint.
        (b) Combined Touch-Forms: tenuto vs. dotted tenuto and portamento.
    3. FINGER INDEPENDENCE. Part-playing in each hand.
    4. INTERVAL, CHORD, AND BROKEN CHORD PLAYING. In each hand.
    5. POSITION. Interlocked hands. Hand crossings: L.H. over.

6. PASSAGE-WORK. Scalar and arpeggio passages in each hand.

7. PEDALLING. Indicated and optional use of the damper.

8. FINGERING PROBLEMS.

B. **Musicianship**.

    1. NOTATION. Clef changes in each hand. Thirty-second notes and double-dotted eighth and quarter notes. Mixed accidentals.

    2. RHYTHM. Subdivision of the beat into eight parts: the quarter note as the pulse unit in 4/4. Change of time: 4/4, 2/4 and 3/2. Syncopation.

    3. EXPRESSION.

        (a) Tempo: change of tempo. Doppio movimento = twice as fast.

        (b) Dynamics: intenso.

        (c) Terms: mesto = pensive, melancholy.

C. **Bartók's Comments**. This is very difficult and requires a pupil who has great control. The sevenths are bells and they emphasize the melody.

D. **Suggestions**. Note the decrescendo that takes place towards each dotted eighth (bar 1ff.). In bar 38, the L.H. crosses over to play D an octave higher than the leger-line D in the R.H. In bar 41 the E♮ and E♭ played by the L.H. should be released on beat 3 and, in bars 41–42, observe the tied notes in the R.H.

No. 145. Chromatic Invention (3).[3]

A. **Technique**.

    1. TOUCH. Non-legato and tenuto.

    2. HAND INDEPENDENCE.

        (a) Counterpoint.

        (b) Combined Touch-Forms: non-legato vs. tenuto.

        (c) Dynamic Contrasts: >, ^, and *sf*.

    3. INTERVAL PLAYING. Octaves in each hand.

    4. POSITION. Hand crossings: R.H. and L.H. over, L.H. under.

    5. ENSEMBLE PLAYING. Parts "a" and "b" together as a piece for two pianos.

B. **Musicianship**.

    1. NOTATION. Clef changes in each hand. Mixed accidentals.

    2. RHYTHM. Change of time. Syncopation.

    3. EXPRESSION.

        (a) Tempo: accelerando sin al fine = increasing in speed up to the end.

        (b) Dynamics: *fff* = extremely loud.

        (c) Terms: con 8 (ad lib.) = with octaves (if the performer wishes to do so).

C. **Bartók's Comments**. Versions "a" and "b" can be played separately, or together on two pianos.

D. **Suggestions**. The two-piano transcription of this piece in Seven Pieces from *Mikrokosmos* (No. 6) contains part "a" as the primo and part "b" as the secondo.

No. 146. Ostinato.

A. **Technique**.

1. TOUCH. Legato, non-legato, tenuto, dotted tenuto, staccato, and staccatissimo.

2. HAND INDEPENDENCE.

(a) Combined Touch-Forms: legato vs. non-legato and tenuto. Non-legato vs. tenuto, staccato and staccatissimo.

(b) Dynamic Contrasts: >, ^ , and *sf*.

(c) Accompanying Figurations: L.H. only.

3. FINGER INDEPENDENCE. Part-playing in each hand.

4. INTERVAL AND CHORD PLAYING. In each hand. Also octaves, and chords with the span of an octave.

5. PEDALLING. Use of the damper.

6. POSITION. Hand crossings: L.H. and R.H. over.

7. PASSAGE-WORK. Scalar passages in each hand.

8. FINGERING PROBLEMS.

B. **Musicianship**.

1. NOTATION. Clef changes in each hand. Mixed accidentals. Leger-line notes in each clef.

2. RHYTHM. Syncopation.

3. EXPRESSION.

(a) Tempo: change of tempo. Non accelerando (non acc.), meno vivo.

(b) Dynamics: leggero

C. **Bartók's Comments**. Ostinato: a ground bass which recurs obstinately throughout the composition. Has a definite Oriental feeling. Dorian mode with alterations. This is not actually a traditional ostinato, because the traditional ostinato was a repeated theme. Also suggests Bulgarian pipes [bars 60–80].

D. **Suggestions**. Take notice of the staccatismo marks in the R.H. of bars 138, 142, and 145. In bar 154, beat 1, the octave of D can be divided between the hands. A transcription of this piece appears as No. 7 in Seven Pieces from *Mikrokosmos*. Although the piece is listed on the back jacket of Bartók's recording of the *Mikrokosmos* (Columbia ML4419), it does not appear in the record itself.

No. 147. March.

A. **Technique**.

1. TOUCH. Legato, non-legato, tenuto, staccato, and staccatissimo.

2. HAND INDEPENDENCE.

(a) Combined Touch-Forms: legato vs. non-legato, tenuto and staccato. Tenuto vs. non-legato and staccato.

(b) Dynamic Contrasts: ^ and *sf*.

(c) Accompanying Figurations: in each hand.

3. FINGER INDEPENDENCE. Part-playing in each hand.

4. INTERVAL AND CHORD PLAYING. In each hand.

5. POSITION. Hand crossing: R.H. over.

6. PASSAGE-WORK. Octaves: in each hand.

7. EMBELLISHMENTS. Octave trill in R.H.

8. FINGERING PROBLEMS.

B. **Musicianship.**

1. NOTATION. Mixed accidentals. Clef changes: in R.H.

2. RHYTHM. Change of time: 4/4, 5/4, 3/2. Subdivision of the beat into two, three, and four parts: the quarter note as the pulse unit in 4/4.

3. EXPRESSION.

(a) Dynamics: *sff* and *fff*.

(b) Terms: sonoro.

C. **Bartók's Comments.** Repetition in L.H. (fourths and fifths:) creates a grotesque effect—like a march of primitive peoples.

D. **Suggestions.** This: piece requires quick hand crossings and judicious use of the damper pedal. In bar 26, the separating sign interrupts the legato (L.H.). Note the fingerings in bars 31–32 and that F♯ is tied over the next three bars. The solo sostenuto pedal can be used in bars 54–55.

No. 148. Six Dances in Bulgarian Rhythm (1).

A. **Technique.**

1. TOUCH. Legato, non-legato, tenuto, dotted tenuto, staccato, portamento, and espressivo (dolce).

2. HAND INDEPENDENCE.

(a) Counterpoint.

(b) Combined Touch-Forms: legato vs. non-legato, staccato, tenuto, dotted tenuto,and portamento. Dotted tenuto vs. portamento. Staccato and non-legato. Espressivo vs. legato, dotted tenuto, and portamento.

(c) Dynamic Contrast: > vs. ^.

(d) Accompanying Figurations: in each hand.

3. FINGER INDEPENDENCE. Part-playing in each hand.

4. INTERVAL, CHORD, AND BROKEN CHORD PLAYING. Octaves in each hand and tenths in L.H. Arpeggiated triads: in L.H. Chords with the span of an octave and a ninth.

5. POSITION. Interlocked hands: L.H. under.

6. PASSAGE-WORK. Scalar passages in each hand.

7. EMBELLISHMENTS. Grace notes, turns, and the Prall-triller (inverted mordent) in R.H.

8. FINGERING PROBLEMS.

B . **Musicianship.**

1. NOTATION. Clef changes: in each hand. The inverted mordent. Mixed accidentals.

2. RHYTHM. Additive rhythm: 4+2+3/8. Syncopation.

3. EXPRESSION.

(a) Dynamics: rinf. = rinforzato = a sudden increase in loudness (in this short passage).

(b) Phrasing: in variation form.

C. **Bartók's Comments**. Hexachord in Dorian mode, repeated in the left hand, which never goes to the octave in range. Changes in accentuation typical of Bulgarian rhythm. The phrase dictated the meter sign, because of accentuation. Odd-numbered groups: heavily accented.

D. **Suggestions**. The inverted mordents are played: ♪♪♩♩, not as sixteenth-note triplets or as grace notes in anticipation of the beat. Pianists with small hands may play the tenth in bars 33 and 52 as broken intervals. The last chord in bar 55 can be shared between the hands.

No. 149. Six Dances in Bulgarian Rhythm (2)

A. **Technique**.
  1. TOUCH. Legato, non-legato, staccato, tenuto, and dotted tenuto.
  2. HAND INDEPENDENCE.
    (a) Counterpoint.
    (b) Combined Touch-Forms: legato vs. staccato and dotted tenuto. Non-legato vs. tenuto.
    (c) Dynamic Contrasts: > vs. *p* and ^, *sf* and *mf* vs. ^.
    (d) Accompanying Figurations: in each hand.
  3. FINGER INDEPENDENCE. Part-playing in each hand.
  4. INTERVAL AND CHORD PLAYING. In each hand.
  5. PEDALLING. Optional use of the damper.
  6. PASSAGE-WORK. Scalar passages in each hand.
  7. EMBELLISHMENTS. Slow trill in R.H.

B. **Musicianship**.
  1. NOTATION. Clef changes in each hand.
  2. RHYTHM. Additive rhythm: 2+2+3/8.
  3. EXPRESSION.
    (a) Dynamics: martellato = hammering = a percussive staccato touch played forte or louder. Usually requires the use of the forearm to achieve the indicated dynamic level.

C. **Bartók's Comments**. The rhythmic figure in the first measure is very important—maintained throughout.

D. **Suggestions**. The value of the eighth note is ♩ = 120

No. 150. Six Dances in Bulgarian Rhythm (3).

A. **Technique**.
  1. TOUCH. Legato, non-legato, tenuto, staccato, and staccatissimo.
  2. HAND INDEPENDENCE.
    (a) Counterpoint.
    (b) Combined Touch-Forms: legato vs. tenuto and non-legato. Tenuto vs. non-legato.
    (c) Dynamic Contrast: ^ vs. *f* and > vs. *p*.
    (d) Accompanying Figurations: in L.H.

3. FINGER INDEPENDENCE. Part-playing in each hand.
4. INTERVAL PLAYING. Legato sixths: in L.H.
5. POSITION. Hand crossing: R.H. under.
6. EMBELLISHMENTS. Grace note in L.H.
7. FINGERING PROBLEMS.

B. **Musicianship**.
1. NOTATION. Clef change in L.H. Mixed accidentals.
2. RHYTHM. Additive rhythm: 5/8 as 2 + 3/8.
3. EXPRESSiON.
   (a) Tempo: change of tempo.
   (b) Dynamics: marcato and leggero
   (c) Phrasing: canonic form in bars 58–78.

C. **Bartók's Comments**. 5/8 time. Very much like other things written before it.

D. **Suggestions**. Play staccatissimo on beat 2 of bar 4 in both hands. Use of the solo sostenuto pedal (or damper pedal) will be required for the L.H. beginning in bar 35 and bar 39. Play the leggero sections without emphasis except as marked, and interrupt the legato as indicated by the comma between bars 92 and 93.

No. 151. Six Dances in Bulgarian Rhythm (4).

A. **Technique**.
1. TOUCH. Legato, non-legato, tenuto, and dotted tenuto.
2. HAND INDEPENDENCE.
   (a) Counterpoint.
   (b) Combined Touch-Forms: non-legato vs. tenuto and dotted tenuto.
   (c) Accompanying Figurations: in each hand.
3. INTERVAL AND CHORD PLAYING. In each hand. Octaves: in R.H.
4. POSITION. Interlocked hands: R.H. over.
5. PASSAGE. Chordal passages in L.H.
6. EMBELLISHMENTS. Grace notes and fast trills in each hand.
7. FINGERING PROBLEMS. Repeated notes.

B. **Musicianship**.
1. NOTATION. Clef changes in each hand. Mixed accidentals. The trill sign.
2. RHYTHM. Additive rhythm: 3+2+3/8. Syncopation.
3. EXPRESSION.
   (a) Tempo: change of tempo.
   (b) Dynamics.
   (c) Phrasing: in variation form.

C. **Bartók's Comments**. Very much in the style of Gershwin. Gershwin's tonality, rhythm, and color. American folksong feeling. Moderate tempo but vital, crisp, and accented.

D. **Suggestions**. Bartók, in his recording of this piece, accents each quarter note of the melody (R.H. beginning bar 1). Note the separating sign (comma) in bar 50 and the fermata between the last two bars. Also note the change in rhythm on beats 1–3 in bars 22–23.

No. 152. Six Dances in Bulgarian Rhythm (5).[4]

A. **Technique**.
  1. TOUCH. Legato, non-legato, staccato, and tenuto.
  2. HAND INDEPENDENCE.
    (a) Counterpoint.
    (b) Combined Touch-Forms: legato vs. non-legato, staccato, and tenuto.
    (c) Accompanying Figurations: in each hand.
  3. FINGER INDEPENDENCE. Part-playing in each hand.
  4. INTERVAL AND CHORD PLAYING. In each hand.
  5. POSITION. Hand crossings: R.H. and L.H. over.
  6. EMBELLISHMENTS. Slow trills in both hands and fast trills: in R.H.

B. **Musicianship**.
  1. NOTATION. Clef changes: in each hand. Mixed accidentals.
  2. RHYTHM. Additive rhythm: 2+2+2+3/8. Syncopation.
  3. EXPRESSION.
    (a) Dynamics: leggero

C. **Bartók's Comments**. Combination of staccato and legato. Mixed key, ending in A. Rhythm—strong accents.

D. **Suggestions**. L.H. sopra in bars 7–10, and R.H. sopra in bars 11–15.

No. 153. Six Dances in Bulgarian Rhythm (6).

A. **Technique**.
  1. TOUCH. Legato and non-legato playing.
  2. HAND INDEPENDENCE.
  3. FINGER INDEPENDENCE. Part-playing in each hand.
    (a) Counterpoint.
    (b) Combined Touch-Forms: legato vs. staccato.
    (c) Dynamic Contrasts: ^ vs f, sf vs. f, and Marc. (marcato) vs. f.
    (d) Accompanying Figurations: in each hand.
  4. INTERVAL AND CHORD PLAYING. In each hand. Octave and broken octave playing in each hand.
  5. PASSAGE-WORK. Scalar passages: in each hand.
  6. FINGERING PROBLEMS. Repeated notes.
  7. PEDALLING. Use of the damper.

B. **Musicianship**.
  1. NOTATION. Clef changes in each hand. Mixed accidentals.
  2. RHYTHM. Additive rhythm: 3+3+2/8. Syncopation.
  3. EXPRESSION.
    (a) Dynamics: marcato, marcatissimo.

(b) Phrasing: canonic writing bars 25–29. In ternary form.

(c) Terms: strepitoso = noisily.

C. **Bartók's Comments**. Polymodal—chords against organ point. Key of E. Especially third group of each measure accented. Bring out accents in left hand of bars 9ff. Buzzing effect in bars 69ff.

D. **Suggestions**. In m. 49, middle C should be played with the thumb of the R.H. Avoid accentuation in the leggero section (bars 75ff.).

PART THREE

Style

12

Bartók's Musical Language

During February 1943, Bartók gave four lectures at Harvard University on "the main characteristics of the 'New' Hungarian art music."[1] The second lecture discussed the importance of the modes and polymodality, and touched on their differences from contemporary techniques of poltonality, atonality, and twelve-tone music. The third lecture was devoted to chromaticism and its rarity in folk music, followed by the fourth one on rhythm.[2]

> So, the start for the creation of the "New" Hungarian art music was given, first, by a thorough knowledge of the devices of old and contemporary Western art music: for the technique of composition; and, second, by the newly discovered [Hungarian] rural music—material of incomparable beauty and perfection: for the spirit of our works to be created. Scores of aspects could be distinguished and quoted in regard to the influence exerted on us by this material: for instance, tonality, melody, rhythm, and even structural influence.[3]

Tonality

When Bartók set out in 1906 to investigate peasant music in the villages of Greater Hungary,[4] he was surprised to find the folk melodies were based for the most part on the five most commonly used modes of the art music of the Middle Ages, instead of the major and minor scales. In fact, the next year he was the first collector to discover the "Old" Hungarian anhemitone (without half-steps) pentatonic melodies during a fieldtrip to a remote enclave of Transylvanian-Hungarians (Ex. 12.1).

The old style melodies are generally based on the Hungarian form of the pentatonic scale: a symmetrical arrangement of two major seconds and two minor thirds. And there are many melodies based on certain folk modes, but Bartók's extensive fieldwork failed to turn up Lydian specimens among autochthonous Hungarian villages.[5] The new style, which began its development during the second half of the nineteenth century, consists of Aeolian, Dorian, and Mixolydian melodies. The latter mode represents a modification of the modern major scale which, together with the modern minor scales predominant in the art music of the West, infiltrated Eastern Europe.[6]

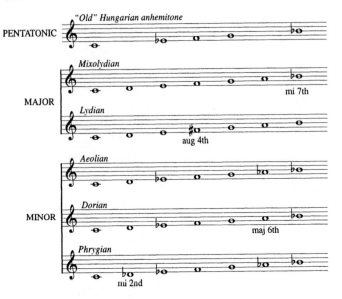

Ex. 12.1. Pentatonic and heptatonic folk modes, based on C as principal tone.

While the Slovak old-style features the Mixolydian mode, the characteristic part of the other material is based on the Lydian mode.[7] In some Hungarian folk songs, and especially in Bartók's vast Transylvanian-Romanian collection of instrumental and vocal melodies, he found scalar formations "absolutely unknown from modal music, and furthermore, scales with seemingly oriental features, that is, having augmented second steps" (Ex. 12.2). [8]

Ex. 12.2. Selected nondiatonic folk melodies from Bartók's Hungarian and Romanian folk music publications.

The last two Romanian scales in this example show semitone-whole tone configurations that are closely related to octatonic formations. Other octatonic melodies include the complementary type—whole tone-semitone structure—that Bartók collected in 1913 during his fieldwork among North African Arab

peasant villages (Ex. 12.3). It should be noted, however, that the principal tones
of the Arab vocal melodies are for the most part "two to three, possibly four
neighboring degrees. . . . The instrumental dance melodies [have] greater range."[9]

Ex. 12.3. Octatonic folk melodies from (a) Bartók, *Chansons populares roumaines du
département de Bihar* (1913), melody No. 199, and (b) *BBSE*, p. 56, scale No. 29. The
Arab instrument is a peasant oboe made of wood.

Long before Bartók began his investigations of the folk music of Hungary
and its national minorities, in 1901—his second year as a piano student at the
Budapest Academy of Music—he prepared Franz (Ferenc) Liszt's Sonata in B
minor for a concert celebrating Liszt's ninetieth birthday, a performance hailed
by the Budapest press and resulting in his award of the Liszt Prize. He later
confessed that although he tried, he could not like the work—that he felt the
first half of the exposition was cold and empty. When he again took up the study
of Liszt's Piano Sonata in 1905, his previous feeling changed: "The few sub-
dued introductory bars, the main thematic group of the exposition. . . . All these
are among the great things in music."[10]
  Examination of the score discloses the unique sequence of pitch collections
that appear in the first seventeen bars: Phrygian mode (bars 2–3), Hungarian-
Gypsy scale (6–7), and octatatonic scale subsets, such as D♯-E-F♯-G-A-A♯ (11–
13). When in 1902 Bartók attended the first performance in Budapest of Richard Strauss's tone poem, *Also Sprach Zarathustra,* he commented that: "At last
there was a way of composing which seemed to hold the seeds of a new life. At
once I threw myself into the study of all Strauss's scores and began again to
write music myself."[11] His study surely disclosed Strauss's use of octatonic scale
subsets as well as the unique, twelve-tone construction of the fugue subject in
the *"Von der Wissenschaft"* ("Of Science") section.[12] Then, in 1903, Bartók composed his symphonic poem, *Kossuth,* stylistically akin to Liszt as well as Strauss,
in which octatonic, pentatonic, and Gypsy scalar constructions are emphasized.[13]
That same year, Bartók composed his Sonata for Violin and Piano, in which the
themes and their motivic variations in the third movement represent a literal
compendium of diatonic and nondiatonic (Gypsy, octatonic, and whole-tone)
pitch collections (Ex. 12.4).

Ex. 12.4. Bartók, Sonata for Violin and Piano (1903), synoptic tabulation of pitch collections in the third movement.

Melody

The first outcome of Bartók's fieldwork in Hungarian villages was the 1906 publication of ten monophonic folk songs, each fitted with a piano accompaniment. One aim of the collection was to introduce the general Hungarian public to autochthonous folk songs, in order to further appreciation of this hitherto unknown music material.

> It is therefore necessary to select the very best songs for adaptation to general taste, and provide them with appropriate treatment. When folk songs are brought from their rustic surroundings into town, a proper musical attire is needed. . . . Be it adapted for singing or piano, the accompaniment must attempt to make up for the lost meadow and village.[14]

Thus, the guiding principle was treatment of the melody as a "jewel" and the accompaniment—derived from the musical qualities of the melody as its setting. Thereafter, Bartók deliberately or subconsciously created themes or phrases in imitation of folk melodies or phrases, used a folk tune as a motto in order to create a highly original accompaniment, or composed abstract melodies which reflect the "atmosphere" or idiom of rural music.[15] In addition to the modal characteristics of Hungarian folk melodies that pervade Bartók's themes are leaps of a perfect fourth, and the combination of that interval with a major second or minor third to evoke a feeling of antique pentatonicism. Structural characteristics include fifth transposition or sequential descent of melody sections or phrases.

Rhythm

Perhaps the most distinguishing stylistic aspect of Bartók's music is his use of "polyglot" rhythms, that is, the characteristic rhythm schemata he observed during his classification studies of instrumental and vocal folk music of Eastern Europe. The so-called Hungarian dotted-rhythm is represented by syncopated patterns such as ♪♩. ♩, ♪♩. ♩.♪ or ♪♩♩♩♪.

The Ruthenian (that is, Ukrainian) round dance (*kolomyjka*) schema, ♫♫|♫♫|♫♫|♩ ♩||, served as a basic pattern in instrumental or vocal melodies performed by rural Hungarians, Slovaks, and Romanians. The highly varied rhythm schemata Bartók found in the Slovak corpus is for the most part represented by combinations of ♩, ♫, and the syncopated pattern, ♪♩♪. A unique feature of Romanian "shifted rhythm" folk melodies involves rhythm patterns of ♫♫, ♫♩, and ♫♫♫, arranged to form short motifs. Since each pattern consists of distinctive pitches, repetition of the motif shifts accents so that accentuated parts lose their accent in the repeat while nonaccentuated parts gain one (Ex. 12.5).[16]

Ex. 12.5. Bartók, *RFM*.i, no. 18c. The letters identify the different pitch content of the patterns, and the accent marks highlight the shifted rhythm.

Bartók also used the asymmetrical rhythms he found in published Bulgarian folk music collections, such as the *pajdushko horo* dance in 5/8 (2 + 3) meter and the *rŭchenitsa* wedding dance in 7/8 (2 + 2 + 3).[17]

Polymodal Chromaticism

Polymodal chromaticism, a term invented by Bartók, is a main characteristic of his "new Hungarian art music." It involves the superposition of two modes with a common fundamental tone, in which the chromaticized degrees have "absolutely no chordal function; on the contrary, they have a diatonic-melodic function"[18] An early example of polymodal superposition appears in Bartók's First Bagatelle (Ex. 12.6).

Ex. 12.6. Bartók, Fourteen Bagatelles op. 6, for Piano, no. 1 (1908), bars. 1–4.

In 1945, the year of Bartók's death, he authorized a reprint edition of the Bagatelles and other early piano pieces, and prepared an introduction in which he states that:

> Some additional explanations seem to be appropriate to the Bagatelles. The first one bears a key signature of four sharps (as used in C sharp minor) in the upper staff and of four flats (F minor) in the lower one. This half-serious, half-jesting procedure was used to demonstrate the absurdity of key signatures in certain kinds of contemporary music. The tonality of the first Bagatelle is, of course, not a mixture of C sharp minor and F minor but simply a Phrygian colored C major.[19]

When the key signatures of the First Bagatelle are removed and the individual degrees are assigned their applicable enharmonic accidentals, the chromaticized degrees thus obtained can be grouped into their respective C-Phrygian (minor) and C-Lydian (major) modes (Ex. 12.7).[20]

Ex. 12.7. Enharmonic notation of Bartók's First Bagatelle, bars 1–6. Elimination of the original key signatures reveals the basic tonality as a C-Phrygian/Lydian eleven-tone polymode (the principal and fifth degrees are common to both modes).

According to Bartók's testimony, his innovative use of polymodal construction as a new approach to twelve-tone tonality stems from Western European art music of the seventeenth and eighteenth centuries. During that period, the two types of the so-called melodic minor scale were used simultaneously in two-part counterpoint, where the ascending type of the scale has major sixth and seventh degrees, and the descending type in which these degrees are minor (Ex. 12.8).[21]

Ex. 12.8. Contrapuntal superposition of the two types of the melodic minor scale.

"This superposition of the two scalar types leads sometimes to rather modern-sounding dissonances. . . . If we consider the two types as modes of the minor scale, for they really *are* modes, then those portions of a work which use them simultaneously would represent a kind of bi-modality,"[22]

Another example of bimodality (or polymodality) Bartók invented was the juxtaposition of diatonic Phrygian (minor) and Lydian (major) modes to achieve a twelve-tone tonality in which the chromaticized degrees are related only to one fundamental tone.[23] The same chromatic relationship also applies to the two complementary nondiatonic modes of the octatonic scale, whose juxtaposition also yields a twelve-tone tonality based on a single fundamental tone (Ex. 12.9).

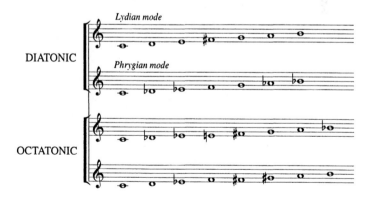

Ex. 12.9. Bartókian twelve-tone tonality as the outcome of juxtaposed diatonic or nondiatonic polymodal pitch collections.

It has been postulated that the most characteristic form of Bartók's "diatonic" system is the (so-called) acoustic or overtone scale, C-D-E-F♯-G-A-B♭, whose tones derive from the natural overtone series.[24] According to the mentioned principles of Bartókian polymodal chromaticism, this pitch collection represents the juxtaposition of two major folk modes, based on a common fundamental (C), in which the Lydian fourth degree (F♯) and the Mixolydian seventh degree (B♭) are the prominent color tones.

Cellular Configurations

In 1950, an essay on Bartók's opera, *Duke Bluebeard's Castle*, for the first time describes a typical aspect of Bartók's art as working out from a basic central idea, from an original musical cell which may be motivic, harmonic, or even rhythmic.[25] The first appearance of motivic cells occurs in Bartók's *Kossuth* symphonic poem, composed in 1903, which commemorates the ill-fated revolution (1848–1849) of the Hungarian people against their King, Francis Joseph I, Emperor of Austria. In the battle section of the work, the first two bars of the Austrian national anthem represent the G-major motif, F♯-G-A-B-C of the Austrian army (Ex. 12.10a).

Ex. 12.10. Bartók, *Kossuth* symphonic poem (1903). (a) Austrian national anthem, bars 1–2, and (b) its octatonic transformation at bar 395, thus forming a characteristic Z-cell tetrachord of two tritones, C♯–G♮ and B♯–F♯.

The grotesque variation of the motif is accomplished by its transformation into an octatonic pitch collection, B♯-C♯-E-F♯-G (Ex. 10b). Another variation of the motif, based on the B♭ whole-tone scale, B♭-C-D-E-G♭-A♭, forms a characteristic Y-cell when the scale is partitioned into a tetrachordal pitch collection (Ex. 12.11). A third type of characteristic cellular structure is the so-called X-cell, a tetrachord of two, juxtaposed minor seconds. This cell, in melodic as well as harmonic form, is the basic, recurrent motif that invariably appears in Bartók's opera, *Duke Bluebeard's Castle*, whenever there is an allusion to blood in the libretto. At R.N. 34, when Judith, Bluebeard's latest wife, opens a door to reveal a room whose blood-stained walls continue to bleed, the flutes play a minor-second trill, B–A♯, while the muted trumpets play sustained intervals of a minor-second, A♮–G♯ (Ex. 12.12).

Ex. 12.11. Bartók, *Kossuth* symphonic poem. Whole-tone transformation of the anthem at R.N. 35, thus forming Y-cell tetrachords.

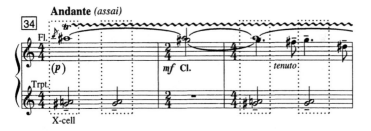

Ex. 12.12. Bartók, *Duke Bluebeard's Castle* op 11 (1911–1918). The X-cell "Blood Motif," G♯-A♮-A♯-B, at R.N. 34 of the vocal score.

Harmony

The *Mikrokosmos* reflects Bartók's ingenious approach to the adoption of nonfunctional harmony and the construction of dissonant vertical sonorities. This approach began in 1908, the year after he had studied Debussy's music and decided to apply the latter's innovative concepts to the harmonization of an old-style Hungarian folk melody (Ex. 12.13a).

Since the principal tones of the pentatonic melody are G-B♭-C-D-F (A and D are passing tones), "not only the third and fifth have to be considered as consonances, but the interval of the seventh, too. On the whole, any intervallic relationship among the five degrees is a consonant one."[26] In Bartók's Fourth Bagatelle, his harmonization treats the pentatonic minor seventh chord and its inversions as consonant structures, thus superseding the resolution requirements of traditional functional harmony. And, like Debussy's practice, this type of consonance appears in the piece as chains of seventh chords in parallel motion (Ex. 12.13b).

Other pentatonic applications involve the use of perfect fourth intervals to create fourth chords such as G-C-F-B♭ and D-G-C-F, or the juxtaposition of the same degrees as major seconds, F-G-B♭-C and C-D-F-G, respectively. A new kind of pyramidal structure was achieved when Bartók juxtaposed modal fourths to form C-Lydian chords, C-F♯-B, G-C-F♯, and F♯-B-E, and C-Phrygian chords,

Ex. 12.13. (a) Bartók, *HFS*, melody No. 7 (collected in 1907), bars 1–4, and (b) Bartók, Fourteen Bagatelles op. 6, for Piano (transcribed in 1908).

Db-G-C, Eb-Ab-Db, and F-Bb-Eb. Note that the juxtaposition of Lydian and Phrygian fourth chords, G-C-F#, and Db-G-C, forms a dual tritone Z-cell, C-F#-Db-G. And the same degrees also constitute a Z-cell partition of the C-octatonic scale, C-Db-Eb-E♮-F#-G-A-Bb.

Another significant tetrachord is a major seventh chord, such as D-F#-A-C#, which appears for the first time as the "Declaration of love" leitmotiv in Bartók's First Violin Concerto (Ex. 12.14).

Ex. 12.14. Bartók, Concerto No. 1, for Violin and Orchestra (1907–1908, op. posth.), first movement, bars 1–4.

The concerto was inspired by and dedicated to Stefi Geyer, a beautiful young Hungarian violinist, and its leitmotiv appears in various transformations in Bartók's piano music after she ended their relationship in 1908.[27] Moreover, the signature intervals of a major seventh and its inversion as a minor second are important constituents of Bartók's musical language.

Form

Analyses of Bartók's themes generally reflect the influence of the varied structural characteristics that distinguish the melodies in his extensive Hungarian, Romanian, Slovak, and Yugoslav folk music collections. Other than the Romanian bagpipe music and other instrumental types, the melodies are structurally related in terms of sectional makeup, for the most part consisting of quaternary sections. Example 12.15 illustrates a quaternary, isometric (same number of syllables) Romanian melody with eight-syllable text lines.

Ex. 12.15. *BBSE*, 23, No. 371. The dotted-rhythm schemata in the fourth section points to a probable Hungarian origin of the melody.

Ex. 12.16 is a quaternary Hungarian variant of a Slovak heterometric folk song, collected by Bartók in 1907, in which the first and second sections are underlaid with ten-syllable text lines, the third section has two six-syllable text lines, and the fourth section has one of four syllables. The syllabic structure of this heterometric melody can be expressed numerically as 10, 10, 6+6, 4.

Ex. 12.16. *HFS*, 283, No. 239. Parlando (or parlando-rubato) means free, declamatory rhythm which does not involve the recurrence of equal values and is nearly the equivalent to recitative style in western European art music.

The *Mikrokosmos* has many pieces in folk song style, in which quaternary sections have heterometric syllabic structure. In Bartók's abstract works, the themes are mainly heterometric, but the syllabic structure is difficult to determine, particularly in the instrumental pieces. In fact, he adapted the indeterminate, nonsectional form of Romanian bagpipe melodies with motif-structure, where one or several two- or four-bar motifs are repeated without any plan or order.[28]

Larger forms of composition in the work consist of discrete parts whose individualized melody sections can be isometric or heterometric syllabic structures. For example, "Variations" (No. 87) is a binary form where part A is in 2/4 time and part B is 3/4. "Boating" (No. 125) is a rounded (architectonic) ABCA type, as is the ABBA structure of "From the Island of Bali" (No. 109). The ABBA form is an indigenous New-Hungarian folk song type.

Counterpoint

From 1923 to July 1926, Bartók's only compositions were the Dance Suite for Orchestra (August 1923) and a transcription of five Slovak folk songs, *Village Scenes*, for Voice and Piano (December 1924). During those years he was preoccupied with the preparation of his Hungarian, Romanian, and Slovak folk music collections for publication, and the performance of his earlier piano pieces for concerts as composer-pianist in Hungary and abroad. In 1924, when Stravinsky began his concert career as conductor and pianist, he featured his new, neoclassical works, such as the Concerto for Piano, with Wind Instruments, Double Basses, and Percussion, which was performed in a Budapest concert attended by Bartók. This work reflects Stravinsky's turn to the so-called classical music of the seventeenth and eighteenth centuries, in which he emulated patterns used by Bach and Handel.[29]

The international success of Stravinsky's appearances prompted Bartók's decision to compose a piano concerto, since his only work for piano and orchestra was the Lisztian-styled Rhapsody op. 1 (1904) he performed in Holland (October 1925) and Germany (January 1926). During Bartók's concert tours in Italy during March 1925 (Milan, Rome, Naples, and Palermo and March 1926 (Bergamo, Cremona, and Florence) he became acquainted with the keyboard works of seventeenth- and eighteenth-century Italian composers, such as Azzolino Bernardino della Ciaia and Girolamo Frescobaldi. He transcribed their pieces for piano and introduced them for the first time during his 1926 concerts on Budapest Radio.[30]

Bartók's study of these works revealed a contrapuntal style significantly different from that of Bach, which led to a distinctive polyphonic dimension in his own works, beginning with the composition of the Concerto No. 1 for Piano and Orchestra in August 1926, and the Nine Little Piano Pieces in October.[31] In the *Mikrokosmos*, the student is provided with a graded, accessible introduction to the study and performance of twentieth-century counterpoint.[32] In view of the broad scope of this subject, the following discussion is limited to a select number of examples that reflect Bartók's use of contrapuntal devices.[33]

Imitation. The majority of pieces in the *Mikrokosmos* is devoted to two-part imitative counterpoint, in which a motive or melody in one part is used successively as the other part. In the first volume, canonic imitation results when the second part is an exact repetition of the first (No. 22). Inversional (contrary motion) counterpoint is produced when the imitation, simultaneously or successively, consists of intervallic inversions of the first part (Nos. 10 and 17).[34] Free canon occurs when the second part deviates to a certain extent from the first part (No. 36). And free counterpoint is the outcome when two, more or less independent melodies are superposed (No. 24).

Ostinato. This device appears for the first time in the second volume, where the melody in the first part is accompanied by a three-bar repetition of perfect fifths throughout the piece (No. 40). Other ostinato accompaniments are the fifths throughout the piece (No. 40). Other ostinato accompaniments are the repetition of triads (No. 69), broken chords (No. 41), dissimilar intervals (No. 61), and single pitches (No. 124).

Pedal Point. This device traditionally is a sustained tone in the bass while harmonic progressions continue above it. In the *Mikrokosmos*, beginning in the second volume, it appears as a pair of drone tones, to a certain extent similar to that of a peasant bagpipe (see No. 138), which serve as a simplified introduction to four-part counterpoint (No. 56).

Stretto. A device in which a musical idea is overlapped by the entry of another musical idea prior to the conclusion of the first one (No. 81).

Retrograde (crab, cancrizans). The repetition of a musical idea in reverse order, that is, the last note begins and the first note ends the repetition (No. 86).

Augmentation. The repetition or imitation of a musical idea by doubling or increasing the its note values (No. 136).

Diminution. The repetition or imitation of a musical idea by reduction of its note values (No. 114).

13

Volume One

(Nos. 1–36)

No. 10 ("With Alternate Hands"): In this simple, five-finger exercise, Bartók introduces the concept of nondiatonic scalar construction: an octatonic pentachord with D as the fundamental tone, D-E-F-G-A♭. The addition of B♭-C♭-D♭ would form an eight-note symmetrical scale based on alternating whole- and half-steps. Transpositions of the same octatonic pentachord occur in Bartók's Arab folk music collection.[1] And the original pentachord, extended in range to B♭-C-D, forms a basic nondiatonic folk mode in Bartók's *Cantata Profana*.[2]

The same type of pentachord, transposed to B as principal tone, accounts for the C♯ key signature in No. 25 ("Imitation and Inversion").

No. 15 ("Village Song"): The modal structure indicates a variant relationship to a melody in Bartók's Slovak folk-song collection (Ex. 13.1).

Ex. 13.1. *SV.*i, no. 128. There are four isometric melody-sections (that is, four six-syllable text lines) in the Phrygian mode.

Bartók's melody shows the same basic syllabic structure, but the third melody-section (bars 7–10) is considered to be a double-section, since it is composed of two metrically equal parts. That is, they are "twin" parts which may be regarded as virtually one section.[3] Expressed as figures, the quaternary structure consists of *6,6,6+6,6* syllables. Another difference is in tonality. The source melody is Phrygian, and, as the small-head notations in No. 15 show, the first and fourth sections are G-major pentachords, the second and third sections are Lydian, G-A-B-C♯-D. Based on G as the principal tone, the juxtaposition of C♮ and C♯ creates a chromatic polymode, an innovative construction typical of Bartók's musical language.

No. 17 ("Contrary Motion" [1]): The architectonic structure, AA⁵A⁵A, is a borrowing from structural characteristics of the new style of Hungarian folk song, which emerged during the nineteenth century.[4] The dotted (syncopated) rhythm, on the other hand, such as 4/4 ♪ ♩. ♩ 𝄾, is characteristic of old and new styles (Ex. 13.2). Note that the chromatic polymode is the same as in No. 15, and that a similar construction appears in the opening bars of Girolamo Frescobaldi's Toccata in G Major.[5]

Ex. 13.2. *HFS,* 47. Old-style Hungarian "dotted-rhythm" melody.

No. 24 ("Pastorale"): The characteristic D-Lydian mode, D-E-F♯-G♯-A-B-C♯, reflects Slovak folk-music influence. The ingenious free counterpoint is a mixture of contrary and parallel motion between the parts.

No. 25 ("Imitation and Inversion"[2]): A nondiatonic stretto canon, beginning with the L.H., and based on a pentachordal partition (whole- and half-steps) of the B-octatonic scale, B-C♯-D-E-F. The inversion is related only to the interchange of parts at bar 21, where the canon begins with the R.H., and not to traditional inversional counterpoint.

No. 27 ("Syncopation"): This polymodal piece, in free counterpoint, juxtaposes the ascending diatonic C-major pentachord with a D-octatonic pentachord, a nondiatonic descending sequence of whole- and half-steps, D-C-B-A G♯.

No. 28 ("Canon at the Octave"): Bars 8–11 illustrate the canonic interaction of the ♩ ♩ | ♩ ♩ rhythm schema. This schema, also notated in shorter values such as ♪ ♩. ♩. ♪, is another example of Hungarian dotted rhythm.

No. 29 ("Imitation Reflected"): A stretto canon in contrary motion, in which the ascending form of the A-melodic minor scale is partitioned into symmetrical pentachords, with E as the dual axis of symmetry. Thus, in bars 1–5, the first five degrees of the whole-tone scale are formed, C-D-E/E-F♯-G♯.

No. 31 ("Dance in Canon Form"): The fourteen-note rhythm schema, ♩♩♩♩|♩♩♩♩|♩♩♩♩| ♩ ♩ ‖, is the characteristic *kolomyjka* (round-dance) rhythm of the Ruthenians (a rural Ukrainian people). This dance schema was adapted for the *kanásztánc* of Transylvanian-Hungarian swineherds and the *Ardeleana* of Transylvanian-Romanian shepherds.[6]

No. 33 ("Slow Dance"): This piece reflects Bartókian fusion of national styles, that is, commingling performance peculiarities which Bartók found in certain Hungarian, Slovak, and Yugoslav melodies. The tonality is based on the Slovak chromatic polymode first encountered in "Village Song" (No. 15). The last bar, however, ends on the dominant perfect fifth, D-A, thus forming a half-cadence, a structural peculiarity of Yugoslav folk music.[7] A somewhat similar cadence, adapted by neighboring Romanian inhabitants of southern Transylvania, ends on the second degree of the scale.[8] The Hungarian influence can be seen in the syncopated, juxtaposed polyrhythmic schemata, ♩ ♪♪♩ and ♪♪♩ ♩, in bars 5–6 and 9–10.

Exercises 1d, 1e, and 1f: It is indeed interesting that Bartók introduces the underlying concept of his unique polymodal chromaticism in the first volume of the *Mikrokosmos*. While such chromaticism involves the juxtaposition of two modes based on a common fundamental tone, it is only when Lydian and Phrygian modes are juxtaposed that twelve-tone tonality is achieved, for example: C-D-E-F♯-G-A-B/C-D♭-E♭-F-G-A♭-B♭.

In order to limit the beginner to simple five-finger exercises, Exercise 1d has A as the fundamental tone of an ascending Lydian pentachord, followed by a descending Phrygian pentachord. Exercises 1e and 1f are transpositions to D and G, respectively, of the same bimodal configuration. Ex. 13.3 illustrates the outcome when the same modes are juxtaposed as tetrachords.

Lydian tetrachords:

Phrygian tetrachords:

Ex. 13.3. Juxtaposition and transposition of Lydian and Phrygian tetrachords.

When the color tritones of the Lydian mode (first and augmented fourth degrees) and the Phrygian mode (minor second and perfect fifth degrees) are juxtaposed, the so-called Z-cell is formed.[9] This innovative cell appears in Bartók's works as a melodic, harmonic, or motivic construction (see Ex. 12.10).

14

Volume Two

(Nos. 37–66)

No. 37 ("In Lydian Mode"): The Lydian mode is also prevalent in the Christmas carol repertory (*colinde*) of the Transylvanian Romanians (Ex. 14.1). The modality, melodic structure, rhythm, and half-cadence ending of such pieces are similar to those in No. 37. The two-part stretto canon, moreover, replicates the so called change song, a performance style in which two alternating groups of village boys—each group singing the various text stanzas in unison—perform in such a way that the entry of one group occurs just before the other finishes, and thus momentarily creates a contrapuntal effect.[1] The same style can be seen in No. 37, where the entry of the upper voice at bar 5 occurs prior to the conclusion of the lower one in the next bar.

Ex. 14.1. Bartók, *RFM*.iv, melody No. 12c.

No. 41 ("Melody with Accompaniment"): The small-head notation and key signature show a polymodal G-major construction which combines the Lydian (C♯) and Phrygian (F♭) degrees.

No. 42 ("Accompaniment in Broken Triads"): A simple example of Bartókian "neutral" tonality, based on A as the fundamental tone, with alternating minor and major thirds (C and C♯) and without the Aeolian or Dorian modal sixths (F or F♯). In addition, the "Yugoslav" cadence (ending on the fifth degree, E) also contributes to the sense of tonal ambiguity.

No. 43 ("In Hungarian Style"): An ironic designation for this two-piano piece, since the form and modality are essentially Slovak in character, although Slovakia was a part of Greater Hungary until the end of the First World War. The basic rhythmic schema of the AA⁵BA melody in Piano I is Hungarian or Slovak isometric six-syllable structure, ♩♩♩♩|♩♩♩𝄾|, in the A sections, and B is a "twin" 6 + 6-syllable double-section (♩♩♩♩ + ♩♩♩♩). A specific Slovak borrowing is the Lydian folk mode in Piano II, D-E-F♯-G♯-A-B-C♯.[2] Here, too, is an interesting treatment in bars 5–8, in which the L.H. descends by a hexachord of alternating half- and whole-steps of the octatonic scale, E-D-C♯-B-B♭-G♯.

No. 51 ("Waves"): This is another example of extracted octave segments as pentatonic tetrachords of the D♭-major scale (bars 1–8, 17–25). The pentatonicism differs from the symmetrical type characteristic of Hungarian folk music. The scalar structure is asymmetrical, consisting of a major second, a minor third and two major seconds, typical of the eastern Russian-central Asian region.[3] The half-cadence ending on the fifth degree of the scale replicates Yugoslav folk-music style.

No. 54 ("Chromatics"): The architectonic quaternary structure is AA³BA, and the chromaticism is based on so-called X-cells—chromatic tetrachords—which Bartók innovated as "Blood" motifs for his opera, *Duke Bluebeard's Castle*.[4] The tetrachords ascend in unison, by half-step (bars 1–5), then occur sequentially (7–8), and in contrary motion to end the piece.

No. 58 ("In Oriental Style"): Although the tempo is Assai lento, ♩. = 46, in 6/8 time, the melody has certain similarities with an Arab *Nuba* (dance) melody Bartók collected in North Africa during June 1913. The *Nuba* also has a scalar pentachord with an augmented second, G-A-B♭-C♯-D, and compound duple meter (6/4), but differs in tempo (♩. = 72).[5] The *Nuba* was performed by an oboe-like wind instrument and by a snare drum played with both hands without sticks.

No. 59 ("Major and Minor"): As the small-head notation shows, the treble staff consists of an F-minor pentachord and the bass staff has an F-Lydian one. The interaction between R.H. and L.H. forms a seven-tone polymode, F-G-A♭-B♭-C/F-G-A♮-B♮-C, with F as the common fundamental tone. Bartók, who innovated polymodal chromaticism as his unique approach to twelve-tone tonality, has specified that the chromatic degrees have no chordal function: such degrees are only diatonic ingredients of one or the other mode to which they belong.[6]

No. 61 ("Pentatonic Melody"): The twelve-tone tonality apparently is achieved by juxtaposition of complementary octatonic scales with the same fundamental tone, notated as A-B♭-C-Df-Ef-E-F♯-G/A-B-C-D-E♯-E♯-F♯-G♯. On the other hand, the same tonality is brought about by juxtaposition of the Lydian and Phrygian modes, also with A as the fundamental tone, A-B-C♯-D♯-E-F♯-G♯/A-B♭-C-D-E-F-G. However, the emphatic rendition of tetrachords and pentachords notated as segments of one or the other octatonic scales (beginning at bar 16) seems to favor an octatonic rather than a bimodal interpretation of twelve-tone tonality for this piece.

The rhythm schema is based on an extended version of the Ruthenian *ko-lomyjka* (cf. No. 31), and the melodic contour has a certain kinship with the first theme in Bartók's Dance Suite for Orchestra.

No. 64 ("Line against Point"): In accordance with Bartók's Hungarian draft, "Wavy Lines and [Pedal] Points" would be a more appropriate designation for the two versions of this piece in four-part inversional counterpoint. In Version (a), the melodic lines in the soprano and bass voices are in contrary motion, and the pedal points are sustained major seconds, D-E. The latent pentatonicism is the symmetrical Hungarian type, E-G-A-B-D, and the chromatic degrees B♭ and F♯, imply a G-major/Dorian polymodality. The juxtaposed fifths in the last two bars are pentatonic degrees that form an inversion of the tonic (E) minor seventh chord, which Bartók considered to be a "consonant" ending.[7]

Version (b) illustrates an innovative Bartókian device, compression of diatonic octave segments into chromatic ones. The pedal points are octaves, with E as the fundamental tone, and the melodic lines may be construed for the most part as X-cells in contrary motion, E-F-F♯-G and D♯-D♮-C♯-C♮. The last two bars consist of an augmented triad in the first inversion, C-E-A♭. Bartók compared his use of chromatic compression—and its converse as diatonic extension of chromatic octave segments—to the Baroque contrapuntal devices of augmentation and diminution of note values. He believed that creating a compressed or extended variant of a melody would yield a new one which would nevertheless retain a hidden yet unified relationship between the two forms.[8]

No. 66 ("Melody Divided"): The melody is based on the diatonic degrees of the G-Lydian mode, G-A-B-C♯-D-E-F♯, which are reordered as a symmetrical pentatonic scale, E-G-A-B-D. The accompaniment is constructed of tetrachords derived from the modal degrees: G-Lydian in the first section, E minor in the second, D-Lydian in the third, and C-Lydian in the fourth. The postlude (bars 25–29) has an interesting sonic effect cause by polymodal juxtaposition of E-Phrygian and G-Lydian tetrachords. The ending, however, is a pentatonic construction, a "consonant" E-minor seventh chord.

Exercise 18: Example 14.2 shows tetrachordal components of Bartók's musical language. Note that the polymodal tetrachord may be interpreted as a C-Phrygian/Lydian construction or a partition of the C-octatonic scale.

Ex. 14.2. Tetrachordal components of Bartók's musical language.

15

Volume Three

(Nos. 67–96)

No. 70 ("Melody against Double Notes"): The use of bitonal key signatures apparently reflects the same kind of "half-serious, half-jesting procedure" used by Bartók in the First Bagatelle for Piano, where the key signatures have four sharps (R.H.) and four flats (L.H.) "to represent a tonality which is, of course, not a [atonal] mixture of C-sharp minor and F minor but simply a Phrygian-colored C major."[1] In the present case, the five sharps in the upper voice and without accidentals in the lower voice do not represent a bitonal mixture of a B-major melody (D♯ is missing!) and a C-major accompaniment. The tonality is based on a D-Lydian/Aeolian ten-tone polymode, D-E-F♯-G♯-A-B-C♯/D-E-F-G-A-A♯ (= B♭)-C.

No. 79 ("Hommage à J. S. B."): A study in polymodal counterpoint, based on the E-Lydian/Phrygian octachordal polymode, E-F♯-G♯-A♯ (= B♭)-B/E-F-G-A. The figurations begin with E-major, minor, and pentatonic octave-segments as triads and tetrachords, in canonic imitation at the fifth (bars 1–8). The midpoint bar consists of the pentachordal octatonic segment E-F♯-G-A-B♭, followed by chromatic compression to an X-cell tetrachord, G-G♯-A-A♯ (10–12).

The last five bars consist of the E-Lydian and Phrygian pentachords, also in canonic imitation but at the octave. The clever use of stretto (L.H. bar 15: the entry of B is a dotted eighth instead of a quarter note), in which E-major and E-minor triads are superposed as harmonic intervals—major thirds and a perfect fourth—provides a momentary "neutral tonality" until the final E-major triad is sounded in the last bar.

No. 80 ("Hommage à R. Sch."): The first occurrence in the *Mikrokosmos* of Bartókian twelve-tone polymodal chromaticism, based on the C-Phrygian/Lydian polymode, C-D♭-E♭-F-G-A♭-B♭/C-D-E-F♯-G-A-B. The accompaniment consists of a twin-bar ostinato whose pitch content is a chromatic scale from B to F♯. This scale, however, is structured as ascending and descending tetrachords which are bounded by the C Z-cell tritones, B–F and F♯-C, respectively (L.H., bars 1–8; R.H., 9–12). The postlude (16–22) consists of an imitative sequence of polymodal tetrachords which end on the fundamental tone.

No. 81 ("Wandering"): An exemplar of twelve-tone linear counterpoint, based on D as the fundamental tone, in which the "wandering" apparently is represented by such contrasting pentachords as major and minor (bars 1–14) and diverse Lydian and octatonic constructions (15–17, 17–21, respectively). The last section (28–35) begins with a variation of the opening bars, and is followed by juxtaposition of the D-Dorian hexachord (R.H.) and octatonic pitch collections, D-C-B-A♭, B-B♭-A-G-F♯ (L.H.). The piece ends with a half-cadence on the dominant triad.

No. 86 ("Two Major Pentachords"): An invention in free counterpoint, without a key signature, which Bartók described as a juxtaposition of the upper voice in C and the lower one in F♯. Although the illustrative small-head notation above the piece illustrates the two pentachords as discrete scalar pitch collections, if certain chromatic degrees are enharmonically treated as ingredients of the mode to which they belong—D♭, A♭, B♭ instead of C♯, G♯, A♯—the outcome is an eleven-tone Lydian/Phrygian polymode based on C as the fundamental tone.

The first section begins with the melodic form of the C Z-cell, F♯-C♯ (= D♭)-C-G. The same cell, in its retrograde construction, G-C-C♯-F♯, appears in the second section (bars 5–8). In this way, the color tones of the Lydian and Phrygian modes (F♯ and D♭, respectively) are introduced as primary degrees of the polymode. The postlude (27–36) begins with another polymodal construction, the harmonic form of an X-cell, F♯-G♯ (= A♭)-F-G, which appears as juxtaposed major seconds rather than a chromatic sequence of minor seconds. The melodic form of an X-cell also appears as major seconds, D-C-C♯-B (33–34), followed by the cadential Lydian tetrachord, C-E-F♯-G.

No. 88 ("Duet for Pipes"): The first composition in the *Mikrokosmos* where polymodal and nondiatonic pitch collections are featured. The first three melody-sections (bars 1–22) are based on the D-Phrygian/Lydian polymode, D-E♭-F-D-A-B♭-C/D-G♭ (= F♯)-A♭ (= G♯)-B. The the pitch collection in the fourth melody-section (Più lento, 23–32) is a heptachord of the D octatonic scale, D-E♭-F-G♭-A♭-A♮-C♭ (29–30). The piece ends, however, with a tonic minor-seventh chord, D-F-A-C, as a Bartókian "consonant" sonority.

No. 89 ("In Four Parts"). The use of C♯ and G♯ as the key signature for an introductory melody section in A major (bars 1–9), without the traditional F♯ included, reflects Bartók's aversion to the use of traditional key signatures in his works. Following the sectional cadence on C♯ minor (bar 9), the piece continues with a tritone transition to the G-Lydian mode. It is interesting that at the change of tempo to Un poco più mosso, Bartók applies accidentals instead of replacing the key signature with a solitary C♯. The final cadence, E minor to A major, returns the tonality to its original key.

No. 91 ("Chromatic Invention [1]"): Since this piece and the following one have a shared title but contrasting tempos—Lento and Allegro robusto, respectively—in common, they may be considered as a contrasting pair—*Lassú-Friss* (Slow-Fast)—in Hungarian folk dance style, a genre that Liszt popularized in his Hungarian Rhapsodies.[2]

The architectonic ternary (A B Av) form is delineated by permutation of cellular components of the theme (Ex. 15.1).

Ex. 15.1. Z-cell and X-cell components of the theme and their inversion, first section (A, bars 1–6).

Section B (bars 6–11) has an ingenious succession of Z-cells whose initial pitches form a descending whole-tone scale, Bb-Ab-F♯-E-D-C. The reprise ends with discrete X-cells in contrary motion, resulting in an unusual deceptive cadence of a major second, E and F♯, thus implying *attacca* treatment to the next piece.

While this invention consists of a chromatic scale based on A as the fundamental tone, the pitch collection can be interpreted as a twelve-tone A-Phrygian/Lydian polymode. On the other hand, however, the emphatic rendition of Z-cells—which represent tetrachordal octatonic partitions—points to a nondiatonic twelve-tone interpretation: complementary octatonic scales (that is, A is the common fundamental tone), A-B-C-D-Eb-F-F♯-G♯/A-Bb-C-Db-Eb-E♮-F♯-G.

No. 92 ("Chromatic Invention [2]"): Although this invention also begins with a Z-cell, the pitch collection is based on E as the fundamental tone of an octachordal Phrygian/Lydian polymode (Ex. 15.2).

Ex. 15.2. E Z-cell and its repetition in retrograde motion.

In the second melody-section (bars 8–12), X-cell components of the polymode, F♯-G♯-A-G♮ are juxtaposed as a stretto. The third section (19–25) begins with the retrograded Z-cell and its original construction. A postlude follows, consisting of a two-part ostinato of juxtaposed minor seconds, B-A♯ and A♯-B. The retrograded Z-cell ends the piece on its fundamental tone.

No. 94 ("Once Upon a Time . . ."): The binary form opens with an unaccompanied theme in the C-Dorian mode, which has a structural similarity to the Hungarian folk song collected by Bartók in 1906 (Ex. 15.3).

Ex. 15.3. Bartók, Twenty Hungarian Folk Songs (1906), No. 6, bars 9–12.

The second section begins with the theme in folk-like Hungarian fifth transposition (bars 6–10). The third section returns to the tonic as a thematic variant. Both sections are harmonically linked by a sequence of descending chromatic thirds (6–14).

The construction of part B is polymodal counterpoint, in which the theme and its stretto transposition juxtapose the C-Dorian and E-Lydian modes (15–19). The stretto continues with a progression of descending octatonic pentachords which end with a whole-tone tetrachord in the lower voice (20–26). The return of the transposed theme is similarly treated in stretto, but with the original version in the C-Lydian mode. This polymodal juxtaposition of tonic minor and major modes is resolved in the codetta (32–35) by a "neutral" cadence of a perfect fifth, C–G.

No. 96 ("Jolts"): A more or less free sectional arrangement, A B C D E F, based on the G-Lydian/Phrygian twelve-tone polymode, with "jolting" strettos constructed of imitative and inversional configurations. The triple meter, ♩ ♩ ♩, is a hemiolic, alternative subdivision of metrical units, ♫♩ ♫♩. The stretto in section B begins with the R.H. an octave lower and the L.H. entry a bar later (bars 18–19). In section C, the stretto is transposed down a fifth to C, beginning with the L.H., the R.H. entry is on the second beat of the same bar, and the section ends on an accented ("jolting") tritone B♭-E (bars 17–18).

Section D is a stretto in inversional counterpoint, in which the configurations consist of major and diminished broken triads (19–23). While the piece ends in G major, it is preceded by two bars of juxtaposed broken triads whose component degrees give the impression of polymodal, broken seventh chords (29–32).

16

Volume Four

(Nos. 97–121)

No. 100 ("In Folk Song Style"): The sectional arrangement of the first half of this binary piece represents a borrowing from a nineteenth-century Slovak folk song which Bartók adapted as No. 8 in Ten Easy Pieces (Ex. 16.1).[1]

Ex. 16.1. Bartók, Ten Easy Pieces, No. 8 (1908), transposed to A for comparative purposes.

The basic similarity is in terms of heterometric syllabic structure. The underlying text of the quaternary folk song consists of two sections of twelve-syllable lines, a double-section—each one with six-syllable lines—and a fourth section also with six syllables. Bartók symbolized the proportion of this type of syllabic structure with different sizes of the letter Z: Z,Z,z+z,z.[2] The extrapolated proportion of No. 100 is of the same heterometric type.

The first half of the binary form combines the Dorian melody with an octatonic accompaniment, A-Bb-C-C#-D#-E-F#-G# (bars 1–10). The addition of F♮ in the lower voice of the double-section confirms the twelve-tone makeup of the A-Dorian/Lydian polymode. The sectional arrangement in part B (lower voice), essentially the same as before, is followed by a postlude (21–24).

No. 101 ("Diminished Fifth"): Bartók's comment: "Probably in the key of D minor, ending on a diminished fifth" [A-Eb]. But this ending apparently forms an irregular (implied?) Phrygian cadence of the D-Lydian/Phrygian polymode. On the other hand, the same type of cadence could be applied to the juxtaposition of nondiatonic pitch collections, namely, the complementary octatonic scales based on D as the fundamental tone (Ex. 16.2).

Ex. 16.2. Comparison of polymodal and nondiatonic pitch collections based on D as the fundamental tone.

The first two sections consist of tetrachordal partitions of the octatonic scale, E♭-F-G♭-A♭ (L.H.) and A-B-C-D (R.H). These partitions are linked by the emphatic rendition of D Z-cell degrees, E♭-A♭-A-D in the first two sections (bars 1–11). The third section is extended to pentachords which are linked for the most part by a C Z-cell, C-D♭-G♭-G♮ (12–18). The D Z-cell returns in the fourth section (bars 19–26), and the fifth one shows a descending sequence of octatonic tetrachords (L.H., 27–35). The piece ends with an extended reprise of the first section, including its cadence on the diminished fifth, E♭–A.

No. 102 ("Harmonics"): The A B C form and its interlude (bars 29–30) coincide with each change of harmonics. Part A is in the B-Mixolydian mode; Part B is Dorian but is chromatically expanded to the twelve-tone B-Phrygian/Lydian polymode (22–27). The piece ends with superposition of seemingly unrelated sonorities: a B-major triad and a D-minor seventh chord. This combination, however, provides the seven degrees of a gapped B-octatonic scale, B-C-D-D♯-F-F♯-[ ]-A. With regard to the harmonics, their nonpercussive rendition eliminates the principal noise elements peculiar to the piano tone. These elements, which are emphasized when the piano is played with the various percussive (that is, key-striking) touch-forms, include the impact of finger against key, key against key bed, hammer against string, and rattling of parts during key descent and ascent. Thus, the use of portamento (portato) touch, as indicated by slurred staccato marks for the D-minor seventh chords (42–43), avoids what would otherwise result in a highly dissonant cluster chord.[3]

No. 103 ("Minor and Major"): A study in additive rhythm and change of time, with A as fundamental tone of a Dorian/Lydian polymode, A-B-C-D-E-F♯/A-B-C♯-D♯-E-F♯. Part A (bars 1–18) begins with four bars of 9/8 time as 4+5 eighths. The following bars illustrate the ways that groups of 2+3/8 and 3+2/8 can be organized as 5/8 and 8/8 meters, similar to Bulgarian-influenced, Romanian *colinde* (Christmas songs).[4] Part B reverts to traditional compound 9/8 time, and the polymodal octave segments are reorganized as pentatonic motifs, consisting of a major second, minor third, and perfect fifth (19–28). The double-bar marks the introduction of 5/8 time as a 2+3/8 Bulgarian *pajdushko* dance rhythm.[5] The ending, in Yugoslav style, is a half-cadence on the dominant fifth, E–B.

No. 107 ("Melody in the Mist"): The mist is created by the alternation of white key and black key tetrachords which are juxtaposed in bars 40–41. The white keys are arranged as pentatonic components, major second, perfect fourth, and perfect fifth, based on G as the fundamental tone of a major scale. The black keys have the same type of degrees a half-step higher. The major melody concludes with a Mixolydian cadence in West-Hungarian (Trans-Danubian) style, C–F♮-G (38–39), in which major and minor sevenths alternate during the performance of a folk song. Another Hungarian borrowing is the dotted rhythms, 3/4 ♩ ♩|♩ ♩ and ♩ ♩|♩ ♩, which represent augmented values derived from 2/4 ♩. ♪|♪ ♩. and ♪ ♩.|♩. ♪. The use of the damper pedal as well as the juxtaposition of the "misty" tetrachords creates a cluster chord of minor seconds similar to the tone clusters invented by Henry Cowell in his piano music.[6] The use of the black key tetrachord as the last sonority creates the effect of a Phrygian cadence, A♭–G.

No. 108 ("Wrestling"): Bartók's impression of a struggle between the tones of a minor second. The section structure is A B Av, and the "neutral" tonality results from the superposition of the major third drone (F♯) and the minor third of its encapsulating tetrachord, D-E-F♮-A, which is resolved by the cadence on the tonic major third, D-F♯ (bar 11). The first half of section B continues the conflict between the Phrygian (minor second) drone (E♭) and the major second degree, where the latter serves as the introduction of a polymodal hexachord, E♮-F-G-A-G♯-F♯ (11–15). The following half of the section superposes the Lydian augmented-fourth drone, D-G♯, and the perfect fourth, D-G♮ (15–19).

In the reprise of section A, the struggle ends in a "deadlock" between the major and minor color tones, since they are superposed as a "neutral" chord, D-F-F♯-A, in the last bar. Noteworthy, however, is the preceding octatonic tetrachord, E♭-F-F♯-Gs (penultimate bar), which therafter combines with the marcato tonic-dominant interval to outline the D Z-cell, D-E♭-G♯-A as a remarkable type of octatonic cadence.

No. 109 ("From the Island of Bali"): The form emulates the indigenous A B B A rounded structure of Hungarian new-style folk songs. The melodic structure illustrates the similarities between nondiatonic and polymodal pitch collections, where D serves as the common fundamental tone. The nondiatonic collection is an octatonic scale, D-E♭-F-G♭-G♯-A-B, organized as discrete Z-cell tetrachords (Ex. 16.3).

Ex. 16.3. Z-cell tetrachords derived from the D-octatonic scale.

Part A, in stretto counterpoint and 6/8 time, superposes the D and F Z-cells as motifs (bars 1–11). The first section of part B, in unison and 4/4 time, is based on the F Z-cell, extended to A♭♭ (12–16). The second section is mostly an attenuated, inverted reprise of Part A (16–22). The third section returns to unisonal structure, but the motif is transformed to a Phrygian tetrachord, A-B♭-D-E♭ (23–30). The octatonic repetition of part A (31–39) is followed by an unusual cadence of nonfunctional chords derived from the D-octatonic scale, D-E♭-F-G♭-G♯-A-B-C.

No. 110 ("And the Sounds Clash and Clang. . ."): In rondo form, A B-A-C-A, based on C as the fundamental tone of a Phrygian/Lydian twelve-tone polymode. The juxtaposition of two perfect fifths at the interval of a minor second, and minor thirds likewise, form discrete bimodal tetrachords. The latter tetrachord, D-F/E♭-G♭ is followed by resolution to a unison E as the section end-tone (bars 1-20). The second section consists of a chromatic melody in unison, with E–B followed by C as the drone tones. The third section is a reprise of the first one, slightly varied. The contrapuntal fourth section, with E as the drone, is a transposed variant of the melody and its stretto inversion (47–59). The last section is another, slightly varied reprise of the first one.

No. 112 ("Variations on a Folk Tune"): The diatonic theme in C major is a variant the Slovak melody collected by Bartók in Northern Hungary (now Slovakia) in 1915 (Ex. 16.4).

Tempo giusto

Ex. 16.4. *SV.*ii, melody no. 84a.

This piece is another *Mikrokosmos* example of thematic variation by chromatic compression of diatonic degrees and diatonic extension of chromatic degrees (cf. No. 64a). Bartók justified this procedure by equating it with Baroque contrapuntal devices of diminution (= compression) and augmentation (= extension).[7] The theme, consisting of the first four degrees of the scale, has the same isometric six-syllable structure of the Slovak folk text. This rhythmic structure is applied to the stretto counterpoint in the first and second variations (bars 9–24). Although the third variation is similarly contrapuntal, the structure is heterometric, consisting of *4,4,7,5* syllables (bars 25–31). In the fourth variation, chromatic compression transforms the theme into the first four degrees of a chromatic tetrachord, B-C-C♯-D, followed by a leap to the tritone, F, to "compress" the syllabic structure from six to five syllables. The stretto counterpoint in the lower voice has the same intervallic and syllabic structure, transposed to G♯ (32–40). Thereafter, a four-bar transition leads to the last variation which is a reprise of the isorhythmic theme in the major tonality but with a four-syllable rhythmic structure (45–52). A heterometric coda in free counterpoint follows, ending as a unison on the fundamental degree.

No. 113 ("Bulgarian Rhythm" [1]): So-called Bulgarian or Turkish *aksak* (limping) rhythm—usually designated by additive time signatures—can be defined as regularly recurring bars which have asymmetrical groups of note values. The 7/8 time signature actually represents the Bulgarian 2+2+3/8 *rŭchenitsa* dance rhythm.[8] The melody, according to Bartók, is Hungarian in origin. Example 16.5, on the other hand, a Bulgarian folk-song incipit in additive 9/8 time, has a certain similarity in terms of melodic as well as rhythmic structure.[9]

Ex. 16.5. First melody section of the Bulgarian folk song, "Ferryman's song."

There is, however, a difference in tonality. The Bulgarian folk melody has an Oriental character, that is, the pitch collection is the Dorian mode with an augmented second, D-E-F-G♯-A-B-C. Bartók's essentially Dorian melody includes the two augmented seconds which are characteristic of the nondiatonic Hungarian Gypsy scale, F-G♯ and B♭-C♯.

No. 115 ("Bulgarian Rhythm" [2]): Bartók made his first contact with Bulgarian peasant music during March 1912, in the Banat region of Hungary (southwestern Transylvania, now part of Romania). Although he made preliminary transcriptions of the eight vocal melodies he had collected in November 1912, it was not until 1935 that he revised them. The revisions were a necessary adjunct to his preparation for publication, beginning in 1932, of his Romanian folk music material: he discovered that about five percent of the latter had a peculiar, 9/16 asymmetrical rhythm that he suspected were derived from Bulgarian types of additive rhythm. He therefore commenced his study and analysis of thousands of Bulgarian folk melodies and rhythm in published collections and published his essay, "The So-called Bulgarian Rhythm, in 1938."[10]

The additive 5/8 time configured as 3+2/8 and 2+3/8, are schemata of the Bulgarian *pajdushko* dance rhythm (cf. No. 103). Each part of the ternary (A B Av) form has a nonarchitectonic section structure: A has four sections, a b c d (bars 1–8), B has three, a b c (9-22), and Av is a variant of part A. The melodic construction is based on pentachordal motifs which form the G-Lydian/Phrygian twelve-tone polymode.

No. 120 ("Triads"): An interesting presentation of nonfunctional chord progressions, beginning in Ukrainian *kolomyjka*-dance style (bars 1–13). Notwithstanding the unusual change of time, the fourteen-syllable rhythm schema—characteristic of the *kolomyjka*—is clearly evident: 5/4 𝄾 ♩♩♩♩ | ♩♩♩. | 3/2 𝄾 ♩♩♩♩♩ | 4/4 ♩ ♩ |. The traditional 4/4 schema appears in bars 20–30, and is followed by the nine-syllable structure of old Hungarian folk song, in augmented values: 4/4 ♩♩♩♩ | ♩ ♩|♩♩ ♩|.

Exercise 33: An example of Bulgarian additive rhythm in 7/8 time, intended as a preparation for No. 113. The R.H. ostinato consists of alternating perfect fifths and fourths which are asymmetrically organized as ♫♫♫ (4+3/8). The L.H. accompaniment, on the other hand, is notated as ♩ ♩ ♩ 𝄿 (2+2+3/8), with a marcato accent (>) on the third quarter note. The tonality is F major, and the harmony—including the ostinato— is composed of triads, seventh chords, and two fourth-chords, C-F-B♮ and G-C-F.

17

Volume Five

(Nos. 122–139)

No. 122 ("Chords Together and in Opposition"): This piece is an advanced sequel to No. 120 ("Triads"). There are two motifs whose rhythm schemata are, respectively, ♪♩ ♪| ♩ ♩| ♪ ♩. | and ⅞ ♫♪ | ♩ ♩| ♫♪♪ |. The motifs, enclosed between ostinato perfect fifths, C–G (L.H.) and G–D (R.H.), consist of scalar trichords in contrary motion and in the C-Lydian mode (bars 1–26). In the second section, the ostinato changes to G–D and E–B, and the contrary-motion motifs are transposed to the G-Lydian mode (27–48). The third section begins in F-Lydian and ends in the Dorian mode (49–59). The following postlude consists of syncopated fifth chords and their inversion as quartal structures, where the pitch collection is derived from the symmetrical Hungarian pentatonic scale, A-C-D-E-G.

No. 123 ("Staccato and Legato (2)"): The theme of this stretto canon has a certain resemblance to the fugue subject which opens Bartók's Music for String Instruments, Percussion, and Celesta. The similarity includes melodic contour, narrow range, and chromatic counterpoint. The entire piece is based on a single, three-bar motif and its variants, including different transpositions and inversions. The pitch collection is the twelve-tone C-Phrygian/Lydian polymode, and both parts (a and b) end with an emphatic rendition of the C-Phrygian mode.

No. 125 ("Boating"): Architectonic A B Av1 Av2 form, with G as the fundamental tone of a Phrygian/Lydian twelve-tone polymode, in 3/4 time. The theme, in the upper voice of section A, consists of the symmetrical Hungarian anhemitone-pentatonic scale, E♭-G♭-A♭-B♭-D♭ (bars 1–14). The accompanying ostinato, a hexachord of the G-Mixolydian mode, is structured as hemiolic trichords of arpeggiated perfect fourths and major seconds. The hemiola, in which two groups of beamed eighths are in nonaccentuated 6/8 time, results in a cross-rhythm with the upper voice. A new theme in the Aeolian mode appears in section B. The same type of intervallic accompaniment becomes a progression of altered degrees, based on the descending chromatic scale from G to A. The arpeggiated trichords of the hemiolic ostinato descend by half-step, as degrees of the chromatic scale, from G to Ab (15–23).[1] The piece ends with a "neutral" (minor/major) tetrachord, G-B♭-B♮-D.

No. 126 ("Change of Time"): The frequent change of time is typical of the Romanian Christmas carols Bartók collected in Transylvania prior to the First World War (Example 17.1)

Ex. 17.1. *BBE,* 121, Example 1, bars 1–4.

The inclusion of the Lydian F♯ and Phrygian D♭ color tones among the other chromatic degrees point to a C-Lydian/Phrygian twelve-tone polymode. The repetitions of the theme, however, provide most of the emphasis on the C-Mix-olydian mode (bars 1–16, 21–32). A four-bar codetta ends on the fifth degree.

No. 127 ("New Hungarian Folk Song"): The piano accompaniment illustrates Bartók's approach to the transformation of folk music into contemporary art music. The pitch collection is the symmetrical pentatonic scale, with B as the fundamental tone, B-D-E-F♯-A, and the source melody is also typical of exclusively monophonic Hungarian peasant music. Thus, Bartók believed that such archaic features could be provided with the most daring harmonies, since the fifth degree, F♯, is not a functional dominant, the fourth degree, E, generally appears as a passing tone, and the seventh, A, assumes the character of a consonance.[2] Example 17.2 shows the varied harmonic treatment of the melodic sequence, D-B-D-E, that opens the first and fourth melody sections. The piece ends on a "consonant" tonic minor-seventh chord, B-D-F♯-A.

Ex. 17.2. Chordal accompaniment to pentatonic sequence in bars 3, 11, 16, and 24.

No. 128 ("Stamping Dance"): The theme is an imitation of old-style Hungarian quaternary folk song: descending section end-tones, seven-syllable structure, and the G-Phrygian mode, G-A♭-B♭-C-D-E♭-F. The variation form, too, is a Bar-tókian innovation, where the theme is preceded by an introduction, its variants are interspersed with transitional interludes (bars 21–27 and 40–50) and followed by a postlude which features a Phrygian cadence (61–66). And the second and third variations are based on motifs, in stretto (28–39), whose altered degrees convert the tonality to the G-Phrygian/Lydian polymode.

No. 130 ("Village Joke"): This programmatic dance piece, whose original French title on Bartók's fair copy MS is "Burlesque rustique," represents his synthesis of East European folk music and West European art music. According to the specific folkloric elements and artificial scales evident in the music, there is a fusion of Romanian bagpipe style, Slovak modal structure, Hungarian fifth transposition, and nondiatonic whole-tone and octatonic partitions.

The form and rhythm are derived from bagpipe accompaniments to Romanian round-dance pieces, in which in the indeterminate form is based on the repetition of two- or four-bar motifs without any plan or order.[3] The diverse rhythm schematas of these motifs include combinations of ♫, ♫♫, ♫♩, and ♫♫♫. The first appearance of the theme is in the C-Lydian mode and its transposition to G, together with their respective tritones, A-E♭ and E-B♭. The Lydian mode and its melodic leaps of a tritone are characteristic of Slovak folk songs. Hungarian influence is not only reflected by the fifth transpositions of the theme throughout the piece but the thematic inversions which result in basically Phrygian pitch collections, a modal property of many Transylvanian-Hungarian folk songs. Perhaps Bartók's "Joke" is a tonal one, such as the mentioned leaping tritones or the prominent whole-tone pentachords which result from alteration of the sixth degree in three, otherwise "pure" Phrygian inversions of the theme (beginning with bars 7, 9, and 11), In addition, there are two minor to major chord progressions which may be interpreted as constituting octatonic scale partitions: E♭-E♮-F♯-G-[ ]-B♭-C (bar 17) and B♭-B-C♯-D-[ ]-F-G (bar 20). Perhaps Bartók's humor also extends to ending his C-Lydian/Phrygian twelve-tone polymodal piece with a functional 1V⁷-V⁷-I cadence in C major.

There is a thematic resemblance between this piece and the second movement of Bartók's Music for String Instruments, Percussion, and Celesta (Ex. 17.3).

Ex. 17.3. (a) *Mikrokosmos* No. 130, bars 1–3, and (b) Bartók, Music for String Instruments, Percussion, and Celesta (1937), second movement, bars 5–8.

No. 131 ("Fourths"): This theme and its variations are based on the Romanian *Ardeleana*, a round-dance genre borrowed from the Ruthenian *kolomyjka*, in which the rhythm schema of fourteen feet: 2/4 ♫♫♩ | ♫♫♫ | ♫♫♫ | ♩ ♩ |, forms a characteristic four-bar bagpipe motif.[4] Bartók's chordal theme, an exact replication of that schema, and its slightly varied repetition form the first section (bars 1–8). Thereafter, other variants of the same schema create five different sections. Moreover, in the fifth section (35–42), the preceding intervals of harmonic perfect fourths appear as sequential melodic fourths, and, in the last section, as alternating fourth-chords.

The quartal harmony consists of discrete perfect fourths in the upper and lower staves, whose juxtaposed intervals form pentatonic, diatonic, and poly-modal fourth-chords. The tonality is the symmetrical E♭ pentatonic scale, E♭-G♭-A♭-B♭-D♭, from which juxtaposed perfect fourths are derived: B♭-E♭ (L.H.) and D♭-G♭ (R.H.). The alternation of these pentatonic fourths with such inter-vals as F♯-B, G-C, A-D, and C♭-F♭, reveals the twelve-tone polymodality. Fur-thermore, as can be seen in the Ossia degrees (46–50), the piece ends with the E♭-Dorian mode, E♭-F-G♭-A♭-B♭-C♮-D♭. In this way, Bartók's integrates three types of pitch collections basic to his tonal system of composition—pentatonic, modal, and polymodal—where each type is based on a common fundamental tone. In fact, as he explained and illustrated during his lecture at Harvard in 1943:

> As the result of superposing a Lydian and Phrygian pentachord with a common fundamental tone, we get a diatonic pentachord filled out with all the possible flat and sharp degrees. These seemingly chromatic degrees, however, are totally dif-ferent in their function from the altered degrees of the chromatic styles of the previous periods. A chromatically-altered note of a chord is in strict relation to its non-altered form; it is a transition leading to the respective tone of the following chord. In our polymodal chromaticism, however, the flat and sharp tones are not altered degrees at all; they are diatonic ingredients of a diatonic modal scale.[5]

No. 132 ("Major Seconds Broken and Together"): The ternary (A B Av) form is for the most part comprised of four sections (a b c d). In part A, the fourth section is a double one (bars 7–10). Part Av, on the other hand, has three sec-tions (L.H., 19–24). The major seconds consist of melodic and harmonic inter-vals. The latter are extended in range to whole-tone trichords in the upper or lower staves, and to tetrachords by juxtaposition between the staves.

The theme, constructed of alternating half- and whole-steps, combined with the accompanying dyads and trichords, establish a twelve-tone pitch collection, namely, the G-Phrygian/Lydian polymode. The emphatic rendition of clustered whole-tone seconds, however, provides an alternate analysis: the pitch collec-tions can be interpreted as nondiatonic, complementary whole-tone scales, G-A-B-C♯-D♯-E♯ and A♭-B♭-C-D-E-G♭. Another resemblance to Bartók's Music for String Instruments, Percussion, and Celesta is illustrated in Ex. 17.4.

Ex. 17.4. (a) *Mikrokosmos* No. 132, first two melody-sections (bars 1–4), and (b) Bartók, Music for String Instruments, Percussion, and Celesta (1937), first movement, fugue subject (bars 1–2).

The chromatic theme and its contour in the first melody-section of Part A (L.H., bars 1–2) is related to the fugue subject in Bartók's Music for String Instruments, Percussion, and Celesta. Furthermore, G as the fundamental tone of a Mixolydian mode is confirmed at the end of part A (bar 10), where that degree is highlighted as a unison. Note, too, the last bar of the piece, in which a G-Mixolydian tetrachord, G-B-D-F♮, appears as a "consonant" closing sonority.

No. 133 ("Syncopation (3)"): The piece may be characterized as a variation form: A (bars 1–8), Avl (9–17), Interlude (18–24), Av2 (25–30), Av3 (31–38). And each variation, moreover, is subdivided into two-bar subsections. The syncopation arising from the combination of syncopated rhythm schematas, non-traditional beamed eighths, and the alternation of 5/4 and 4/4 time result in performance difficulties which can be addressed by converting the meters to so-called Bulgarian rhythm, that is, using the eighth note as the denominator and as additive numerators. As a case in point, 5/4 and 4/4 in the first two bars could be converted to 10/8 (3+3+4/8) and 8/8 (3+3+2/8), respectively. Other additive conversions: 4/4 as 3+2+3/8 (bar 8) and 3/4 as 3+3/8 (15–17).

The tonal ingredients of Bartók's musical language are apparent in the repetition of X-cells, such as F♯-F♮-E-E♭ and B♭-B♮-C-D♭ (3-4), and the Y-cell (whole-tone tetrachord), D♭-E♭-F-G (13–14). The X-cell as a vertical sonority, D-E♭-E♮-F (R.H., 23–24), is juxtaposed with melodic forms (L.H., 22–24). Polymodality is also manifest in the chordal leap of a tritone from E♭ minor to A minor (9–11) and the repeated alternation of a pentatonic chord, A♯-C♯-E♭-F♯, with the tonic Mixolydian seventh chord, G-B-D-F♮ (25–26).

No. 138 ("Bagpipe Music"): The composed motifs in this piece simulate the structure and performance style of bagpipe melodies or their imitations on the violin and peasant flute. Bartók collected specimens of this genre in northern Hungary (now Slovakia) in 1910, and in Transylvanian-Romanian villages of then Greater Hungary (now Romania) from 1910 to 1917 (Ex. 17.5).

Ex. 17.5. Bartók, *RFM*.i, (a) No. 61a, is from a Christmas dance melody played by a violinist, and (b) No. 562, is from a dance for couples, played by a bagpiper. The tonic drone is a sustained G (not shown), sounding an octave below the middle pipe.

The instrument, now obsolete, has three pipes: the drone, a low-pitched pipe, always sounding the fundamental tonic; middle-pipe, similarly sounding the dominant or alternating with the higher tonic; and chanter, whose imprecise scale, the tonic Mixolydian mode, can be chromatically lowered.[6] Bartók's imaginative bagpipe has G as the drone, and two middle-pipes with sustained dominant and supertonic degrees, thus producing the fifth chord, G-D-A, as the accompaniment. The chanter plays an "imprecise" G-major/minor melody in which the third and seventh degrees are chromatically lowered (bars 1–27). In terms of Bartókian polymodal chromaticism, the pitch collection is a G-major/Dorian nine-tone polymode.

The rondo-variation form, A Av1 B C Av2, is based on the two-bar motifs which are characteristic of Romanian bagpipe melodies. However, the motifs in A and Av1 have three-bar, a b c d, subsections (1–15 and 16–27, respectively), and Av2 has five-bar subsections (52–76). It is noteworthy that the L.H. accompaniment in A and Av1 includes a hemiola in Romanian "shifted" rhythm. The hemiola results when the syncopated (e q e) and juxtaposed dotted-rhythm (q. e) schematas in 2/4 time are sonically converted to 3/8 (♪♩) by "shifting" bar lines. In other words, the hemiola shifts the rhythm in each three-bar subsection, so that the successive accentuation of the fundamental, G, falls on the first, fourth, third, and second beats.

Part B reverts to the traditional two-bar motif structure, and its two motifs are accompanied for the most part by a simple dominant-tonic "middle-pipe" ostinato (28–39). Part C is somewhat similar, but it begins with a tetrachordal ostinato, G-D-E-F♯, juxtaposed with a Mixolydian motif (bars 40–45). The second motif in Av2 and its ostinato introduce another altered degree, the Lydian augmented fourth, Cs (61–75). This addition creates the G-Dorian/Lydian ten-tone polymode, G-A-B♭-C-D-E-F/G-A-B-C♯-D-E-F♯. The piece ends, however, with the tonic Mixolydian tetrachord, G-D-A-F.

No. 139 ("Merry-Andrew"): This program music—title, rhythm schematas, and jocularity—recalls similar characteristics in Richard·Strauss's *Til Eulenspiegel's Merry Pranks*. The most striking commonality in the latter work is the emphatic rendition of the ♫♩ schema (Ex. 17.6).

Ex. 17.6. Strauss, *Til Eulenspiegels lustige streiche,* op. 28 (1894–1895), full score, six bars after R.N. 33.

Repetition of the same schema is not only the signature of the first theme and its extension (bars 1–8), but it appears in a substantial number of melodies in Bartók's large collection of Romanian instrumental music.[7] The second theme has a different rhythm schema, ♫♫ ♫ | ♫♫♫ ♩ , introduced contrapuntally during the repetition of the first theme (13–19) and thereafter repeated with its own accompaniment (43–46). In bars 22–23, there is an interesting cadenza-like configuration of sixteenths, where its pitch collection shows a concatenation of an octatonic pentachord, E♭-D-C-B-A, with a whole-tone one, A-G-F-E♭-D♭. Pentachords from the complementary whole-tone scales appear in the accompaniment and are followed by a variant repetition of the mentioned sixteenth-note configuration (45–48). The penultimate bar ends on C as the fundamental tone, a pentatonic tetrachord, C-E♭-G-B♭, and the ♫♩ schema.

18

Volume Six

(Nos. 140–153)

No. 140 ("Free Variations"): The rondo-variation form can be analyzed as A Av1 B C Cv Av2 coda, and the twelve-tone tonality is based on octatonic and other partitions of the chromatic scale, where the fundamental tone, A, appears throughout as the primary ostinato (Ex. 18.1).

Ex. 18.1. Octatonic pitch collections in (a) part A, bars 1–12; (b) parts Av1 and Av2, bars 13–23 and 65–72; and (c) part C, bars 52–57.

It is noteworthy that the hexachordal structure of each pitch collection is bounded by the tritone tetrachords which form the A Z-cell, A-G♯-E♭-D, and its inversion, A-B♭-D♯-E. Moreover, the latter cell is emphasized at the end of part B (44–50). The repetition of another, chromatic tetrachord in the coda, points to X-cell formations which appear as harmonic dyads with the ostinato subdominant, D, or tonic degrees (72–81).

Change of time and metronome mark imply Bulgarian rhythm schemata which are based on the eighth note as the denominator and additive numerators (♩/160 = ♪/320). Thus, 3/8 and 2/4 in part A and its variants may be construed as 3+2+2/8, 3/8 and 5/8 as 3+3+2/8, 7/8 as 4+3/8, 8/8 as 3+3+2/8, and 9/8 as 4+3+2/8. Part B, in 2/4 time, includes Ruthenian *kolomyjka* rhythm (34–41).

No. 141 ("Subject and Reflection"): In this rondo-variation form, each theme and its inversion appear simultaneously. Structural analysis indicates the organization of parts as A B Av1 Av2 Av3 C Av4 coda. The change of time and rhythm schemata in part A and its variants have a striking resemblance to a melody in Bartók's collection of Transylvanian-Romanian Christmas songs (Ex. 18.2). While the theme is a major pentachord with B♭ as the fundamental tone, the mirror inversion adds the lowered sixth and seventh degrees, G♭ and A♭. The resultant pitch collection is a B♭-Mixolydian/Aeolian octachordal polymode (bars 1–14).

Part B is a transposition of the same polymode to B♮ as the fundamental tone, but the theme is based on the rhythm schema, 2/4 ♩ ♪ | ♫ ♪ | ♬♬ | ♫ ♩ ‖, which may have been derived from heterometric melodies in Bartók's Slovak folk song collection.[1]

Ex. 18.2. *RFM*.iv., melody No. 62t.

Following the successive transpositions of part A variants (23–46), part C introduces a new, simple theme in the ascending form of the C melodic minor scale. This pitch collection, rhythm schema, and intervallic leaps are reminiscent of children's play songs (47–59). Although part Av4 returns to repetitions of the tonic pentachord, the first stretto "reflection" is an octatonic pentachord (63–66), and the second one is a larger partition of the chromatic scale (66–69). Thus, the pitch collection is extended to a basically Bb-Mixolydian/Lydian nine-tone polymode, Bb-C-D-Eb-F-G-Ab/Bb-C-D-E-[F♯]-G-A. A further extension, to the eleven-tone Bb-Phrygian/Lydian polymode, occurs in the coda, where the lowered (Phrygian) second degree appears in the R.H. octatonic pentachord, Cb-C♮-D-Eb-Fb. Note, too, the X-cell cluster chord, A-Bb-Cb-C♮ (bars 74–81).

No. 142 ("From the Diary of a Fly"): In this programmatic piece, Bartók describes the sound of a fly when it is caught in a spider's web but manages to wriggle free before it is devoured.[2] From the theoretic-analytical aspect, the music is based on cellular constructs derived from the F-Phrygian/Lydian twelve-tone polymode, F-Gb-Ab-Bb-C-Db-Eb/F-G-A-B-C-D-E .

The free sectional form, A B C D E F, generally follows the composer's story line. Section A begins with a G X-cell, in which the otherwise contiguous minor seconds of the tetrachord, Gb-G♮-Ab-A♮, are reorganized as discrete major seconds, G-A and Gb-Ab. The extension of this X-cell from F to C (beginning at bar 8) not only establishes F as the fundamental tone of the mentioned polymode but creates a Y-cell tetrachord of contiguous major seconds, Gb-Ab-Bb-C (15–22).

Section B begins with transposition of the X-cell to F, and its extension completes the polymodal pitch collection to twelve tones (26–34). The linear counterpoint in the second half of this section masks the ingenious organization of six X-cells, where the interaction between upper and lower parts of each bar creates a sequence of ascending major seconds, from G-F/Ab-F♯ to F-D♯/F♯-E. The sequence, moreover, outlines the complementary whole-tone scales (35–40), and the following episode is based on emphatic rendition of the dual tritones comprising the A Z-cell, A-Eb-E♮-Bb (44–48).

Section C (*molto agitato e lamentoso*) depicts the fly's surprise and reaction when it is unexpectedly caught in the spider's web. Its struggles to escape are marked by successive hexachordal clusters of minor seconds, beginning with inversion of the A Z-cell to form a B♭ Z-cell (B♭-E♭-E♮-A), and the addition of C♭ and G♯ (49–51). Chromatic compression of the outer cellular degrees (B♭ and A) converts the cellular cluster chord to a gapped octatonic configuration, B-C-[ ] E♭-E♮-[ ] G-A♭ (52–54). Further chromatic compression of the outer scalar degrees converts the configuration to a hexachordal partition of the C-octatonic scale, C-D♭-E♭-E♮-F♯-G, whose dual tritones are those of the C Z-cell (55–59).

Section D (*con gioia*) describes the fly's escape and flight from the web before it is eaten. Here, too, the sequence of major seconds outlines the complementary whole-tone scales—now in descending order and without the previous interaction between upper and lower parts—from A♭ to D (R.H) and G to D♭ (L.H.), respectively (59–68).

Section E juxtaposes the minor seconds, G and A♭, as sustained tones in the L.H. and R.H, respectively, while the interaction of arpeggiated white-key tetrachords and black-key pentachords creates diverse kinds of intervallic dyads (76–87). The last section, a more or less reprise of Section A, in which F returns as the fundamental tone of a Phrygian/Lydian polymode, F-G♭-A♭-B♭/F-G-A-B. The surprise ending, however, is on G, together with the Phrygian trichord, G♭-A♭-B♭, in the penultimate bar.

No. 143 ("Divided Arpeggios"): Essentially a tour de force of symmetrical and asymmetrical arpeggios, based on C as the fundamental of a Phrygian/Lydian twelve-tone polymode. The more or less free sectional form, A B C D, includes a pentatonic introduction, three interludes, and a coda.

The introduction consists of symmetrical tetrachords whose Phrygian degrees, D♭-E♭-A♭-B♭, are organized as a perfect fourth bounded by minor thirds (bars 1–4). The intervallic construction of tetrachords in section A is the same, beginning with C-E♭-A♭-B♮, then successively transposed upward in major seconds until a matrix of two complementary whole-tone scales is formed (Ex. 18.3).

Section B also begins with symmetrical tetrachords—delimited to a gapped hexachord of the A octatonic scale, A-B♭-C-C♯-[ ]-E-F♯—which appear as a two-part stretto in inversional counterpoint (14–21). A short interlude follows, in which syncopated, contrary-motion scalar configurations, together with the sustained F♯-minor seventh chord, create an A-Phrygian/Lydian eleven-tone polymode (22–25).

In section C, the tetrachordal degrees are organized as minor and major thirds (30–32), then as disjunct broken chords whose intervals are extended to augmented fourths and perfect fifths (bars 32–38). The section continues with the alternation of arpeggiated diminished and minor seventh chords in contrary motion between the hands, based on A♭ as the principal tone of a Lydian/Dorian octachordal polymode (39–43). The second interlude follows, consisting of dissonant, nonfunctional chord sequences which not only serve as a transition but also provide the remaining four degrees, A-Db-E♮-F♮, which convert the preceding pitch collection to a twelve-tone Lydian/Phrygian polymode.

Ex. 18.3. Matrix of complementary whole-tone scales formed by sequential transposition of tetrachordal degrees, bars 6–11.

Section D shows a stretto-like contrapuntal treatment of the motivic rhythm schema, ♩. ♪ ♫♫, somewhat similar to the structure of section B. The intervallic construction of tetrachords, on the other hand, replicates the section A matrix of complementary whole-tone scales, in the inverse direction, beginning with C-A-E-Db (Ex. 18.4). The third interlude is a variant of the first one, except that the sustained, nonfunctional Af minor seventh chord is enharmonically notated as a pair of augmented seconds, Ab-B/Eb-F♯, and the pitch collection is the C-Lydian/Aeolian eleven-tone polymode (63–67). With regard to the use of enharmony, Bartók thus indicates that chromaticized degrees "have absolutely no chordal function; on the contrary they have a diatonic melodic function" (*BBE*, 376). Such degrees, moreover, enable the analyst to group them into the modes to which they belong.

The coda begins with the section A opening tetrachord, C-Eb-Ab-B♮, followed by the above-mentioned Ab minor seventh chord (68–74). The last two bars form a "neutral" C tonality, that is, major and minor third degrees.

Ex. 18.4. Inverse matrix of complementary whole-tone scales formed by sequential transposition of tetrachordal degrees, bars 50–55.

No. 144 ("Minor Seconds, Major Sevenths"): The emphatic repetition of D clearly indicates that tone as the fundamental of the twelve-tone Phrygian/Lydian polymode, D-E♭-F-G-A-B♭-C/D-E-F♯-G♯-A-B-C♯. The content structure could be loosely categorized as free sectional form, A Aᵥ B C Bᵥ D coda, with an interlude between sections B and C. On the other hand, however, the sections are based on one or several motifs, stylistically similar to the indeterminate motif-structure of bagpipe pieces in Bartók's collection of Transylvanian-Romanian instrumental music.[3] The assumption of a folkloric connection is strengthened by the parlando-rubato (free rhythm) tempo changes which are commonplace in the performance of certain instrumental and vocal folk music.

In regard to structure of the motifs, they are for the most part melodic and harmonic tetrachords derived from partitions of the chromatic scale. The first bar of section A consists of a chromatic X-cell (Ex. 18.5a) and its extension to an octatonic configuration (18.5b). The second bar shows a further extension to a Z-cell (18.5c) and its embedded X-cell, a simultaneity that not only delineates the bimodal color tones, E♭ and G♯, but also results in a hexatonic cluster chord. A third motif is based on discrete, symmetrical (Hungarian type) pentatonic scales, C-A-G-F-D and D♭-B♭-A♭-G♭-E♭, that are juxtaposed as major sevenths in parallel motion (bars 6–8).

Ex. 18.5 (a) The juxtaposition of inversional minor seconds, A-Bb/G#-G♮, form the contiguous half-step intervals of an X-cell motif. (b) The half-step extension of G to F# and Bb to B♮ forms an octatonic tetrachord of a half-step bounded by two whole-steps. (c) The tritones Eb-A and G#-D form a tonic Z-cell motif.

Section B begins with a syncopated melody in four-part counterpoint, followed by a sustained harmonic Z-cell, C-F-F#-C#, and its reconfiguration as a melodic motif (19–25). An interlude or subsection ensues, in which a series of diverse cluster chords are featured, each cluster ranging from five to eight tones (26–33).

Section C alternates major sevenths with chordal X-cell motifs. The latter are reconfigured as interlocked major thirds between the hands, Fs-As/G-B (35–38).[4] The last section alternates major sevenths with tonic Z-cells, followed by a reprise of pentatonic scales juxtaposed as parallel major sevenths (55–59). The coda is based on a variant of the same tonic Z-cell with its embedded X-cell that appeared in section A (second bar): the configuration is organized as a melodic motif with an X-cell extended to six chromatic degrees. The piece ends with yet another configuration of the tonic Z-cell, a major seventh, Eb-D, in each hand, sustained with the damper pedal, while the minor second, Gs-A, is embedded.

No. 145 ("Chromatic Invention [3]"): While this two-part invention continues the cellular constructions developed by Bartók in Nos. 91 and 92, the thematic rhythm schema, ♪♪♪♪ ♪♪♪♪ | ♩ ♩ ♩ ♩ |, is similar to the schema, in doubled values, of the subject in Bach's Two-Part Invention No. 1 (Ex. 18.6).

Ex. 18.6. J. S. Bach, Fifteen Two-Part Inventions, No. 1.

The binary form (A B) has three motifs and their variants: (1) ♪♪♪♪ , derived from the first bar of the theme, (2) ♩. ♪ ♩. ♪, and (3) ♪♪ ♩ ♪♪ ♩. The tonality is the D-Lydian/Phrygian twelve-tone polymode, D-E-F#-G#-A-B-C#/D-Eb-F-G-A-Bb-C. Part A begins with a stretto in which the theme is replicated at the interval of a tritone (bars 1–4). Motif 2 appears in the R.H. as a chromatic tetrachord (that is, as a B♭ X-cell) while motif 1 in the L.H. is assigned D and C♯ X-cells (5–6). Motif 3 follows, as C X-cells (L.H., 13–14).

The combination of ♩. ♪ and ♫ rhythm schemata, together with tritone intervals, not only form individual or interlocked nonfunctional "V–I" (A–D) Z-cells (17–21), but also result in sequences of complementary whole-tone scales: R.H. A♯-G♯-F♯-E-D-C; L.H. A-G-E♯-E♭-D♭-B (19–21). Part B begins with the same stretto, now with the theme in the upper staff and transposed a fifth higher to A (at bar 27). The piece ends with contrapuntal ascending and descending chromatic pentachords, based on the fundamental tone and its polymodal Phrygian and Lydian degrees (43–49).

No. 146 ("Ostinato"): This piece continues Bartók's exploration of Transylvanian-Romanian bagpipe melodies as a source for composition (see Nos. 130, 131, 138, and 144). Here, too, the structural medium is a free sectional form but substantially extended, A Av1 B C D E F G Av2 coda, and, moreover, by the insertion of interludes throughout the work—perhaps a stylistic borrowing from the practice of North African Arab instrumentalists during their performance of folk dances.[5] Certain sections incorporate one or more two-bar motifs whose rhythm schematas are based on different combinations of ♫, ♫♫, ♫♫, and ♫♫♫, the same values typical of Romanian bagpipe pieces of indeterminate structure (Ex. 18.7).

Ex. 18.7. Twin-bar motifs in Transylvanian-Romanian bagpipe style.

In regard to tonal language, the basic pitch collection is the D-Lydian/Phrygian twelve-tone polymode, in which the prominent color tones, F♯ (Lydian augmented fourth) and Ef (Phrygian minor second), are combined with the common fundamental and fifth degrees to form the Z-cell tetrachord. This Z-cell is implied in the introduction, where the L.H. ostinato appears as a Lydian trichord, D-F♯-G. Section A, a quaternary R.H. melodic structure, begins with motif 1 and ends on the Phrygian second (E♭) in juxtaposition with the ostinato trichord to complete the Z-cell tetrachord (bars 5–14). Motif 2 represents the fourth subsection of the quaternary (15–16). It should be noted that the pitch collection of section A consists of nine tones, and that the variant reprise adds C♯ as the tenth degree of the polymode (bar 23).

Section B is preceded by an interlude whose ostinato is a Z-cell trichord transposed to A as the fundamental tone, A-D♯-E (L.H, 28–31). The section begins with motif 3 in the R.H., and the emphatic rendition of C♮ adds the eleventh degree to the basic D-polymode (bar 53). The ostinato tonic and dominant degrees not only simulate the drone and middle pipe (respectively, A-E) of a Transylvanian bagpipe, but combine with the Lydian degree as tied, syncopated trichords. Their juxtaposition with motif 3 creates a polyrhythmic accompaniment (32–57).

The following interlude shows the L.H. Z-cell trichord transposed to B♭ as the fundamental tone, thus completing the basic twelve-tone tonality of the composition (58–63). Section C, structured in Romanian *Ardeleana* dance style (see No. 131), begins with motif 4 and ends on the fundamental tone, D. Since B♮ is the first tone of the motif, its juxtaposition with the accompaniment forms the complete Z-cell, B♭-B♮-E-F (64–73). The next, extended interlude serves as a syncopated transition to section D, in which the melody consists of sixteenth-note tetrachordal partitions of the D major scale, and the polymodal accompaniment includes C♯-, B♯- and E♯-minor seventh chords, thus creating a twelve-tone polymode (81–91). The next interlude is limited to the alternation of minor triads between the hands.

Section E returns to motif 1, followed by motifs 5 and 6, with the simple accompaniment being a sustained E♭ seventh chord. This juxtaposition between the hands creates an E♭-Phrygian/Mixolydian nine-tone polymode (96–103). Another short interlude, transposed to E as the fundamental tone, leads to section F, where reconfigured motif 5 and its accompaniment of noncellular trichords constitute an E-Lydian/Phrygian eleven-tone polymode (108–115). The motif, however, leads abruptly to another extended interlude in which the emphatic repetition of the fundamental D is juxtaposed with a sequence of nonfunctional triads. The chromatic degrees of these sonorities contribute to the eleven-tone polymodality of the interlude (116–125).

Section G repeats the *Ardeleana* dance style introduced in section C, but with motif 1 instead of motif 3 (126–132). And the previous polyrhythmic accompaniment of syncopated trichords is changed to D-minor triads. Another difference is the transposition of motif 1 to the G-Lydian mode, thus creating a G-Lydian/Dorian octachordal polymode. An attenuated motif 7, ♩♫♩, appears in the last six bars of the section in "shifted" rhythm (Ex. 18.8).

Ex. 18.8. Repetition of motif 7 in "shifted" rhythm, bars 132–137. The accent marks are added as a guide for the reader.

This type of rhythm, a peculiarity of certain *Ardeleana* dance music, occurs when a motif is repeated with shifted accents so that accentuated parts lose their accent in the repeat and nonaccentuated parts gain one.[6] Section Av2, somewhat similar to Av1 with regard to alteration of motif 1, returns to the tonic twelve-tone polymode. The accompaniment is a syncopated repetition of fourth chords (138–151). The coda returns to the original tempo, based on a slight alteration of motif 2, in which the R.H. features tetrachordal partitions of the D-Dorian mode. The syncopated accompaniment consists of dyads and trichords whose chromatic degrees and the inversional pentachords of the cadence complete the twelve-tone tonality.

No. 147 ("March"):[7] Although Bartók referred to this composition as a march of primitive peoples, because the L.H. intervallic repetitions and tonality create a grotesque effect (p. 105), there is decided relationship to rhythm schematas of the nineteenth-century Hungarian *verbunkos* style (Ex. 18.9).

Ex. 18.9. Extracts from The Rákóczi March (Ference Erkel's elaboration, 1840).[8]

The structural concept is a theme and four variations, with interludes following certain variants. The rhythm schemata of the theme, ♫ ♪ | ♫ ♪ | and ♫ ♩ | ♩ ♩ | ♩ |, have commonalities with those of the Rákóczi March. Octatonic and scalar tetrachords alternate with X-cells. The twelve-tone tonality is the E-Phrygian/Lydian polymode, and the ostinato accompaniment consists for the most part of alternating fifths and fourths.

The first five notes of variant 1 form a whole-tone pentachord (bars 7–8), followed by a sequence of X-cells (9–11). The transitional interlude temporarily establishes a C-Lydian tonality (12–15). Variation 2 consists of another sequence of X-cells, ending on G, the fifth degree (15–20). Thereafter a two-bar interlude shows the ostinato as octave trichords in each hand, in which C♯ and F♯ are given prominence.

The inverted parts in the noncellular variant 3 have F♯ as the fundamental of a Mixolydian/Aeolian nine-tone polymode. The R.H. ostinato is in Romanian style "shifted" rhythm, where the accentuation is created by octave leaps of the trichords, thus shifting the sequential accents to beats 4, 3, 2, 4; 3, 1, 4, 3; and, 4, 2, 1, 4, respectively (22–31). Another short, transitional interlude leads to variant 4, where the parts are restored to their original form. The L.H. ostinato consists of alternating fifths and major thirds, with D as the fundamental of a Lydian/Aeolian nine-tone polymode (34–38). The ostinato is discontinued, and the theme is treated as imitative and inversional strettos between the hands (38–41). The last interlude has half-note intervals in contrary motion, that end on a sustained G-major/minor trichord, G-B-A♯ (L.H., 42–45).

The structure of the unique coda gives the impression of a miniaturized ternary form, in which section A has thematic transformations of rhythmic (♫♩) and broken fourth-chord elements while the sustained L.H. major/minor trichord changes to chromatic dissonances. Section B returns to the type of juxtaposed ostinatos in the interlude preceding variant 3 (21–22), but the coincidence of discrete trichords produces cluster chords with five or six degrees that eventually resolve to a simple G-major triad (49–52). Section Av is a reprise of the thematic tetrachord as Y-cell (whole-tone) constructions, ending on a Phrygian cadence, C♯-D♯-F♮-E.

Six Dances in Bulgarian Rhythm

No. 148 ("Bulgarian Dance [1]"): In order to avoid redundancy, the reader will find an introduction to aspects of Bartókian Bulgarian rhythm in the analyses of *Mikrokosmos* Nos. 113 and 115.[9] The structural makeup is a more or less architectonic form, A Av B A coda, the tonality is the E-Phrygian/Lydian twelve-tone polymode, and the 9/8 additive meter is organized as ♫♫ ♫ ♩. (4+2+3/8).

The part A motif is based on the E-pentatonic scale, E-G-A-B-D (C is a passing tone), and the syncopated rhythm schema, ♪ ♩. ♩ ♫♫ , in the R.H. The L.H. is assigned the 9/8 additive meter as a scalar ostinato in E major (bars 4–13). Section Av is transposed to the C as the fundamental tone: the ostinato is in the Lydian mode—the Phrygian minor second (D♭) appears there as an intervallic addition—while the R.H. motif consists of C-Aeolian degrees (14–17). The latter modality continues when the L.H. ostinato is transposed to the A-Lydian mode (18–21).

Part B begins with variations of the scalar ostinato as a descending configuration, including a new rhythmic motif in the R.H, ♩ ♩ ♩ ♩ ♪ (22–28). The reprise of part A, essentially in the tonic polymode, consists of three sections, beginning with the new motif as the L.H. accompaniment of intervals and trichords (29–32). In the second section, the same type of accompaniment takes on its own life as independent sonorities in two-part, free counterpoint with the R.H. variant motif, ♩. ♪♫ ♫♫ (33–41). The third section begins with an ingenious two-part stretto in the R.H., based on the syncopated rhythm schema, while the accompaniment consists of arpeggiated triads (42–45). The coda (50–54) features another syncopated rhythm schema, ♪ ♩. ♩ ♩. , and ends with scalar configurations in the E-Phrygian mode.

No. 149 ("Bulgarian Dance [2]"): Perhaps the formal plan, A B Av Bv1 Bv2 coda, represents the influence of Beethoven, "who revealed to us the meaning of progressive form."[10] The tonality is the C-Phrygian/Lydian twelve-tone polymode, and the additive 2+2+3/8 meter shows three rhythm schemata: ♫ ♫ ♫♫ (the ostinato), ♩♩♩♪ (part A motif), and ♫♫♩ ♫♫ (part B motif). The form also includes an introduction, interludes, and a postlude (the coda), based on the ostinato and its variant pitch collections.

The thematic construction of part A is the pure C-pentatonic scale, C-E♭-F-G-B♭ (L.H.), while the R.H. imitates the theme as an antiphony (bars 4–8). The interlude, a temporary transposition to the F-pentatonic scale, returns to the tonic as a two-bar, polymodal pitch collection of the unisonal part B theme (16-21). Although the polymode is a ten-tone C-Phrygian/Lydian collection, it is rotated by fifth transposition to G, where the accentuation of the dual tritones, G–D♭ (=C♯) and C–G♭ (= F♯), outlines the related Z-cells (Ex. 18.10).

Ex. 18.10. (a) The ten-tone, C-Phrygian/Lydian polymode (the dual tritones are shown in large-head notation), and (b) rotation of the polymode to G (the dual tritones are shown with enharmonically altered degrees).

Part B ends with a sequence of alternating major and octatonic tetrachords, and the following interlude leads to the reprise of attenuated part Av and its fourth-chord accompaniment (bars 21–30). Another interlude shows the ostinato as an F♯ drone (bagpipe imitation?) with trichordal degrees. Part Bv2 has alternating major and octatonic tetrachords in the R.H., while the accompaniment consists of triads (44-49) and whole-tone sonorities (50–53). The coda is for the most part an extended reprise of the introductory ostinato.

No. 150 ("Bulgarian Dance [3]"): Another example of progressive form, in Bulgarian 2+3/8 *pajdushko horo* dance meter.[11] The rhythmic units in 2/8 are ♩ and ♫; in 3/8 are ♩., ♪♩, ♩♪, and ♫♩. These units are combined to form the quintuple additive meter as well as the distinctive motifs of the part form and its interludes. The tonality is the A-Lydian/Phrygian twelve-tone polymode. Excluding variants and interludes, the basic binary form may be interpreted as an architectonic plan: A B I A A B A I B A (= coda?).

Part A has the distinctive R.H. rhythm schema, ♫ ♫♫, that defines motif 1. Together with its accompaniment, the motivic pitch collection is an E-Lydian pentachord with a minor and major seventh degree (bars 1–4). The thematic content of part B, on the other hand, is based on a three-bar, symmetrical arrangement of rhythm schemata, ♩ ♩. I ♩ ♪♩ I ♩♩., and the pitch collection is an A-major pentachord (5–12). Bv1 is extended to a hexachord by the addition of D♯, the Lydian fourth degree (13–19). The following interlude, transposed to the dominant, has juxtaposed sustained and repeated perfect intervals and ♩ ♩. as the motivic schema.

Av1 is extended to a complete E-octatonic scale (23–26),[12] and Av2 follows with chromatic descent of motif 1 and its accompaniment of major sixths (27–30). Bv2, a rotation of A-Aeolian to G-Mixolydian, shows its theme in contrary motion between the hands (31–42). Thereafter, a three-bar reprise of the interlude, transposed to C♯, leads to Av3, in which motif 1 appears as chromatic tetrachords and pentachords, together with its accompaniment of a chromatic progression of major sixths (48–57).

The contrapuntal Bv3 presents motif 2 as a stretto (58–73), and, in similar counterpoint, the third interlude as a ♩ ♩. ♩ schema. The interlude ends with a leading tone (G♯) Z-cell, G♯-C♯/D-G♮ (77–78), thus providing a transition to the coda, where the reprise of part A, in the A-Lydian/Phrygian twelve-tone polymode, ends with a simple A-major triad.

No. 151 ("Bulgarian Dance [4]"): According to Bartók's explanation this piece is "Very much in the style of [George] Gershwin's tonality, rhythm, and color. American folk song feeling." The additive 3+2+3/8 meter as ♫♩ ♫ ♫♩ occurs in the first movement, second theme, of Gershwin's Concerto in F for Piano and Orchestra (1927) as 4/4 ♪ ♩♩♩ ♪. The form is a rondo-variation type, A B A C D E Av, the parts are generally subdivided into four-bar sections, and the pentatonic theme, A-C-D-E-G, is based on the old-Hungarian anhemitone (symmetrical) scale.

The chordal accompaniment in the first section of part A consists of trichords whose degrees form the C-Lydian/Phrygian hexachordal polymode. In the second section, the pentatonic theme is played an octave higher, the sonorities appear as triads, and their roots are organized as a whole-tone tetrachord followed by an octatonic pentachord (bars 1–8). In part B, the theme appears in the L.H., transposed to Fs, in the first section. The section, transposed to G♯, is an octave lower. The asymmetrical third section is subdivided into 3+3+2 bars, and its pitch collection is the F-Phrygian/Lydian twelve-tone polymode (9–24).

The reprise of part A is followed by part C, in which the characteristic pentatonic intervals of a perfect fourth, major seconds and minor thirds are delimited for the most part to thirds and occasional seconds in the L.H. The accompaniment consists of ostinato-like, dissonant trichords (R.H., 25–40). A three-bar interlude of descending thirds is followed by part D, in which the basic schema appears in eighth-note values, ♫♩ ♫ ♫♩, and in asymmetrical 2+2+3 bars.

Part E has a single, four-bar section, the L.H. accompaniment is a sequence of ascending scalar triads, and the schema of the R.H. theme is ♫♩ ♩ ♩. (51–54). The first section of the coda-like part Av returns to the original rhythm schema as R.H. octaves, and is accompanied by various nonfunctional triads which feature the tritone degree, F♯. The construction of the polymodal second and third sections is quite different from the sections in the preceding parts. The R.H. has minor-sixth intervals which are accompanied by octatonic and other scalar configurations (55–64). The plagal cadence ends on the tonic with a functional IV⁷–I progression.

No. 152 ("Bulgarian Dance [5]"): Although this composition has an architectonic A B C A design, there are a number of attributes similar to those of Romanian bagpipe pieces in indeterminate form, such as two- and four-bar constructions, tonic-dominant ostinatos, and sections with diverse rhythm schemata. The tonality is the A-Lydian/Phrygian twelve-tone polymode, and the additive meter, 2+2+2+3/8, appears in three basic rhythm schemata, 1. ♫ ♫ ♫ ♫♫, 2. ♩ ♩ ♩ ♩ ♪, and 3. ♫♫♩ ♩ ♫♫.¹³ Part A has a 4+2+4 symmetrical arrangement of bars, and the accompanying ostinato, an A-Lydian tetrachord, is followed by the intervallic tritone B-C (bars 1–10). The functional resolution of this interval marks the transition to a C-major hexachord in part Av1, where there is an asymmetrical, 2+3 arrangement of bars. Part B alternates rhythm schemata 1 and 2 as a rounded (*a b a*) arrangement of two-bar sections. The melodic structure of section *a* consists of chromatic configurations that are juxtaposed in stretto-like inversional counterpoint, ending on a G-major triad (16–24).

Part C returns to the tonic polymode with a new, distinctive theme, introduces schema 3, and features an octatonic tetrachord, A-G♯-F♯-F♮, as an ostinato accompaniment (25–30). The Phrygian (A-B♭) tremolo in the last four bars could be construed as an interlude (R.H., 31–34). In any event, the sectional structure is *a b a c*, 2+2+2+4 bars. Part Av2 begins with a two-bar, A major hexachord and is thereafter altered to Lydian construction. The cadence in the last two bars consists of a perfect fourth, G♯-C♯, the leading tone and major third degrees, respectively, of the fundamental pitch collection.

No. 153 ("Bulgarian Dance [6]"): During a 1939 interview in Paris, Bartók pointed to Debussy's influence in "reawakening an awareness of harmony and all its possibilities."¹⁴ At an earlier interview in Budapest, and with greater specificity, he stated that "Debussy totally and strictly persisted in tonality. He used with greater freedom, of course, strange notes in the harmony without preparation and resolution."¹⁵ It seems apparent that Bartók was referring to the fifth door scene in his opera, *Duke Bluebeard's Castle*, when Bluebeard's domain is tonally described as a progression of nonfunctional chord sequences, including a leap of a tritone. The chordal motifs—triads and dyads—in this, the last *Mikrokosmos* piece, reflect Bartók's Debussyian approach, and their additive rhythm schema is 3+3+2, ♩. ♩. ♩| ♩. ♪. ♪|. The ostinato schema is ♫♫ ♫♫ ♫, the tonality is based on the E-Lydian/Phrygian twelve-tone polymode, and the large ternary form can be represented as A Av1–2 B Bv1–2 Av3 (Interlude) Av4–5 coda.

Part A consists of four two-bar sections, with the chordal melody in the R.H. and the tonic ostinato as the accompaniment (bars 1–8). In the following eight bars of part Av1, the R.H. takes up the ostinato on the third degree. Av2 continues the ostinato on C♮, while the L.H. melody is constructed of dyads with dominant and tonic sustained tones (17–23).

Part B is a canonic stretto at the tritone, consisting of a motif in the ostinato rhythm schema, ♫♩ ♫♩ ♫, in which two descending octatonic configurations thereafter appear as a nonoctatonic collection, bounded by a C Z-cell, C/G–F♯/Cs (at bars 28–29). The following G-octatonic scale has an inverted form of the same Z-cell, G/F♯–C♯/B♯ (29–30). In Bv1, the partially octatonic motif reverts to an ostinato in both hands, but with a superposed tetrachord, in sustained values, which completes the pitch collection (R.H., 31–35). Bv2 begins with nonoctatonic sequences of the motif, based on an A-Lydian-Phrygian eleventone polymode (36–42), but ends with a stretto of alternating octatonic pentachords (43–45).

Part Av3 is a combination of free, imitative, and inversional counterpoint, in which the R.H. triadic melody is contrasted with L.H. dyads (46–60). A six-bar ostinato, on C in the L.H., serves as a transitional interlude. Av4 has the same ostinato accompaniment for the symmetrical pentatonic melody, F-A♭-B♭-C-E♭, whose individual degrees are harmonized for the most part by inverted major triads (75–80). Av5 returns to the tonic polymode, where the chordal melody appears in the L.H. and the ostinato, B, is assigned to the R.H. (81–90). The coda ends with an emphatic rendition of the E-Mixolydian seventh chord.

Notes

PART ONE

Genesis

Chapter 1: Bartók as Pianist

1. *BBE*, 408.

2. Ibid.

3. János Demény, ed. *Bartók Béla levelei* (Béla Bartók's letters). Zeneműkiadó (1951): 203–17.

4. *BBLW*, 15.

5. Ibid., 16.

6. *BBE*, 408.

7. Christian Altdorfer, credited by Bartók as having discovered his talent.

8. *LMBB*, 17.

9. Another source indicates that Bartók played the opening movement of Beethoven's C Major Sonata op. 2, no 3. See *BBLW*, 268n. 18.

10. *LMBB*, 6.

11. *BBLW*, 19.

12. *BBE*, 408.

13. *LMBB*, 11.

14. Ibid.

15. Ibid., 12.

16. Serge Moreux, *Béla Bartók*. Preface by Arthur Honegger. Trans. G. S. Fraser and Erik de Mauny. London: The Harvill Press (1853): 22–3.

17. *BBLW*, 26–7.

18. *LMBB*, 15.

19. *BBE*, 408.

20. Interviews with Ernő Balogh, July–August 1954. He was a pupil of Bartók from 1909 to 1915.

21. *LMBB*, 15.

22. Ibid., 17.

23. Moreux, *Bartók*, 33. At the time of his graduation from the Academy, Bartók had produced an unusual quantitative and qualitative output as a composition student.

24. *LMBB*, 20.

25. Moreux, *Bartók*, 29.

26. *LMBB*, 20–1.

27. Moreux, *Bartók*, 145.

28. Béla Bartók, "Some Early Letters," in *Béla Bartók: A Memorial Review*. New York: Boosey & Hawkes, Inc. (1950): 13.

29. *BBE*, 409.

30. Zoltán Kodály, *The Selected Writings of Zoltán Kodály*. Trans. Lili Halápy and Fred Macnicol. London: Boosey & Hawkes Ltd. (1974): 104.

31. Moreux, *Bartók*, 78.

32. *BBE*, 410.

33. Ibid., 410–1.

34. Interview with Lili Balint Weinberger, 21 December 1954. See also János Demény, "The Pianist" in *BC,* 64–78.

35. Moreux, *Bartók*, 141-2.

36. Letter to the *New York Herald Tribune*, 4 December 1927.

37. Olin Downes, *The New York Times,* 23 December 1927.

38. Interview dated 21 December 1954.

39. *BBLW,* 107–9.

40. Lajos Hernádi, "Béla Bartók, le pianiste, le pédagogue, l'homme," *La Revue Musicale* 224 (1955): 84.

41. Ibid.

42. *LMBB*, 77.

44. Ibid., 93–4.

45. Interviews with Ernő Balogh and György Sandor. They agreed that Bartók's basic concepts of piano playing did not change in the years they knew him.

46. Margit Varró, Unpublished notes to her lecture given at the Wisconsin Conservatory of Music, 29 September 1950. She taught piano at the Budapest Academy of Music

during Bartók's tenure there as professor of piano.

47. Hernádi, 84.

48. Moreux, *Bartók,* 69, 145.

49. Wilhelmine Creel Driver, personal letter dated 6 May 1954. She studied with Bartók from 1936 to 1937.

50. Interview, 8 January 1955.

51. Willi Apel, *Masters of the Keyboard.* Cambridge: Harvard University Press (1947): 292. He also states that the earliest example of the new percussive style in piano literature is Bartók's *Allegro Barbaro* (1911).

52. Aaron Copland, *What to Listen for in Music.* Rev. ed. New York: McGraw-Hill (1957): 86. He defines the nonvibrating piano as one where "little or no use of the pedal is made. This results in a hard, dry piano tone which has its own particular virtue."

53. William Murdoch, "Pianoforte Music," in *A Dictionary of Modern Music and Musicians.* London: J. M. Dent & Sons (1924): 385–7. In the same publication (p. 243), Bartók describes the cimbalom as "Steel wires spread out on a wooden board like the strings of a piano, but they are not placed in order of pitch. Its compass is fifty notes, the wires are struck with cloth-covered wooden sticks, and a pedal damper is attached to instrument."

54. Interview dated 21 December 1954.

Chapter 2: Bartók as Teacher

1. *LMBB,* 9–10.

2. Letter from Bartók to his mother, dated 16 January 1900. The original Hungarian text appears in János Demény, *Bartók Béla levelei* (Béla Bartók letters). Budapest: Zeneműkiadó (1976): 19. The English translation will be found in Serge Moreux, *Bartók.* London: Harvill Press (1953): 21-2.

3. Interview with Elisabeth Lang, 21 December 1954.

4. Interview with György Sandor, 8 January 1955.

5. The specific works are listed in *BBLW, 354–9.*

6. *LMBB,* 43.

7. *BBE,* 432.

8. Ibid., 426.

9. Published under the title of Thirteen Little Piano Pieces from the "Notebook for Anna Magdalena Bach."

10. Sándor Reschofsky, personal letter dated 6 June 1954.

11. Ibid.

12. Ibid. Reschofsky's comment was intended to refute certain published opinions that Bartók's only contribution to the collaboration was to furnish illustrative compositions.

13. Personal letter, dated 12 December 1954.

14. Ibid.

15. *BBLW,* 124.

16. *BBE,* 426–30.

17. Canadian pianist who studied with Bartók for several years in Budapest.

18. Agnes Butcher, unpublished script prepared for her broadcast on Radio Free Europe (Munich), 21 January 1954.

19. Ernő Balogh, "Personal Glimpses of Béla Bartók," *Pro-Musica* (June 1928): 18.

20. Interview with Peter Bartók, 28 July 1954.

21. Ibid. The son was twelve years old when he began the study of the piano in 1936, continuing his lessons until 1939.

22. The introductory aural exercises appear on pp. 6–9 in the English translation of *Zongora Iskola* (Piano School). The 1968 revised edition, titled *Bartók-Reschofsky Piano Method* and edited by Leslie Russel, was published by Editio Musica (Budapest) and Boosey & Hawkes (London).

23. Émile Jaques-Dalcroze, *Rhythm, Music and Education.* New York: G. P. Putnam's Sons (1921): 62-3.

24. Ibid., 103.

25. Andor Földes, "My First Meeting with Bartók," *Etude* (March 1955): 12.

26. Interview with Dorothy Parrish, 14 April 1955.

27. Interview with Ann Chenée, July 1954.

28. *LMBB,* 39.

29. In *Zenei Szemle* 11, no. 3 (March 1927): 344-7.

30. *BBE,* 400. An illuminating presentation of Liszt's piano technique and pedagogy is given in Derek Watson's book, *Liszt.* New York: Schirmer Books (1989): 171–9.

31. Edwin Hughes, "Solving Piano Problems." *Etude* 73, no. 10 (October 1955): 60–1. See also Malwine Brée [Leschetizky's assistant], *The Groundwork of the Leschetizky Method.* New York: G. Schirmer, 1930 (the first, German edition appeared in 1902).

32. See Tobias Matthay, *The Act of Touch in All Its Diversity: An Analysis and Synthesis of Pianoforte Tone-Production.* London and New York: Longmans, Green, 1926.

33. See *The Physical Basis of Piano Touch and Tone.* New York: E. P. Dutton and

Company, 1925. See also *The Physiological Mechanics of Piano Technique*. New York: E. P. Dutton, 1929 and reprinted in 1981 by Da Capo Press, New York. Ortmann was a member of the piano faculty and later the director of the Peabody Conservatory of Music in Baltimore.

34. Ortmann, *The Physiological Mechanics of Piano Technique*, 246.

35. Ibid., 342–4.

36. *BBE.*, 432.

Chapter 3: Background and Development of the Mikrokosmos

1. *BBLW*, 103.

2. Denijs Dille, *Béla Bartók*. Antwerp: N.V. Standaard-Boekhandel (1939): 89-91. A photostatic copy of the pamphlet is on file at the *PBA* in Homosassa, Florida. The date listed for the *Mikrokosmos* is 1926-1937.

3. *PBA* 62TVPFC2.

4. There is no apparent relationship between the other incomplete sketches in Bartók's MS ZI32 and the *Mikrokosmos* MS 59S1 as finally constituted by me during my tenure as curator of the New York Bartók Archive.

5. He completed Nine Little Piano Pieces on 31 October 1926, in Budapest, and the work was published by Universal-Edition A.G. (Vienna) in 1927.

6. During one of my visits to the Budapest Bartók Archívum (*BBA*), I had the opportunity to browse the composer's library, where I found the quotation among other, underscored texts in his personal copy of *Faust*. For further details, see my remarks in *BC*, 209n.1.

7. Mátyás Seiber, personal letter dated 9 October 1954. During my interview with Peter Bartók on 28 July 1954, he remarked that his father taught him popular pieces composed by Seiber: "We played foxtrots, rhumbas, and so forth, as duets in which my father improvised a bass part."

8. Interview dated 28 July 1954. See also *BBE*, 426–30 and the jacket to Bartók Record No. 919 (*For Children* for Piano).

9. Margit Varró, unpublished paper read at the Wisconsin Conservatory of Music, 29 September 1950. Another unpublished paper, "Contributions to Béla Bartók's Biography," was presented to the Midwest Chapter of the American Musicological Society in March 1949, and contains a similar statement.

10. *PBA*, Bartók Program File.

11. *LMBB*, 83.

12. Ralph Hawkes, "Béla Bartók: A Recollection by His Publisher," *Béla Bartók: A Memorial Review*. New York: Boosey & Hawkes, Inc. (1950): 17.

13. Dated from May 1938. See in *PBA* Correspondence Files.

14. *BBGM*, 75. Letter dated 29 April 1938.

15. Ibid., letter dated 8 May 1938.

16. Ibid., letter dated 13 May 1938.

17. Later changed to 3 P.M.

18. The document is undated and unsigned.

19. *BBGM*, 77. Letter dated 6 April 1939.

20. Ibid., letter dated 17 April 1939.

21. *BBGM,*, 78. Letter dated 25 April 1939.

22. Bartók also suggested that not all pieces should have sketches and that the illustrations should be in Vol. I for the most part.

23. *BBGM*, 79. Letter dated 8 July 1939.

24. Ibid., correspondence of 14–21 July 1939. The draft, prepared by his editorial assistant, Dr. Ernst Roth, was annotated by Bartók and returned on 19 July.

25. *BBGM*, 80.

26. Ibid., letter dated 21 July 1939.

27. *BBGM*, 81.

28. Ibid.

29. *BBGM*, 82. Letter dated 7 January 1940.

30. *BBGM*, 84. Letter dated 5 February.

31. *BBGM*, 86. Letter from Ernst Roth to Ralph Hawkes.

32. New York University, 1956.

33. See also Victor Bator, *The Béla Bartók Archives: History and Catalogue*. New York: Bartók Archives Publication, 1963. My editorial contribution is represented by the catalogue of Bartók estate holdings (pp. 22–39), facsimiles of manuscripts, *Mikrokosmos* annotations, and selected photographs. The catalogue, moreover, was based on the two volumes of my Master Index of *NYBA* manuscripts.

34. The letter *P* in the MS numeric designation is the abbreviation for the *Piano*.

35. Thus the manuscript consists of first and second intermediary drafts and was filed as *NYBA* 59PID/ID2, since the individual variants could not be separated without irreparable damage.

36. A comprehensive description of this heterogeneous collection of manuscripts will be found in the *NYBA* Master Index.

37. Of the circa fifty-nine pages of transparencies, their page proofs numbered 9–12 and 33–36 were missing.

38. See also Benjamin Suchoff, "History of Bartók's *Mikrokosmos*," *Journal of Re-*

search in Music Education 7, no. 2 (Fall 1959): 185–96.

39. *PBA* Program File. The pieces are listed by title on the program, and the timings were noted by Bartók in pencil.

40. *BBGM*, 76. Letter from Bartók to Hawkes, dated 13 May 1938.

41. *BBE*, 426–30.

42. Given at Oberlin Conservatory, Mills College, University of Washington, and University of Kansas City. The Mills College program also included Nos. 140, 142, 144, 137, and 146.

43. At the New Jersey College for Women, Swarthmore College, and Vassar College.

44. At the Detroit Institute of Arts, Stanford University, Wells College, and the University of Oregon. Nos. 148–153 were also played at Stanford, Wells, and Oregon.

45. At Oberlin Conservatory, Princeton, and Brigham Young Universities, University of Washington, Reed College, and the Wilshire Theater in Los Angeles.

46. Titles and numbers appear on the American Columbia (ML 4419) recording. The jacket lists thirty-five titles, but Nos. 122, 72, and 146 do not appear on the recording.

Chapter 4: Technique and Musicianship.

1. *BBGM*, 60.

2. From the Bartók-Reschofsky, Piano School (*Zongora Iskola*). London: Boosey & Hawkes, 1968. See also Bartók's comments in his edition of J. S. Bach, Well-tempered Clavier. Budapest: Editio Musica (reprint).

3. Ibid. See also Bartók's edition of J. S. Bach, Thirteen Little Piano Pieces from the "Notebook for Anna Magdalena Bach." Zeneműkiadó, Budapest, 1950.

4. Not listed here is tenuto, the weakest of accents, in order to emphasize its basic function as a nonpercussive touch.

Chapter 5: Format and Definitions

1. Chapters 5–11 are a revised version of pp. 16–142 in my book, *Guide to Bartók's Mikrokosmos*. London: Boosey & Hawkes, 1971. Reprint. New introduction by György Sandor, New York: Da Capo Press, 1983).

2. In 1944, Bartók's publisher, Boosey & Hawkes, asked the composer to participate in a promotional scheme to stimulate sales of the *Mikrokosmos*. It was suggested that he give lessons on the pedagogy of the work to Ann Chenée, president of the Piano Teachers Congress of New York, as a "typical American teacher," who would later write articles and present lectures to other music educators about the value of the *Mikrokosmos* in piano pedagogy. In 1945, Ms. Chenée provided me with a copy of Bartók's comments and responses to her queries while she played through the work for him. She recalled that Bartók reluctantly came to her studio, since he could not understand why the *Mikrokosmos* needed promotion. In fact, he stated that his compositions spoke for themselves and if they did not catch on then, they would later.

PART TWO

Pedagogy

Chapter 6: Volume One

1. The notes in Part Two include selected corrigenda which were the outcome of my comparative study of Bartók's manuscripts (beginning in 1956), the first edition (1940), Winthrop Rogers Edition (1968), and the current New Definitive Edition (1987). The reader should also consult Stuart Thyne's findings in his essay, "Bartók's *Mikrokosmos*: A Reexamination." *The Piano Quarterly* 27, no. 107 (1979): 43–46.

2. The rhythm can be illustrated in this way:

Chapter 7: Volume Two

1. That is, staccatissimo (shorter) and staccato (longer) types.

2. In bar 24, the interval in the bass clef lacks a staccato dot.

Chapter 8: Volume Three

1. This is a teasing song to pair off a courting couple. An earlier, different setting, without text, appears as No. 68 in Bartók and Sándor Reschofsky, *Zongora Iskola* (Piano School)—a method intended as instructional material from the beginning to the highest degree of piano study—which was published in Budapest in 1913. In 1929, Bartók reprinted the piece as No. 10 in his First Term at the Piano (see *Piano Music of Béla Bartók, Series II*. The Archive Edition, 1981, 138).

2. The rhythm schemata consist of eighth note-sixteenth note patterns typical of Romanian bagpipe melodies: ♫♫, ♫♫, and ♫♫. They are also notated in 7/8 additive meter (2+2+3/8) in Exercise 29.

Chapter 9: Volume Four

1. Staccato dots under B♯ in both hands would be consistent with bar 12

2. In bar 27, the R.H. dotted quarter note should be changed to a staccato quarter note (7/8 = 2+2+3 = ♩♩♩.).

3. In bar 23, the dot should be deleted from the L.H. half note.

Chapter 10. Volume Five

1. In part (a), bar 9, the R.H. eighth notes should have staccato dots.

2. The posthumous Boosey & Hawkes Ltd. publication appeared in 1947. It is interesting that the title given the arrangement (No. 4) is "Short Canon and Its Inversion."

Chapter 11: Volume Six

1. In bar 15, the finger number 3 should be positioned above the soprano voice. In bar 74, the finger numbers 1/2 should be inverted to read 2/1 (see also bar 76, etc.).

2. In bar 38, the meter sign should be changed from 1/2 to 1/4.

3. In 145 b), L.H. bar 2, beat 4, a natural sign should be inserted before D. In bar 7, R.H., the eighth rest should be replaced by a quarter rest.

4. In bar 11, L.H. beat 2, the chord should read C-F-G, not C-G-A.

PART THREE

Style

Chapter 12: Bartók's Musical Language

1. The complete texts appear in *BBE,* 354–92.

2. *BBLW*, 152.

3. *BBE,* 363.

4. At that time a substantial number of minority peoples—Slovaks, Romanians, and Serbo-Croatians—inhabited their own villages in more or less close proximity to Hungarian enclaves.

5. *BBE*, 85.

6. Ibid., 96.

7. Ibid., 131–2.

8. Ibid., 363.

9. *BBSE,* 31–2.

10. *BBCO*, 21, 37.

11. *BBE*, 409.

12. See *BBCO,* 23–4.

13. Ibid., 23–7.

14. *BBSE,* viii.

15. *BBE*, 343–4.

16. *RFM*.i, 45.

17. See *BBSE*, vi–xiii and *BP*, 198.

18. *BBE*, 376.

19. Ibid., 432-3.

20. The absence of the major second degree (D♮) underscores the coloring of the Phrygian minor second (D♭).

21. *BBE*, 364.

22. Ibid., 364–5.

23. Ibid., 367.

24. Ernő Lendvai, *Béla Bartók. An Analysis of His Music*. London: Kahn & Averill (1971): 67.

25. Sándor Veress, "Bluebeard's Castle." In *Béla Bartók: A Memorial Revue* (New York: Boosey & Hawkes (1950): 44. The most comprehensive theoretic-analytical treatment of cellular structures in Bartók's music is given in *MBB*, 67–137.

26. *BBE*, 74.

27. Ibid., 328.

28. *BBCO*, 56–7, 366–7, 171.

29. *BBE*, 360.

30. Benjamin Suchoff, "The Impact of Italian Baroque Music on Bartók's Music." In *Bartók and Kodály Revisited*, ed. György Ránki. Budapest: Akadémiai Kiadó (1987): 188–9.

31. Ibid., 191–6. See also *BBCO*, 84–6, and Vernon H. Taylor. "Contrapuntal Techniques in the Music of Béla Bartók." Ph.D. diss., Northwestern University, 1950.

32. See the relevant music examples in William Dale Dustin. "Two-voiced textures in the *Mikrokosmos* of Béla Bartók." Ph.D. diss., Cornell University, 1959.

33. The majority of pieces in the *Mikrokosmos* are limited to two-part counterpoint, in which the individual voices are divided between the hands and on separate staves.

34. Bartók also uses "inversion" to indicate when the melody is transferred from one hand to the other (see No. 23).

Chapter 13: Volume One

1. *BBSE*, 50, no. 12. See also *YFM*.i, 190-3, No. 36; *TFM*, 23-4, No. 12; and *RFM*.ii, No. 639a.

2. *BP*, 66.

3. *YFM*.i., 28.

4. *HFS*, 52. Western influences are indicated by the rounded ABBA structure (ibid.).

5. Béla Bartók, *XVII and XVIII Century Italian Cembalo and Organ Music Transcribed for Piano*. Carl Fischer, New York, 1930. (Reprint 1990, with introduction by László Somfai): 59.

6. *HFS*, 74.

7. *YFM*.i., 59–61.

8. *RFM*.ii, 18.

9. See "Explanation of Terms" in *BBCO*, 247.

Chapter 14: Volume Two

1. *RFM*.iv, 25.

2. *BBE*, 128.

3. Ibid., 363–4.

4. Sándor Veress, "Bluebeard's Castle." In *Béla Bartók: A Memorial Review.* New York: Boosey & Hawkes (1950): 45–9.

5. *BBSE*, 67, no. 49.

6. *BBE*, 367.

7. Ibid., 364–5.

8. Ibid., 381.

Chapter 15: Volume Three

1. *BBE*, 432–3.

2. Ibid., 504.

Chapter 16: Volume Four

1. *Piano Music of Béla Bartók: Archive Edition Series I*, ed. Benjamin Suchoff. New York: Dover Publications, Inc. (1983): x.

2. *BBSE*, 245, subgroup 5, no. 6.

3. *BBGM*, 58–64.

4. See *RFM*.iv, 31–2 and melody nos. 25, 59d, and 95b.

5. *BBE*, 44. See also *BP*, 198–9.

6. *BBLW*, 101.

7. *BBE*, 381.

8. Ibid., 44–5. See also *BP*, 198–9.

9. *Südslawische Volkslieder*, ed. Heinrich Möller. Mainz: B. Schott's Söhne (1923): 100–1.

10. *BBE*, 40–9.

Chapter 17: Volume Five

1. A graphic explanation of "hemiola" is given in *BBCO,* 246.

2. *BBE,* 371–4.

3. *RFM.*i, 50.

4. Ibid., 666–9.

5. *BBE,* 367.

6. *BBE,* 244–6.

7. An excellent example is *RFM.*i, no. 14, a dance piece played on the violin.

Chapter 18: Volume Six

1. SV.ii, nos. 687–8.

2. The original source of Bartók's description is in his letter to the London office of Boosey & Hawkes, dated 18 December 1939. See *BBGM,* 81.

3. *RFM.*i, 13–4.

4. At bar 37 in the 1987 edition, the editor has attempted to rectify the error in the manuscripts and earlier editions in which Bartók placed a supernumerary eighth rest in the R.H., without a compensating reduction of values in the last group of notes preceding the bar line. While the editorial adjustment to read ♫ instead of ♫. in the soprano voice is the proper analytic solution, the truncated dotted eighth, B, is carried over as a tied note on the first beat in bar 38. Similarly, the alto quarter note, A, is changed to an eighth and likewise carried over to the following bar. The sonic effect of this peculiar insertion is an atypical vertical sonority, Eb-F♯-G-A-B, instead of the composer's scalar configuration. The editor's reconstruction is based on "Bartók's own recorded performance of the piece in Columbia ML 4419" (see notes, p. 64). Bartók, on the other hand, refuted such reliance in his essay, "Mechanical Music," stating that:

> The composer himself, when he is the performer of his own composition, does not always perform his work in exactly the same way. Why? Because he lives; because perpetual variability is a trait of a living creature's character. Therefore, even if one succeeded in perfectly preserving with a perfect process a composer's works according to his own idea at a given moment, it would not be advisable to listen to these compositions perpetually like that. . . . Because it is conceivable that the composer himself would have performed his compositions better or less well at some other time—but in an case, otherwise (*BBE,* 298).

5. See the several music examples in *BBSE,* 69–75.

6. *RFM.*i., 45–6.

7. A simplified version of No. 147, in Bartók's autograph, is published on p. 2 of the 1987 edition.

8. Bence Szabolcsi, *A Concise History of Hungarian Music.* Budapest: Corvina Press (1974): 171–2. See also *BBLW,* 10–1, 36.

9. See also *BBE*, 44–9 and *BP,* 197–201.

10. Serge Moreux, *Bartók*, 92.

11. See *BP,* 198–9.

12. See *MBB*, 253.

13. *BP,* 199–200.

14. Moreux, Bartók, 92.

15. In *Esztendó* (Budapest, 1918), 144-7.

Select Bibliography

Ameringer, Silvia, 'Teaching with Bartók's 'Mikrokosmos'," *Tempo* (London), Autumn, 1951, 31-5.

Antokoletz, Elliott. *The Music of Béla Bartók: A Study of Tonality and Progression in Twentieth-Century Music*. Berkeley and Los Angeles: University of California Press, 1984.

————. *Twentieth-Century Music*. Englewood Cliffs, N. J.: Prentice Hall, 1992.

————. *Béla Bartók: A Guide to Research, Second Edition*. New York: Garland Publishing, 1997.

————. "The Music of Bartók: Some Theoretical Approaches in the USA." *Studia Musicologica* 24 (1982): 67–74.

Antokoletz, Elliott, Victoria Fischer, and Benjamin Suchoff, eds. *Bartók Perspectives*. New York: Oxford University Press, 2000.

Apel, Willi. *Masters of the Keyboard*. Cambridge: Harvard University Press, 1947.

Balogh, Ernő. "Personal Glimpses of Béla Bartók," *Pro-Musica*, 1928, 18.

Bartók, Béla. *Slowakische Volkslieder*. Ed. Alica Elscheková, Oskár Elschek, and Jozef Kresánek. Bratislava: Academia Scientiarum Slovaca, vol. I, 1959; vol. II, 1971; vol. III, unpublished.

————. *Rumanian Folk Music*. Ed. Benjamin Suchoff, trans. E. C. Teodorescu et al. Foreword by Victor Bator. The Hague: Martinus Nijhoff, 1975. 5 vols. The five volumes appear as vols. 2–6 of the New York Bartók Archive Studies in Musicology series, ed. Benjamin Suchoff: 2) I. Instrumental Music (1967); 3) II. Vocal Melodies (1967); 4) Texts (1967); 5) Carols and Christmas Songs (*Colinde*) (1975); 6) Maramureş County (1975).

————. *Turkish Folk Music from Asia Minor*. Ed. Benjamin Suchoff. Princeton and London: Princeton University Press, 1976. Appears as vol. 7 of the New York Bartók Archive Studies in Musicology series, ed. Benjamin Suchoff.

————. *Béla Bartók Essays*. Selected and edited by Benjamin Suchoff. London: Faber & Faber; New York: St. Martin's Press, 1976. Reprint. Lincoln and London: University of Nebraska Press, 1992. Appears as vol. 8 of the New York Bartók Archive Studies in Musicology series, ed. Benjamin Suchoff.

————. *Yugoslav Folk Music*. Ed. Benjamin Suchoff. Albany: State University of New York Press, 1978. 4 vols. Appear as vols. 9–12 of the New York Bartók Archive Studies in Musicology series, ed. Benjamin Suchoff: 9) I.

Serbo-Croatian Folk Songs (with Albert B. Lord); 10) II. Tabulation of Material; 11) III. Source Melodies: Part One; 12) IV. Source Melodies: Part Two.

———. *The Hungarian Folk Song.* Ed. Benjamin Suchoff, trans. M. D. Calvocoressi, with annotations by Zoltán Kodály. Albany: State University of New York Press, 1981. Appears as vol. 13 of the New York Bartók Archive Studies in Musicology series, ed. Benjamin Suchoff.

———. *Piano Music of Béla Bartók.* The Archive Edition, ed. Benjamin Suchoff. New York: Dover Publications, 1981. Series I appears as vol. 14, Series II as vol. 15 of the New York Bartók Archive Studies in Musicology series, ed. Benjamin Suchoff.

———. *XVII and XVIII Century Italian Cembalo and Organ Music Transcribed for Piano.* Ed. László Somfai. New York: Carl Fischer, 1990.

———. *Studies in Ethnomusicology.* Ed. Benjamin Suchoff. Lincoln and London: University of Nebraska Press, 1997.

Bartók, Béla, and Sándor Reschofsky. Piano School (*Zongora Iskola,* 1913). Reprint, ed. Leslie Russell. London: Boosey & Hawkes, 1968.

Bator, Victor. *The Béla Bartók Archives: History and Catalogue.* New York: Bartók Archives Publication, 1963. Cataloging preparation (pp. 22–39) by Benjamin Suchoff.

Béla Bartók: A Memorial Review. New York: Boosey and Hawkes, 1950.

Brée, Malwine. *The Groundwork of the Leschetizky Method.* New York: G. Schirmer, 1930.

Copland, Aaron. *What to Listen for in Music.* Rev. ed. New York: McGraw-Hill, 1957.

Demény, János, ed. *Béla Bartók Letters.* Trans. Péter Balabán, et al. New York: St. Martin's Press, 1971.

———. *Bartók Béla levelei* (Béla Bartók letters). Zeneműkiadó, 1951, 203–17.

———. *Bartók Béla levelei.* Zeneműkiadó, 1976, 19.

Demény, János. "The Pianist." In *The Bartók Companion,* ed. Malcolm Gillies. London: Faber & Faber, 1993, 64–78.

Dille, Denijs, *Béla Bartók.* Antwerp N.V.: Standaard-Boekhandel, 1939, 89-91.

Downey, John W. *La musique populaire dans l'oeuvre de Béla Bartók.* Preface by Jacques Chailley. Paris: L'institut de Musicologie de l'Université de Paris no. 5, 1966.

Dustin, William Dale. "Two-voiced textures in the *Mikrokosmos* of Béla Bartók." Ph.D. diss., Cornell University, 1959.

Fassett, Agatha. *The Naked Face of Genius; Béla Bartók's American Years.* Boston and New York; Houghton Mifflin Company; Cambridge: Riverside Press, 1958. Reprinted as *Béla Bartók–the American Years.* New York: Dover Publications, 1970.

Földes, Andor. "My First Meeting with Bartók," *Etude* (March 1955): 12.

Gillies, Malcolm, ed. *The Bartók Companion.* London: Faber & Faber Ltd., 1993.

———. "The Teacher." In *The Bartók Companion*, ed. Malcolm Gillies. London: Faber & Faber, 1993, 79–88.

Hawkes, Ralph. "Béla Bartók: A Recollection by His Publisher." In *A Memorial Review.* New York: Booseyand Hawkes, 1950, 17.

Heinsheimer, Hans W. "Béla Bartók: A Personal Memoir," *Tomorrow* (October 1949), 30–4.

Hernádi, Lajos. "Béla Bartók, le pianiste, le pédagogue, l'homme."*La Revue Musicale* 224 (1955): 5, 84.

Hughes, Edwin. "Solving Piano Problems" *Etude* 73, no. 10 (October 1955): 60–1.

Jaques-Dalcroze, Émile. *Rhythm, Music and Education.* New York: G. P. Putnam's Sons, 1921.

Kodály, Zoltán. " Bartók the Folklorist." In *The Selected Writings of Zoltán Kodály.* Ed. Ferenc Bónis. Trans. Lili Halápy and Fred Macnicol. London: Boosey & Hawkes, 1974.

Kroó, György. "Bartók Concert in New York on July 2, 1944." *Studia Musicologica* 11 (1969): 253–7.

Lendvai, Ernő. *Béla Bartók. An Analysis of His Music.* London: Kahn & Averill, 1971, 67.

Matthay, Tobias. *The Act of Touch in All its Diversity: An Analysis and Synthesis of Pianoforte Tone-Production* (London and New York: Longmans, Green, 1926.

Moreux, Serge. *Béla Bartók.* Preface by Arthur Honegger. Trans. G. S. Fraser and Erik de Mauny. London: Harvill Press, 1953.

Murdoch, William. "Pianoforte Music." In *A Dictionary of Modern Music and Musicians.* London: J. M. Dent (1924): 243, 385-7.

Ortmann, Otto. *The Physical Basis of Piano Touch and Tone.* New York: E.P. Dutton, 1925.

———. *The Physiological Mechanics of Piano Technique.* New York: E.P. Dutton, 1929. Reprint. New York: Da Capo Press, 1981.

Rice, Timothy. "Bartók and Bulgarian Rhythm." In *Bartók Perspectives,* ed. Elliott Antokoletz, Victoria Fischer, and Benjamin Suchoff. (New York: Oxford University Press, 2000): 196–210.

Stevens, Halsey. *The Life and Music of Béla Bartók.* 3d ed., prepared by Malcolm Gillies. New York: Oxford University Press, 1993.

Suchoff, Benjamin. "Errata in the *Mikrokosmos* Publication." *Piano Quarterly Newsletter* 16 (summer 1956): 11, 24.

———. *Béla Bartók and a Guide to the Mikrokosmos.* Ann Arbor, MI: University Microfilms, 1957.

———. "History of Béla Bartók's *Mikrokosmos.*" *Journal of Research in Music Education* 7, no. 2 (fall 1959): 186-96.

———. *Guide to Bartók's Mikrokosmos.* London: Boosey & Hawkes, 1971. Reprint, with foreword by György Sandor. New York: Da Capo Press, 1983.

————. "Bartók's Musical Microcosm." *Clavier* 16, no. 5 (May–June 1977): 18–20.

————. "Béla Bartók: the Master Musician." *Music Educator's Journal* (October 1981): 34–7, 57.

————. "Introduction to *Piano Music of Béla Bartók.*" The Archive Edition, ed. Benjamin Suchoff. New York: Dover Publications, Inc., 1981. Series 1: vii–xii, 2: vii–xxv.

————. "Folk Music Sources in Bartók Works." In *"Weine meine laute."* *Gedenkschrift Kurt Reinhard*, ed. Christian Ahrens, et al. Laaber: Laaber-Verlag, 1984: 197–218.

————. "Ethnomusicological Roots of Béla Bartók's Musical Language." *The World Of Music* 29, no. 1 (1987): 43–65.

————. *"The Impact of Italian Baroque Music on Bartók's Music."* In *Bartók and Kodály Revisited*, ed. György Ránki. Budapest: Akadémiai Kiadó, 1987, 188.

————. "Fusion of National Styles: Piano Literature 1908–1911," and "Synthesis of East and West: *Mikrokosmos.*" In *The Bartók Companion*, ed. Malcolm Gillies (London: Faber and Faber, 1993): 124–45, 189-211.

————. "The Genesis of Bartók's Musical Language," and "Bartók's Odyssey in Slovak Folk Music." In *Bartók Perspectives*, ed. Elliott Antokoletz, Victoria Fischer, and Benjamin Suchoff (New York: Oxford University Press, 2000): 15–27, 113–28.

————. *Béla Bartók: Life and Work.* Lanham, MD: Scarecrow Press, 2001.

Szabolcsi, Bence. *A Concise History of Hungarian Music.* Budapest: Corvina Press, 1974.

Taylor, Vernon H. "Contrapuntal Techniques in the Music of Béla Bartók." Ph.D. diss., Northwestern University, 1950.

Thyne, Stuart. "Bartók's *Mikrokosmos*: A Reexamination." *The Piano Quarterly* 27, no. 127 (1979): 43–6.

Vargas, Lajos. "Bartók's Melodies in the Style of Folk Songs." *Journal of the International Folk Music Council* 16 (January 1964): 30–4.

Veress, Sandor. "Bluebeard's Castle." In *Béla Bartók: A Memorial Review.* New York: Boosey & Hawkes, Inc., 1950, 36–53.

Vinton, John. "Toward a Chronology of the *Mikrokosmos.*" *Studia Musicologica* 8, nos. 1–4 (1966): 41–69.

————. "Bartók on His Own Music." *Journal of the American Musicological Society* 19, no. 2 (summer 1966): 232–43.

Waldbauer, Ivan. "Polymodal Chromaticism and Tonal Plan in the First of Bartók's 'Six Dances in Bulgarian Rhythm.'" *Studia Musicologica* 32, nos. 1–4 (1990): 241–62.

Watson, Derek. *Liszt.* New York: Schirmer Books, 1989.

Index

About the Author

Benjamin Suchoff is adjunct professor in the Department of Ethnomusicology at the University of California, Los Angeles, and a member of the American Society of Composers, Authors, and Publishers (ASCAP, 1960–). Dr. Suchoff was curator of the New York Bartók Archive (1953–1967), successor-trustee of the New York Bartók estate (1968–1984), and editor of the thirteen volumes comprising the Bartók Archive Studies in Musicology series and the two volumes of piano works in the Bartók Archive Edition. His most recent books are *Bartók: Concerto for Orchestra: Understanding Bartók's World* (1995), *Béla Bartók Studies in Ethnomusicology* (1997), *Bartók Perspectives* (coeditor, 2000), and *Béla Bartók: Life and Work* (2001). He was awarded the Béla Bartók Diploma and Memorial Plaque from the Hungarian Republic in 1981 for his "great contribution to the understanding of Bartók's oeuvre" and is generally recognized as the dean of Bartók scholars.